INDIANA

HISTORICAL SOCIETY

PUBLICATIONS

VOLUME 25

NUMBER 1

FURNITURE MAKERS OF INDIANA

1793 TO 1850

BY

Betty Lawson Walters

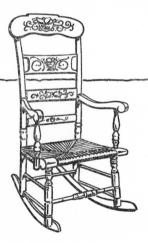

Indianapolis

INDIANA HISTORICAL SOCIETY

1972

PREFACE

In Discussions of American furniture made prior to 1850, it has been usual to consider the craftsmen of the East Coast centers of New York, Philadelphia, Providence, Boston, Baltimore, and Charleston, with occasional mention of the "back country" areas.[1] These areas are usually no farther west than western Pennsylvania, western Connecticut, or western New Hampshire. It may well surprise students of American furniture manufacture to discover that even on the frontier of the United States, in out-of-the-way places such as Brookville, Indiana, furniture was being made in a style probably not too inferior to that made in the East. Indeed, if advertisements are to be believed, many an Indiana craftsman was himself fresh from the shops of the East, bringing with him mahogany and other materials not to be found in the Midwest, together with the latest fashions of furniture design.

It must be admitted, of course, that a great many furniture makers working in Indiana before 1850 were minor craftsmen, making country furniture styles rather than high fashion. But the fact remains that a great deal of furniture was being made in Indiana long before 1850, and that not all fine furniture of the period found in Indiana today was imported from elsewhere. A great deal of it must have been of local manufacture.

This work is intended to be an introduction to furniture making in Indiana before 1850. It is hoped that it will awaken students of American furniture to the hitherto unexplored fields beyond the Appalachians and students of Indiana history

---

[1] See for example, Charles F. Montgomery, *American Furniture, The Federal Period* (New York: Viking Press, 1966) ; and *Antiques*, XCIII, No. 3 (March, 1968), issue devoted to country furniture.

to the relatively unexplored subject of the state's craftsmen. Persons living in Indiana, with the opportunity to visit local museums, historic houses, and historical societies, would undoubtedly discover many pieces of documented Indiana-made furniture in addition to the few mentioned herein. At the time that I was preparing this work I was serving as Museum Specialist in the Division of Cultural History of the Smithsonian Institution in Washington, D.C. My distance from Indiana made it impossible for me to obtain information on, and photographs of many of the pieces that have been identified as to the maker. This study, therefore, is restricted to the workmen and records of their work and is not a treatise identifying characteristics of Indiana craftsmanship.

The assistance of the following persons was most helpful and is gratefully acknowledged: Mrs. Estelle Bell of the Children's Museum, Indianapolis; Mrs. Horace D. Cook, Curator of the Miami County Historical Museum, Peru, Indiana; Mr. Thomas S. Emison, Vincennes; Mr. and Mrs. John L. Goldthwaite, Indianapolis; Miss Fannie H. Hall, Vincennes; Mrs. Charles A. Hamke, Curator, Francis Vigo Chapter, Daughters of the American Revolution, Vincennes; Mrs. Daniel M. Immel, Assistant Curator, Tippecanoe County Historical Museum, Lafayette; Mr. Frank A. Lindsey, Indiana State Museum; Mr. R. Gerald McMurtry, Director, The Lincoln National Life Foundation, Fort Wayne; Mrs. William E. Satori, President, Pennington Family Association, Louisville, Kentucky; Mrs. Robert I. Clark, Museum Curator, Vigo County Historical Society, Terre Haute; Mrs. C. B. Zeller, Indianapolis.

Particular acknowledgment is due Mrs. Noble W. Hiatt, Indianapolis; Miss Martha Merrill, Assistant Curator, Northern Indiana Historical Society, South Bend; Mr. Frederick P. Griffin, former President of the Harrison County Historical Society; and Mrs. John Seville, President, Parke County Historical Society, Rosedale, who have supplied substantial information for the check list appended to this paper. Special thanks go to Miss Caroline Dunn, librarian of the Indiana Historical Society, to Mr. and Mrs. Robert Montgomery, and especially to Frederick R. Walters, for their helpful suggestions and encouragement.

BETTY LAWSON WALTERS

April 1969

CONTENTS

A BRIEF SURVEY

ALTHOUGH INDIANA did not become a state until 1816 furniture makers and other craftsmen were active there long before that date. In 1793, for example, Gilbert Imlay in *A Topographical Description of the Western Territory of North America* wrote of Indiana manufactures:

> Linen and woolen cloths, leather, and hats, for home consumption, are manufactured with considerable success. The two first articles are only made in families for their own use; but the latter are made by men of profession in that business, and are of a quality that would not disgrace the mechanics of Europe. Blacksmiths' work of all sorts, even to making fire arms, is done there; as is also cabinet work, . . . in short, all the trades, immediately necessary to the promotion of the comforts of new settlements, are to be found here.[2]

By 1818, William Darby was writing that

> Tables, chairs, and bedsteads, are made in all the large towns in the valleys of Ohio and Mississippi, with all the requisite qualities of elegance and strength.[3]

Indiana's virgin forests made it prime territory for settlers who were craftsmen in wood. In 1818, *The Emigrant's Guide, or Pocket Geography of the Western States and Territories* provided the following inducement to eastern cabinetmakers when it described Indiana in part as follows:

> The hills are commonly the best timbered; in rich soils, the principal growth, is ash, walnut, sugar maple, hackberry, buckeye, elm, poplar, box elder, locust, &c. . . . The poorer sort of land is timbered principally with the various kinds of oak and hickory. . . . At this time emigrants have it in their power to acquire

---

[2] George [Gilbert], Imlay, *A Topographical Description of the Western Territory of North America* (London: J. Debrett, 1793), p. 96.

[3] William Darby, *The Emigrant's Guide to the Western and Southwestern States and Territories* (New York: Kirk & Mercein, 1818), p. 217.

prairie lands with a suitable proportion of timber, at the rate of 2 dollars per acre.[4]

Some idea of the number of skilled craftsmen working in Indiana in the prestatehood and early statehood periods can be gained from examining various cities and towns of the period. For example, Brookville in 1817 had one silversmith, two cabinetmakers, and one chairmaker, among other craftsmen noted by Samuel R. Brown in *The Western Gazetteer or Emigrant's Directory,* who remarked of Franklin County that ". . . the principal timber [is] white oak, hickory and black walnut. The oak trees are remarkably tall and handsome."[5] In 1819, Andrew Miller said that Brookville "is pleasantly and advantageously situated for trade, manufacturing and agriculture . . . ," its lumber being "beech and maple, oak, hickory, ash, elm, poplar, buckeye, &c.," and its craftsmen still comprising two cabinetmakers, one silversmith, and one chairmaker.[6]

One of these two cabinetmakers was Joseph Meeks, member of the prominent Meeks family of cabinetmakers, who came to Brookville in 1818 from New York City.[7] On February 5, 1819, he advertised in the *Enquirer and Indiana Telegraph*:

JOSEPH MEEKS
CABINET-MAKER,
Late from the City of N. York,
where he has conducted a small business for the last eight

---

[4] *The Emigrant's Guide, or Pocket Geography of the Western States and Territories* (Cincinnati: Phillips & Speers, 1818), pp. 108, 248.

[5] Samuel R. Brown, *The Western Gazetteer or Emigrant's Directory* (Auburn, N. Y.: H. C. Southwick Printers, 1817), p. 52.

[6] Andrew Miller, *New States and Territories* (n.p., 1819), p. 63.

[7] See John N. Pearce, Lorraine W. Pearce and Robert C. Smith, "The Meeks Family of Cabinetmakers," in *Antiques,* LXXXV, No. 4 (April, 1964), pp. 414-20; and John N. Pearce and Lorraine W. Pearce, "More on the Meeks Cabinetmakers," in *Antiques,* XC, No. 1 (July, 1966), pp. 69-73; also *Antiques,* XCVIII, No. 1 (July, 1970), p. 127.

years, takes this method of informing the inhabitants of
Brookville, and the vicinity, that he intends following
the above Business at this place. He has brought with
him a quantity of *Superior Mahogany,* which he will
manufacture in the newest fashion and workman like
manner; likewise other woods natural to the growth of
this country. His residence at present is at the House of
Mrs. Cooper, in the rear of Mr. Ray's tavern.

N.B. An Apprentice wanted immediately.

Presumably, Meeks brought with him the latest styles and
patterns popular in New York as well as the mahogany.
Although he is referred to as a "woodworking genius" in one
local history, no evidence of his work thus far has been dis-
covered by the author. Meeks built his own home on North
Main Street in Brookville, and as recently as 1915 it was
said, "There are many pieces of his handiwork to be seen in
the homes of Brookville people today."[8] His son Theodore
continued the business after his death until 1854.

From the 1820s onward there was an ample number of
cabinetmakers to supply the demands of the inhabitants of
Indiana. In 1822 Indianapolis had four cabinetmakers; by
1829 there were five or six of them in addition to two chairmakers.[9] By 1836 the *Indiana Democrat* of April 16 was
reporting of Indianapolis that "Luxury and the semblance of
extravagance are holding a strong rule in their sphere, and the
hum of business is heard from street to street."

Terre Haute had about fifty buildings, five stores, one
grocery, three taverns, two boot and shoe stores, two black-
smiths, one gunsmith, three tailors, "several carpenters,
joiners [and] cabinet-makers" in 1823.[10] The economic

---

[8] August J. Reifel, *History of Franklin County, Indiana* . . . (Indianapolis: B. F. Bowen & Co., 1915), p. 196.

[9] *The Indiana Gazetteer* (Indianapolis: Douglass & Maguire, 1833),
p. 92.

[10] C. C. Oakey, *Greater Terre Haute and Vigo County* (Chicago: Lewis
Publishing Co., 1908), I, 99.

breakdown of Richmond, given in the *Public Leger* on March 6, 1824, was as follows: ". . . 7 blacksmiths, 4 hatters, 4 cabinet-makers, 6 shoe-makers, 3 tailors, 3 coopers, 3 potters, 1 gunsmith, 1 saddler, 1 pump maker, 1 bake shop, and a steam distillery, besides a large number of carpenters, brick and stone masons, plasterers, &c." To which were added on March 13, 1824, "1 silver-smith, 1 coverlid and diaper weaver, 1 last maker, 1 painter, 1 brewer, 3 large tan yards, and since our last another saddler has commenced business in this place." By 1833 the *Indiana Gazetteer* mentioned five cabinetmakers and two chairmakers in Richmond.[11]

New Harmony, the Owenite community, really does not fit the mold of the usual Indiana community, for it was established as a social experiment in communal living. Although it was called a failure by its leaders in 1827, under the direction of William Maclure the second industrial school in the United States had been established there, at which were taught "taxidermy, printing and engraving, drawing, carpentry, wheelwrighting, wood-turning, blacksmithing, cabinet-making, hat-making, shoemaking, agriculture, washing, cooking, sewing, housekeeping, dressmaking and millinery."[12]

In the *New-Harmony Gazette* of October 22, 1825, there is a description of the industries conducted by the community, and they form a significant list in a study of Indiana manufactures. Following a long description of its textile processing plant, there are mentioned a dye house, soapmaking, candle making, glue making, a rope walk, hat manufactory, pottery,

boot & shoe department . . . [employing 17 men]; 36 farmers, 4 tanners, 2 gardeners, 2 butchers, 2 bakers, 2 distillers, 1 brewer, 1 tinner, 2 watch-makers, 4 black and white smiths, 2 turners, 1 machine maker, 4 coopers, 3 printers, 1 stocking weaver, 3 sawyers,

---

[11] *The Indiana Gazetteer*, 1833, p. 149.
[12] George B. Lockwood, *The New Harmony Movement* (New York: D. Appleton & Co., 1905), p. 243.

7 tailors, 12 seamstresses and mantua makers, 9 carpenters, 4 brick-
layers, 2 stone cutters, 4 wheel wrights, 1 cabinet maker and 3
cloth weavers.

Although *The Indiana Gazetteer,* 1826, gives a total of
21 cabinetmakers and 5 chairmakers in Indiana towns, plus
"several" cabinetmakers in Indianapolis and Connersville,[13]
the industrial census of 1820 had previously recorded as
many as 28 cabinetmakers and 7 chairmakers.[14] The *Western
Annotator* of Salem reported on September 29, 1829, that
there were in that town ". . . 3 Cabinet Makers shops, . . .
2 Brass Clock Makers, 1 Watch Maker and Silversmith,
. . . 2 Chair Makers, 1 Painter . . . ."

The Indiana Gazetteer of 1833 did not enumerate all the
craftsmen in each city it discussed, and some of its entries are
tantalizing. For example, it records two cabinetmakers and a
chairmaker for Putnam County, while the check list appended
to this paper records no such craftsmen for Putnam County
who are known to have been working there prior to 1850.
The county was said to have ample supplies of "beech, poplar,
ash, sugartree, walnut, hickory, and oak."[15]

Rising Sun numbered among its inhabitants in 1835
four cabinetmakers, and it also claimed a chair factory and two
stoneware potteries in addition to other manufactories.[16] The
number of inhabitants and furniture makers in Indiana
gradually swelled until in the 1840 census furniture making
ranked third (after house construction and leather industries)
among Indiana's leading industries and the 1850 census re-

[13] John Scott, *The Indiana Gazetteer or Topographical Dictionary,* 1826
(Reprinted as Indiana Historical Society *Publications,* XVIII, No. 1, Indianapolis, 1954), *passim.*

[14] Fourth Census, Industry, Indiana, 1820 (microfilm, National Archives
and Records Service, and Archives Division, Indiana State Library).

[15] *The Indiana Gazetteer,* 1833, p. 146.

[16] *History of Dearborn and Ohio Counties, Indiana* (Chicago: F. E.
Weakley and Company, 1885), p. 362.

corded 1,872 persons engaged in the cabinet- and chairmaking trades.

The industrial census of 1820 disclosed a great deal of information about the volume and type of products made by Indiana craftsmen of all types. In addition to those named in the check list here, there were many unnamed persons listed as cabinetmakers, particularly in Clark County (see Appendix I). In this census, cabinetmakers would list their raw materials (amounts of cherry, walnut, poplar, hickory or oak, or simply "plank and scantling"), as well as their equipment. This was often simply "1 Sett of Cabinet maker Tools" and occasionally a lathe, although some ambitious census takers were more specific, as was the man who interviewed John G. Henderson of Salem, and recorded for him: "58 planes General assorted four screw gages, two dozen screw Clamps, Six Iron screw Clamps, One Brace & thirty bits, thirty chisels & gouges, nine saws of various kinds, one turning lathe, three benches."

Where a lathe was indicated, the source of power for it was given. Uzziel Church of Brownsville had a "Turning Lathe going by Water," with which he made flax wheels, clock reels, knot reels, quill wheels, and bedsteads. Usually horse power was indicated, but Hosea C. Buckley of Haddon Township, Sullivan County, among others, had "Dogs for turning." In this period dogs would have been used as demonstrated in Plate II.

It seems unlikely that dog power would have been sufficient to power extensive machinery; even operating a turning lathe with dog power might seem to be relatively unreliable. Perhaps several dogs were used together, running within a large wheel; the wheel's rotation in turn powered a small apparatus. However, it is interesting to note that in the Rappite community which preceded the Owenite community at New Harmony the water which supplied the distillery was pumped by a large dog running in a wheel and one of the bellows in the smith shop was moved in the same manner.[17]

Horse power was far more prevalent and more dependable. The horse (or horses) walked in a circle, drawing a sweep which turned wheels providing motive power to the machinery. This system is shown in Plate I, operating a cider mill.

It is in the lists and prices of products manufactured included in the 1820 industrial census that one sees the full spectrum of the Indiana furniture-making industry of 1820. One of the more complete lists was that of Sydnor Dale of Connersville:

Side Boards Average $100; Secretaries Average $75; Bureaus Dto $32; Desks Dto $32; Cupboards Dto $18; Tables Best per set $45; Tables Dining & Breakfast $8; Clock Cases Each $25; Bedsteads Best quality $18; Dto Common $3.50; Coffins Raised lids $10; Candle Stands $4; Book Cases $7.

Abijah Shields of Jennings Township in Fayette County also made wheat fans for $25 and wool carding machines for $400, in addition to cabinet furniture. Some frontier cabinetmakers, such as James Cutter of Paoli, were dubious about this Federal inquiry into their affairs, and would only state "Good sale and you gess at the rest."

The condition of the cabinetmaker in Indiana in the 1820s must have been tenuous. A fire, such as that described in the Corydon *Indiana Gazette* of March 12, 1823, was probably a complete disaster to its cabinetmaker victim:

FIRE!!

The citizens of this place were alarmed by the cry of Fire! on Tuesday morning about 4 o'clock. The building was occupied by Jesse West as a Cabinet Shop, which was well stowed with Furniture and tools; all of which were consumed by the devouring

[17] Henry R. Schoolcraft, *Travels in the Central Portions of the Mississippi Valley* (New York: Collins and Hannay, 1825), p. 168.

element:—The damage is considerable, especially to a poor man whose all, is but little at the most.

This disaster did not keep Mr. West unoccupied for long. On August 13, he published the following advertisement:

NOTICE

THE subscriber informs his friends and the public, that he has just commenced the Cabinet business in the town of Corydon again since the devouring element of fire consumed his shop and tools on the 11th day of March last, and he will on the shortest notice furnish any person who wishes to purchase furniture of him. He will sell furniture as follows, to wit:

Large Pannel Beaura's neat		$14,00
Small Beaura's	do	4,00
Dining Tables 4 feet large at		10,00
Breckfast tables three feet		
4 inches long at		6,00
Corner Cupboards		14,00
Desk,		22,00
Curtain Bedsteads at		14,00
Coffins 6 feet long of raised led		8,00

and all other work in proportion.
All mountin [mountings] must be furnished by the purchaser.

JESSE WEST.

Aside from the hazards of fire, there was also the very real hazard of bankruptcy, which seems to have befallen Henry Rice of Corydon. The *Indiana Gazette* of May 26, 1834, advertised for sale at a sheriff's sale to settle a suit against him:

Eight Beds and bedding, and bedsteds, two pair of and irons, nine chairs, one large Kettle, two tables, all the cupboard furniture in two cupboards, consisting of plates, tea-cups and saucers, knives and forks,—one tea board, three dutch-ovens, one waffle iron, three buckets, and all the other kitchen furniture in said Rices kitchen,—three saws and all other Cabinet tools in said

Rices shop, about two hundred feet of Cherry plank, two fire shovels, and two pair of tongs, one grind stone; . . .

Others doubtless suffered similarly. At least one furniture maker was listed as a pauper in the 1850 census.

One is tempted to think of the craftsmen on the Indiana frontier as being industrious, thrifty, hardy souls, but the following notice, placed in the Brookville *Enquirer,* September 11, 1824, shows that at least one itinerant chairmaker fell short of the local standards:

LOOK OUT FOR WOLVES IN SHEEP'S CLOTHING.

A Man (as he called himself) by the name of
Seth Sumpter,
A chair maker by trade, boarded with me for five weeks past, and promised that I should have my demand for all incidental expenses knowing his employers to be men of stability, every attention was rendered unto him: Notwithstanding the aforesaid Seth, has absconded and to my loss ten dollars. . . .

Cabinetmaking establishments enumerated in the manufacturers' census of 1850 often included in their list of raw materials such items as varnish, paint, hardware, and "chair stuff" (seating materials such as rush or cane). Most establishments had several employees, whereas most entries in the 1820 census had been for a single craftsman. The increased volume of products from single shops reflected the impact of improved, mechanized techniques on the work of Indiana craftsmen. Although steam power was indicated for some establishments, horse power and water power were more prevalent, and hand power was listed often.

As early as the 1830s, due to improvements in machinery, the coming of genuine industrialization to Indiana, and an increased supply of labor, shops began to advertise that they were keeping on hand a supply of furniture. Previous advertisements had only indicated that objects could be made on short notice. So we find an increasing number of advertisements for furniture "ware rooms." Such advertisements should not be interpreted to mean that these establishments sold imported furniture, for they were usually accompanied by an indication that cabinet work was being done on or near the premises. They may also, of course, have handled imported pieces for sale.

Benjamin Price, a cabinetmaker in South Bend from 1834 to 1884, began his work as did other Indiana craftsmen, in a log house, where he devoted most of his energy to making bedsteads. Later he worked on the upper floor of a new home which he built, and eventually, as a result of making many coffins, he became South Bend's first undertaker.[18] Mr. Price's story is fairly typical. He and Andrew Gardner of Vincennes (see below) were but two of many Indiana cabinetmakers who, called upon often to make coffins, decided to fill that need in the community as a second occupation. Coffins are frequently listed in advertisements as well as census reports of cabinetmakers' products. By the 1840s it is not uncommon to see newspaper advertisements such as the following from *The Lafayette Free Press* of October 27, 1840:

CABINET MAKING

H. J. MULFORD respectfully informs the citizens of Lafayette and vicinity, that he still continues to carry on the *CABINET MAKING* in the stand on the south side of Main street. . . . He keeps constantly on hand a good supply of *BUREAUS, TABLES, STANDS* and *BEDSTEADS,* and is prepared to manufacture to order, all kinds of Furniture needed in this country . . . . he is provided with a Hearse and will attend at all times to the business of an Undertaker.

---

[18] Obituary, South Bend *Tribune,* October 22, 1887. For a discussion of the combination of cabinetmaking and undertaking activities, see Robert W. Habenstein and William M. Lamers, *The History of American Funeral Directing* (Milwaukee: Bulfin Printers, 1962), pp. 226-34.

Since furniture makers often combined their primary trade with other allied industries, such as undertaking, one finds notices of combinations such as William Bullock's Chair and Spinning Wheel Manufactory in Lafayette; Richard Burk's wheat fan and cabinet furniture shop in Richmond, and Eratus Smith in the same town making wool carding machines, repairing clocks, and producing furniture (see check list). Osgood & Dennett of Lafayette set up a window sash and blind factory, at the same time doing "joinering, carpentering, turning, sawing, etc. . . . keeping constantly on hand Sashes, Bedsteads, Split Bottom Chairs, &c," according to the *Indiana Eagle* of May 8, 1839. A more common combination of crafts was chairmaking and sign and ornamental painting, although Edward H. Hudson of Brookville added to these the manufacture of a patent spinning wheel (*Enquirer,* August 13, 1822).

Another characteristic of the Indiana pioneer as well as the Indiana furniture maker is frequent moving from place to place. The 1850 census records show the westward progression of many men who were born in Europe, Virginia, New Jersey, or New England and whose children were born in Ohio, Pennsylvania, or Kentucky as well as in Indiana. Once in Indiana, many of them moved about the state.

Cabinetmaking and chairmaking, like pottery making and other crafts, appear to have been family enterprises. Craftsmen with sons trained them in their trade. It is not unusual for a cabinetmaker to be listed in the census with two or three sons living in the same household also listed as cabinetmakers. Because of this familial trade tendency, one suspects that persons of the same surname, though scattered about the state, may well have been related (for example, see in check list, below, Caleb Scudder and Mathias S. Scudder).

Recent arrivals advertised, as had Joseph Meeks, that they brought eastern materials with them. Samuel S. Rooker of Indianapolis advertised his Chair Manufactory in the *Indiana*

Democrat of July 17, 1835, concluding: "Having just received a supply of materials from the city of New York, he will be able to execute fancy work in a style superior to any before offered in this place."

George Stephens opened his new "Cabinet, Chair Making and Upholstery" establishment in Mishawaka, which he advertised in the *South Bend Free Press* of June 16, 1838, including the note that he had "obtained in the East Mahogany, Black Walnut & French Veneers," in addition to "hard wove curled hair and hair cloth." Other establishments noted with pride their acquisition of eastern workmen, as did Lucius Taylor of Lawrenceburg, who concluded his advertisement in the *Indiana Palladium* of January 30, 1830, by boasting: "He flatters himself, from the experience he has had in the business, and from the fact of his having employed a first rate workman, directly from New York, that he will be able to give general satisfaction."

The activities of the cabinetmaker in Indiana closely parallel the activities of cabinetmakers on the East Coast, which have been discussed at length elsewhere.[19] But heretofore, little note has been made of the work in the Midwest. It has generally been assumed that furniture made in Indiana must have been of a primitive or common style and that any elaborate furniture there must have been brought from the East by immigrants. A typical statement, made in 1941, proclaims

. . . it is doubtful if Indiana produced anything outstanding in the field of the minor arts. Furniture design reflected the models brought in from the South and East, which in turn were based on European prototypes; carpenters and woodcarvers used the same books of plans as their Eastern colleagues, and pottery was designed for utility rather than beauty.[20]

---

[19] See sources cited footnote 1.

[20] Federal Writers' Program, Indiana, *Indiana, A Guide to the Hoosier State* (New York: Oxford University Press, 1941), p. 128.

The very fact that Indiana-made furniture reflected eastern models indicates that outstanding works must have been created in the state.

It is unfortunate that American furniture makers did not always mark their products with identifying labels or stamps. Eastern furniture makers sometimes applied a printed paper label to their wares, or burned a mark or painted a stenciled label on them. No such labels or marks have been found on Indiana-made furniture of the period covered in this study. Paper was scarce in Indiana in the early period, as evidenced by the local newspapers, which would frequently skip an issue and remark later that the issue had been omitted because the paper supply had not been received. Perhaps the combination of a scarcity of paper and a lack of printers (except in the larger cities) combined to make labeling furniture too cumbersome a project, as well as an expensive one for the small businessman. The single mark illustrated herein, the carved initials "T L" of Thomas Lincoln (Plate IV), occurs on a cupboard made by Mr. Lincoln in Kentucky prior to his arrival in Indiana. The mark is shown here, nevertheless, because it is possible Mr. Lincoln may have so marked pieces he made following his move to Indiana.

The account books of three Indiana cabinetmakers reinforce the theory that plain as well as high-style furniture was being made early in Indiana, and that the latest styles being made in the eastern furniture shops were also being produced beyond the Alleghenies. Although the Indiana cabinetmaker had to manufacture virtually every wooden household item that could not be made by the head of the household himself, it is evident that he made elaborate pieces of furniture as well.

David Thomas, writing his *Travels Through the Western Country* in 1816, noted the following craftsmen in Vincennes:

. . . 4 Black-Smiths' Shops, 2 Gun Smiths' Shops, 3 Shoemakers' shops, 3 Saddlers' shops, 4 Tailors' shops, 2 Cabinet Makers, 3

Hat Factories, 1 Silver Smith, 1 Tin Factory, 1 Chair Maker, . . .
1 Limner . . . .[21]

One of the two cabinetmakers listed must have been
Andrew Gardner, who came to Vincennes from Boston in
1814. After an extensive career as a cabinetmaker, he turned
to undertaking as a natural extension of his coffin-making
activities. The firm he established in 1816 is still in business
as a funeral home, now known as Dexter Gardner & Sons.
The accounts kept by Andrew Gardner & Son from 1816 to
1853 provide a good insight into the activities of a pioneer
cabinetmaker in Indiana, disclosing the diversity of his
product.[22]

The greatest volume of Gardner furniture was beds and
tables. The accounts list 115 beds, mostly of unspecified types,
but including high post, trundle, "fancy," and low post bedsteads. He also made "Teaster frames," paneled headboards,
and cornices for beds, as well as turning numerous sets of
bed posts. He made tables of all kinds, including dining,
breakfast, kitchen, and toilet tables, pairs of side tables, a
lady's work table, a table for the priest, a square table with a
drawer, and a small table with a drawer. He also produced
walnut, cherry, and mahogany front stands.

Gardner's shop made few chairs, for only three sets are
listed (a set being four or six, usually), together with an
arm chair and a high chair. His "crib cradle" and "rocking
crib" may also have been products of the chairmaking part of
his shop.

Cabinet furniture included 27 bureaus, as well as bookcases, chests made of walnut or poplar, corner cupboards,
counting-house desks and one plain desk, and a sideboard. In

[21] David Thomas, *Travels Through the Western Country in the Summer
of 1816* (New York: David Rumsey, 1819), p. 190.
[22] Gardner Mortuary, Account Book [1816/1853], Vincennes (Microfilm, Indiana State Library, Indianapolis).

the account for A. L. Badollet on April 17, 1824, is the entry "To 1 Secratory [$]35 00." Several presses are listed in the account book, among which are a large "close press," presses of poplar, cherry, or walnut; a china press, and a large wardrobe press as well as a press with drawers. Perhaps the French heritage of Vincennes caused the wardrobe, or press, to be popular there. Few references were found to show presses being made elsewhere in Indiana.

The only evidence of painted furniture is a listing of "1 painted Trunk [$]3 50" and the references to "fancy" beds which, like fancy chairs, may have been painted.

It is in the diversity of minor items made by Gardner that the flavor of early nineteenth-century Indiana life is revealed. Gardner made numerous kitchen items such as a dough tray, bread board, "bread pele & oven rake," knife box, salt box, rolling pins, sausage stuffers, and a churn dasher and top. He made "2 Lions Heads" in 1823 and a squirrel cage in 1827 for Hiram Decker. He made a child's wagon, a whip stock, corset boards, checkers, and a mace stick. For the local businessmen and industries he produced such items as "press furniture" [that is, parts for the printing press] for the shop of Indiana's first publisher Elihu Stout, editor of *The Western Sun*; hat blocks for Richard P. Price; "1 Sett brickmoulds [$]3 00" for Josiah L. Holms; and pumps for boats, rulers and yardsticks, and currying boards. For women's use he made quilting frames, lace forms, and a bead loom.

Andrew Gardner was also called upon for miscellaneous services in the home. He screwed up and unscrewed bed cords, varnished mantels and furniture, glued a fiddle, added rockers to chairs, put shelves in a shoe box, put bottoms in canisters, and added wheels to a wheelbarrow. He also turned handles for augers, files, hoes, and hammers. For local buildings he made newel posts, "32 lights of walnut sash & hinging," and laundry and bath equipment such as "1 box and barrel for bath," a bottom for a bathing tub, a washing board, a washing machine, "brackets & roler for towel," and a press board. He also repaired and painted wagons and carriages, and occasionally made shoes.

Woods mentioned were primarily poplar and walnut, with cherry, sycamore, oak, and mahogany also employed. Among the supplies purchased by Gardner from local businessmen were the following in an account with William J. Heberd:

1838	Nov 25	To 4 Setts Glass Knobs	4 00	
1839	Feby 19	" Brass Tacks	1 00	
. . .				
	May 10	" 1 Cupboard Lock	69	
. . .				
	" 14	" 1 doz Table Hinges	4 68	
	" 25	" 1 Sett Glass Knobs	1 25	
. . .				
	" 31	" 1 Sett File Locks	25	
	June 27	" 4 Chest Locks	50	
1840	April 4	" 1 File Lock	13	

and from J. & S. (?) Wise he bought:

1835	April 28	To 1 doz. escutcheons	12½	
	Dec 5	" 1 Sett Castors	37½	50
	9	" 2 pr Small Shoes		1 37½
	Feb 18	" 1 Cubbard Lock Self	31½	
	20	" 6 brass Secretary bolts	75	
	Sept 24	" 1 Cubbard Lock Self	25	
	Oct 3	" 1 Cubbard Lock	25	

A typical account, reflecting some of the variety of work Gardner performed for a single person, is that of Robert L. Reynolds, an excerpt of which follows:

1824	March 10	To 1 Beureau	25 —
	Augt. 24	" repairing waggon	2 —
	Oct 5	" 1 Cradle	6 —
	23	" 1 high post Bedstead	35 00
	"	" 1 p^r. Tables	30 00
	"	" 1 Breakfast Table	9 00

	Oct	30	”	Screw up Glass	50
	”	”	”	Bread Board	75
	”	”	”	1 Rolling pin	25
	Dec	29	”	1 high post Bedstead	15 00
1826	June	1	”	1 Trundle Bedstead	5 00
	Nov	8	”	1 Crib Bedstead	6 00
	. . .				
1830	Jany	21	”	turning sasuage stuffer	25
	April	12	”	1 large wardrobe	**23 00**
	August	21	”	1 Beadstead	6 00

From the twenty-five cent sausage stuffer to the thirty-five dollar high post bedstead, Andrew Gardner was making everything conceivably needed in the Indiana home. Often the final entry in a Gardner account was for the coffin made for the customer's estate.

The last dated entry for furniture in the Gardner account book was in 1843. However, the 1850 manufacturers' census indicates that "A. Gardner & Sons," cabinetmakers, that year produced 60 bedsteads valued at $360; 40 tables worth $200; 13 bureaus for $223; and 60 coffins totalling $480. A letter from Evansville dated December 16, 1853, indicating that John S. Mitchell was shipping "50 pkgs furniture & chairs" to Gardner, suggests that Gardner was selling wares from other sources by that time.

Prices for Andrew Gardner's products give some indication of their style. In 1827 a bedstead sold to John B. Bonhomme for $10; a small bedstead sold in 1827 for $3.00; a high post bedstead in 1821 sold for $20.00, in 1831 for $23.50. Other expensive items were a pair of tables for $30, the $35 Badollet secretary mentioned previously, and a walnut sideboard sold to Samuel Judah between 1826 and 1829 for $45. The difference in price reflects more than simply the size of the object; it is indicative both of the varied values of the woods used and of the hours of labor involved in its manufacture.

Several pieces of furniture made by Andrew Gardner and

his descendants are still in existence, including a Windsor rocking chair, a chest, a chest or bonnet box, a cradle, a secretary, and a grandfather's clock case. See Plates VI and IX.

A ledger kept by Samuel Goodrich Benedict from 1833 to 1837 throws additional light upon the work of Indiana's cabinetmakers.[23] Benedict appears to have been a journeyman cabinetmaker; if not a journeyman, he was certainly itinerant, for the ledger covers his work in the Muncie area, in Elizabethtown in Bartholomew County and Middletown in Henry County. He was born in 1810 and moved to Portland, Indiana. He died in 1844. No extant examples of his work are known to the author.

Benedict's ledger lists 53 beds, including some forms not made by Gardner such as "French" (empire style) and "field" beds. Fourteen of the beds are called "fancy." He made 50 tables and stands, including cherry work stands, "2 draw" work stands, and a work stand with a lock. (A work stand was a sewing table.) He made dining tables with casters, writing tables, and in 1837 he made for L. J. Leisser "one Center table" worth $62.50. A dollar or less per day was his daily wage for logging and sawmill work, and the indications in the 1837 portion of the ledger are that he could well have spent several weeks in making this table. If so, it must have been most unusual, perhaps with a good deal of carving or inlay.

Cabinet furniture in the Benedict accounts show 24 bureaus including bureaus with "half columns," "half column, 7 drawers," "plane front" and "strate frnt" styles, and dressing bureaus, most costing from $4 to $6. He also made a "washing dresser," a desk, chests, one set of chairs, bookcases with glass doors, a mahogany cradle, and other cradles.

Among the miscellaneous items that Samuel Benedict pro-

---

[23] Samuel Goodrich Benedict, Account Book [1833-1837] (MS, Indiana Historical Society Library, Indianapolis).

duced are a fireboard, an instrument box for a doctor, and bird cages.

Many entries in the accounts record the purchase of lumber, usually in small quantities. In 1833 he bought from William Mulford "two veneers at 25 each" and twelve feet of mahogany. In 1834 he paid Philip Oliver $3.75 for "halling three load of cherry from Clear Crick" and "one load from Little Miami." In 1835 his account with Zibe Wilson included

to nine feet of oak plank	.18¾
to fourteen feet of popular [sic] plank	.21
to six feet of ash plank	.12
to two pieces of oak strips	.10

and from Daniel Doty he bought "three hundred and sixty three of Cherry boards."

In the account book of Sidney B. Goodwin of Terre Haute, covering the period 1823 to 1856, we learn a few more details about the wares being made by Indiana cabinet-makers.[24] His descriptions of pieces he made more often include the material used as well as dimensions and an indication of the decoration used. For example, the entry for March 26, 1828, in his account with Stephen B. Hoffman, reads "To one cherry table 3½ feet [long] with turned legs [$] 7 00," and he made for Samantha Robinson on July 14, 1824, "two maple tables three feet with twist reeded legs [$]14 00." Among entries for beds are found a "turn up beadstead," sold to Eleizar Lewett for $9 and a "french bedstead with caps," sold to Albert G. Brown for $6. He lists a butternut bureau, chests including one of pine, a clock case, cradles of pine or maple, a pine portable cupboard, a birch cabinet, a commode, a desk for a store, and a case of pigeon holes.

---

[24] Sidney B. Goodwin, Account Book [1823-1856] (MS, Indiana Historical Society Library, Indianapolis). Also in the Indiana Historical Society Library is a microfilm copy of the account books of the McBride family, 1837-1917 (see check list below).

His tables show the greatest variety, however. They are listed as being made of maple, birch, cherry, or pine with reeded, turned, or "twist reed" legs, some with pulls (indicating drawers), a "tip [tilt-top] table," and one with a round top. Miscellaneous items not found in the other account books are a "close hors" and a spice pot.

Goodwin made some painted furniture, including a cupboard, a bookcase, and a chest, and he also painted some signs. Only ten chairs are listed, which sold for one dollar each. The most expensive items were "a commode without trimmings," sold to Albert G. Brown on October 1, 1824, for $38, and a birch cabinet sold to John Truax on February 28, 1829, for $40.

Woods listed in Goodwin's wares were butternut, pine, maple, birch, and cherry. In addition to these, he records a purchase of one branch of mahogany. His supply purchases included nails and screws, table buts (hinges), "bead stead caps" for his "french" beds, brass buts, chest buts, linseed oil, and varnish.

Toward the end of the Goodwin account book the entries for work on house construction become more and more numerous. He built porticoes, put on cornices, and made window blinds, but furniture is listed as late as 1856.[25]

It is obvious from the list of types of furniture made in Indiana during this period (Appendix II), that frontier life need not have been primitive. Undoubtedly some log cabins were the ultimate in simplicity and the householder would have fashioned crude furniture for himself in a makeshift way,

---

[25] Unfortunately, no pieces known to have been made by Benedict, the McBrides, or Goodwin have come to light. Some idea of their wares may be gained, however, by studying books devoted to nineteenth-century furnishings, such as Celia Jackson Otto, *American Furniture of the Nineteenth Century* (New York: Viking Press, 1965) ; or style manuals such as John Hall, *The Cabinet Makers' Assistant* (Baltimore: John Murphy, 1840).

but there were professional furniture makers available as early as 1820 in nearly every area which had inhabitants. Probate records of the period reveal all levels of household furnishings from the simplest to the most elaborate. The Indianapolis *Indiana Journal* of April 19, 1824, indicated that in the House of Representatives chamber in Indianapolis, a painted Windsor chair and a table with a drawer were provided every member. These were undoubtedly of local manufacture.

A partial survey of probate records of Fayette County, a county selected at random, revealed that the furnishings of the average Fayette County household were slim indeed prior to 1833.[26] For example, John Lair possessed only "Bed stead Two chairs" in his inventory of November 9, 1821. Account books of Indiana cabinetmakers indicate that beds, chairs, and tables were their most numerous products; this is also reflected in the probate records.

Inventories consulted show an average of three beds per household, ranging from "high post" to "under beds" (trundle beds), or "Bed & Curtains," which would indicate a canopy or tester bed. Price valuations indicate that some beds must have been of elaborate workmanship; whereas an "old" bedstead might be worth 50 cents, and the usual bed worth $7 to $10, Minor Thomas, whose inventory was recorded July 31, 1830, had a bedstead worth $20, and the "Large bed & bedding" of Patience Helm, 1830, was worth $25. Joseph Moffett, a doctor whose very elaborate household inventory was entered October 11, 1833, had "1 Rocking Crib [$] .50" and six other beds.

By far the most abundant piece of furniture listed was the chair. Chairs were usually made by chairmakers rather than

---

[26] Fayette County Probate Records (Microfilm, Indiana State Library, Indianapolis).

by cabinetmakers, although by the 1830s many cabinetmakers had partners or workmen who were chairmakers, so that their advertisements included both products. With the exception of Joseph Moffett's "Super Settee with Rockers $5.00," no form of seating furniture other than chairs was mentioned in the inventories studied. Numbers of chairs in a single household ranged from thirteen to two, including Windsor chairs, sets of Windsor chairs, arm chairs, rocking chairs, and chairs painted yellow, red, or brown. Patience Helm had "6 frame Chairs [$] 2.25."

The other essential item was table furniture. Joseph Moffett's inventory disclosed the following tables and stands (not consecutive in the original):

1 Small Table	[$] .50
1 Large Kitchen Table	2.00
1 Breakfast Table	.75
1 Small Stand	.12¼
1 Dining Table	3.50
1 Small Table	1.00
1 Small Stand	.50
1 Super Do.	2.00
1 circler [circular] Table	4.00
1 Wash Stand	1.00
1 Toilet Table	.12½

George Smith's inventory of May 3, 1830, included "One common square table 1.50," while the effects of John Tyner, recorded July 9, 1830, included "One falling leaf table 3.00." One puzzling entry in the inventory of Archibald Reid, August 13, 1832, is "1 Set maddison tables 14.00." Whether these would have been made in Madison, Indiana, or whether they were of a style connected with President Madison is uncertain.

Cabinet furniture was less abundant. Households with larger inventories might possess a bureau, and Joseph Moffett had a "super Bureau" worth $10. The most expensive items were clocks and their cases, but the value probably lay more in the clock works than in the clock cases. Minor Thomas had "One Clock & Case 22.50." Two tall clocks, with works made by Humphrey Griffith of Indianapolis (working 1825-1835) are known; one illustrated here (Plate VII) and the other in the museum of the Daughters of the American Revolution in Washington, D.C. It is probable that the cases of both were made in Indianapolis. Other cabinet furniture listed in the probate records included cupboards, chests, and clothes chests or presses. Mr. Thomas, in addition to the clock and case, had a desk and bookcase worth $20. Only one "sugar desk" was found in the records consulted. All of the furniture forms listed in these inventories were types that were being made in Indiana (see Appendix II).

Conclusions

The check list appended to this paper contains the names of over two thousand men who were employed in the furniture crafts in Indiana up to and including 1850. The reasons for this large number are various: the frontier offered a new and unexploited market for the products of furniture makers; the influx of settlers provided in addition to an eager market, a supply of labor; and plentiful virgin timber was easily available. The small craftsmen were also escaping from the throes of the industrial revolution, which by 1820 was beginning to make itself felt in the large eastern cities. The small businessman of the large eastern cities found himself in competition with increasingly mechanized, larger firms rapidly becoming factories. Such men eagerly sought a less competitive location on the frontier.

The diverse forms of furniture and household objects made by the Indiana furniture craftsmen prove that the cabinetmakers and turners were making virtually every wooden object needed in the frontier household that could not be readily made by the home owner himself, from paneled bureaus to sausage stuffers.

The Indiana furniture maker was also versatile in the woods he used, and the following were mentioned in the references consulted as being used by these men in their work: ash, birch, butternut, cherry, gum, hickory, mahogany, maple and curly maple, oak, pine, poplar, sycamore, walnut, and "veneers."

These men initially worked in primitive conditions—in log shops, using dog power to turn their machinery. But gradually one sees in the advertisements boasts of new brick shops, new machinery, new workmen recently arrived from the East, and further signs of prosperity and improvement in working conditions. These men branched out into making agricultural implements, textile-processing utensils, and archi-tectural elements as well as offering undertaking services to supplement their previous single line of furniture making.

The concentration of workmen in the towns along the Ohio and Wabash rivers and their tributaries not only reflects the general settlement pattern of the state, but also suggests that the craftsmen in those locations were in a good position to import materials such as mahogany and hardware and had the opportunity to ship their wares elsewhere. The river towns were probably quite up-to-date in styles current in the East, and new workmen would naturally have arrived first in these locations.

A CHECK LIST OF INDIANA
FURNITURE MAKERS WORKING
IN 1850 AND BEFORE

THE FOLLOWING is an alphabetical list of cabinetmakers, chairmakers, upholsterers, and allied craftsmen working in Indiana up to and including 1850. The cut-off date of 1850 was selected for two major reasons: first, the 1850 population census and the manufacturers' census of the same year provide the most extensive records of Indiana furniture makers by name to that date; second, after 1850 the furniture industry became so mechanized and factories were working on such a large scale that the individual craftsman had largely disappeared. Extensive consultation with local historians and local historical societies, together with searches of available newspapers and local history publications have supplemented these basic sources. The manufacturers' census of 1820 was also helpful, although in the case of Clark County no names were recorded for the furniture makers listed (see Appendix I). Newspapers and town and county histories have been searched, but the search should not be regarded as exhaustive.

Many men are listed here whose appearances in the census lists as cabinetmakers or allied craftsmen are unsupported by supplementary evidence. The names of all such men are included because additional information was found for a sufficient number of them to make it likely that extensive genealogical study would prove most of these men to have been making furniture as well as doing routine cabinet work. In an era of strict apprenticeship standards any man listed as a cabinetmaker would have been capable of making furniture whether or not he did so. Should a maker's mark or label be found on existing furniture, the most complete list possible will be the best reference tool for identifying the maker.

It should be pointed out that certain discrepancies exist

in the official records. Some craftsmen listed in the manufacturers' census were not listed as furniture makers in the population census, and vice versa. In many cases in the manufacturers' census the same man was listed twice in the same county but in different townships; I have interpreted this to mean that such a man was probably a journeyman worker and that he was accidentally recorded twice. In many cases, difficulty in deciphering names in manuscript materials has resulted in varied spellings; all variations found are listed herein. No attempt has been made to consolidate material from various sources on persons bearing the same name unless proof exists that such information pertained to the same craftsman. Thus one may find dual listings for the same name, while birthplaces or other details may vary; the reader may draw his own conclusions whether the two listings should be one.

No apprenticeships are indicated unless specific information was found proving that status. The presence of a seventeen-year-old worker in the household of an older craftsman was not considered sufficient evidence of apprenticeship.

It should be remembered that the working dates given for these men are simply the only dates documented. The man who advertised in 1840 may have been working long before and long after that date as well. Many of the men listed here as working in 1850 were still making furniture long after 1850 No attempt has been made here to cover their later careers When later information was readily available, it was included.

Spellings of geographic locations are based primarily on the U.S. Post Office Department's *Directory of Post Offices* (1961 edition). When no post office exists for the locality mentioned, spellings were verified with *Maps of Indiana Counties in 1876* (reprinted by the Indiana Historical Society in 1968 from *Illustrated Historical Atlas of the State of Indiana,* published by Baskin, Forster & Company, Chicago, 1876).

ABBREVIATIONS USED IN CHECK LIST

AGI   Indiana Federation of Art Clubs, *Art Guide to Indiana* (*Bulletin* of the Extension Division, Indiana University, Bloomington, 1931).

adv.   advertised, advertisement

c.   circa (about)

C   census (population)

CD   city directory

CH   county history; number following refers to numbered bibliography, pp. 230-33

Co.   county

est.   established

FWP   Federal Writers' Program, *Indiana, a Guide to the Hoosier State* (New York: Oxford University Press, 1941).

MC   Manufacturers' or Industrial Census, 1820, 1850

q.v.   which see

TH   town (or city) history; number following refers to numbered bibliography, pp. 230-33

Twp.   township

w.   working

-1825   1825 and before, etc.

1825-   1825 and after, etc.

1
ABBOT, JOHN. Cabinetmaker.
Born c. 1800, North Carolina; w.
1850, Driftwood Twp., Jackson Co.
(C)

2
ACRES, DANIEL. Chairmaker.
Born c. 1828, Ohio; w. 1850, Law-
renceburg, Dearborn Co. (C)

3
ACRES, NATHANIEL.
Chairmaker.
Born c. 1821, Ohio; w. 1850, Law-
renceburg, Dearborn Co. Lived
with Cyrus Armstrong, furniture
merchant and manufacturer, q.v.
(C)

4
ADAMS, CHRISTIAN.
Cabinetmaker.
Born c. 1814, Germany; w. 1850,
Evansville, Vanderburgh Co. (C)

5
ADAMS, GEORGE. Chairmaker.
Born c. 1802, New York; w. 1850,
Washington Twp., Elkhart Co. In
same household, George W. Ad-
ams, painter. (C)

6
ADAMS, GEORGE W. Painter.
Born c. 1829, New York; w. 1850,
Washington Twp., Elkhart Co.
Because he lived with George
Adams, chairmaker, it seems like-
ly that he painted chairs as well
as other items. (C)

7
ADAMS, THOMAS.
Cabinetmaker.
Born c. 1827, Indiana; w. 1850,
Saluda Twp., Jefferson Co. (C)

8
ADAMSON, NATHANIEL.
Chairmaker.
Born c. 1814, North Carolina; w.
1850, Stony Creek Twp., Henry
Co. (C)

9
ADMIRE, ROLAND T.
Cabinetmaker.
Born c. 1825, Kentucky; w. 1850,
Hensley Twp., Johnson Co. (C)

10
AKERS, SYRUS. Cabinetmaker.
Born c. 1822, Ohio; w. 1850, Ris-
ing Sun, Ohio Co. (C)

11
ALDRICH, NEAL & CO. Cabinet
and chair factory.
——— Aldrich and Israel Neal;
w. 1840, Logansport, Cass Co.
Adv. in *Logansport Telegraph* 26
December 1840, that they operated
a machine shop and sash factory
and also did cabinet- and chairmaking; they had invented a new
and cheap corn shelling machine.
See also NEAL & BURCH.

12
ALLEN, HARVEY. Cabinetmaker.
Born c. 1824, Ohio; w. 1850, Blue
River Twp., Johnson Co. In same
household, Gideon M. Dehart, cab-
inetmaker. (C)

13
ALLEN, JAMES. Cabinetmaker.
Born c. 1824, England; w. 1850,
Cedar Creek Twp., Lake Co. In
same household, Aaron Fuller,
cabinetmaker. (C)

14
ALLEN, JOHN. Cabinetmaker.
Born c. 1811, Pennsylvania; w.
1850, Covington, Fountain Co. (C)
See ALLEN & VICKERS.

15
ALLEN, SAMUEL.
Cabinet workman.
Born c. 1824, Ohio; w. 1850,
Parke Co. (C)

16
ALLEN, SOLOMON.
Wheelwright and cabinetmaker.
Born 20 October 1796, Virginia;
in 1826 came to Parke Co. and
settled in Reserve Twp. (CH 10)

17
ALLEN, STEPHEN.
Cabinetmaker.
Born c. 1829, Indiana; w. 1850,
Blue River Twp., Johnson Co.
(C)

18
ALLEN, THOMAS. Cabinetmaker.
Born c. 1794, Maryland; w. 1850,
Dudley Twp., Henry Co. (C)

19
ALLEN, THOMAS. Cabinetmaker.
W. 1832, Dublin, Wayne Co. (CH
34). *See* PECK & MATTHEW.

20
ALLEN, WILLIAM.
Cabinetmaker.
Born c. 1829, Indiana; w. 1850,
Greenville Twp., Floyd Co. (C)

21
ALLEN, WILLIAM.
Cabinetmaker.
Born c. 1821, Ohio; w. -1843-
1850-, Winchester, Randolph Co.

Adv. in *Winchester Patriot* 27
October 1843, illustrates a sideboard. In 1850 four men were
working in his shop, annually producing "30 Bureaus $360; 250
Bedsteads $1250; 30 Tables $150;
Other Articles $500." (MC, C)

22
ALLEN & VICKERS.
Cabinetmakers.
John Allen and Christian S.
Vickers; w. 1850, Covington,
Fountain County. Five men work-
ing in shop; annual product "110
Bureaus & Bedsteads $668; Tables
& other Shop Work $1332."
(MC)

23
ALLEY, ENOCH. Chairmaker.
Born c. 1820, Ohio; w. 1850,
Vernon Twp., Jennings Co. (C)

24
ALLEY, GRANVILLE.
Cabinetmaker.
Born c. 1812, North Carolina; w.
1850, Jefferson Twp., Switzerland
Co. (C) *See* ALLEY & COCH-
RAN.

25
ALLEY & COCHRAN (COCK-
RAN). Cabinetmakers.
Granville Alley and John W.
Cochran; w. 1850, Jefferson Twp.,
Switzerland Co. Annual product:
"Bureaus, Tables, &c, $600." (C,
MC)

26
ALLISON, CHARLES.
Cabinetmaker.
Born c. 1827, Ohio; w. 1850,
Wayne Twp., Henry Co. (C)

CABINET MAKING.

As Cheap as the Cheapest, and as Good as the Best.

The undersigned takes this method of tendering his thanks to his friends and the citizens generally for the liberal manner in which they have patronized him heretofore, and would just say that owing to the increased demand for furniture, he has made arangements to procure sufficient help to supply any demand in his line of business. Persons wishing to purchase Furniture would do well to call and examine his work before purchasing elswhere. Beef Cattle. Hides, Pork. Wheat, Corn, Oats, in a word all kinds of Produce will be taken in exchange for Furniture.

WILLIAM ALLEN.

Winchester. Oct. 23rd, 1843.   I–3m.

Fig. 1.   From *Winchester Patriot*

27
ALLISON, SAMUEL C.
Cabinetmaker.
Born c. 1812, Kentucky; w. 1850, Franklin Twp., Johnson Co. (C)

28
ALPHA, ALONZO A.
Cabinetmaker.
Born c. 1824, Indiana; w. 1850, Vienna, Scott Co. (C)

29
ALSPAUGH (ALSBAUGH),
GEORGE. Chairmaker.
> Born c. 1821, Pennsylvania; w.
> 1850, Henry Twp., Henry Co.
> Annual product: chairs worth
> $750. Later joined firm of Brene-
> man & Beam, q.v. (C, MC,
> *Indianapolis Star* 7 July 1940)

30
ALTER, CHRISTIAN.
Cabinetmaker.
> Born c. 1783, Maryland; w. 1850,
> Rush Co. (C)

31
ALVEY, LOUIS. Cabinetmaker.
> Born c. 1817, Kentucky; w. 1850,
> Sugar Creek Twp., Vigo Co. (C)

32
AMICK, ALFRED. Cabinetmaker.
> Born c. 1810, North Carolina; w.
> 1850, Lexington, Scott Co. In
> same household, Milton Robert-
> son, cabinetmaker. Two men
> working in shop, making annually,
> "150 Bureaus, Tables &c.," worth
> $700. (C, MC)

33
AMOS, BENJAMIN.
Cabinetmaker.
> Born c. 1827, Ohio; w. 1850,
> Vermillion Twp., Vermillion Co.
> (C)

34
AMOS, JAMES. Chairmaker.
> Born c. 1833, Indiana; w. 1850,
> Vermillion Twp., Vermillion Co.
> Lived with Nathaniel Amos, chair-
> maker. (C)

35
AMOS, NATHANIEL.
Chairmaker.
> Born c. 1798, Maryland; w. 1850,
> Vermillion Twp., Vermillion Co.
> In same household, James Amos,
> chairmaker. (C)

36
AMOS, WILLIAM. Chairmaker.
> Born c. 1826, Virginia; w. 1850,
> Jennings Twp., Scott Co. (C)

37
ANDERSON, DANIEL.
Cabinetmaker.
> Born c. 1828, Indiana; w. 1850,
> Pine Twp., Warren Co. (C)

38
ANDERSON, EDWARD. Chair
factory.
> W. 1850, Wayne Twp., Henry
> Co. Two men in shop, annually
> making "50 doz. Chairs" worth
> $600. (MC)

39
ANDERSON, JNO. M.
Cabinetmaker.
> Born c. 1829, Indiana; w. 1850,
> Shawswick Twp., Lawrence Co.
> Lived with Levi B. Nunnally,
> cabinetmaker. (C)

40
ANDERSON, JOHN S.
Cabinetmaker.
> Born c. 1815, Kentucky; w. 1850,
> Tipton, Tipton Co. (C)

41
ANDERSON, SAMUEL.
Chairmaker.
> Born c. 1796, Pennsylvania; w.
> 1850, Michigantown, Clinton Co.
> (C)

42
ANDERSON, SANFORD D.
Cabinetmaker.
> Born c. 1813, Kentucky; w. 1850, Haw Creek Twp., Bartholomew Co. (C)

43
ANDREWS, ALEXANDRE.
"Cabinet workman."
> Born c. 1828, Virginia; w. 1850, Brandywine Twp., Hancock Co. (C)

44
ANSHUTZ, GEORGE.
Cabinetmaker.
> Born c. 1804, Pennsylvania; w. 1850, Pleasant Twp., Switzerland Co. (C)

45
APPLE, GEORGE.
Chairmaker.
> Born c. 1829, Ohio; w. 1850, Lawrence Twp., Marion Co. (C)

46
ARMENT, WILLIAM.
Cabinetmaker.
> Born c. 1824, Pennsylvania; w. 1850, Dalton Twp., Wayne Co. (C)

47
ARMFIELD, HENRY. Apprentice cabinetmaker.
> Born c. 1833, North Carolina; w. 1850, New Castle, Henry Co. Apprenticed to Adam Beam, cabinetmaker, q.v. (C)

48
ARMSTRONG—*see* MAPES & ARMSTRONG.

49
ARMSTRONG, CYRUS. Furniture merchant and manufacturer.
> Born c. 1800, Ohio; w. -1839-1858-, Lawrenceburg, Dearborn Co. Prior to 11 December 1839 in partnership with —— Uel (*see* ARMSTRONG & UEL). In 1850 he was recorded as a furniture merchant, chair- and cabinetmaker with three employees, his annual product being 3,000 chairs worth $1,500 and other furniture valued at $300. At the same address were listed chairmakers Nathaniel Acres, —— Hayhs, and Henry Peterman, and cabinetmaker William Griffith. As late as 1858 he was a manufacturer of chairs and furniture. (C, MC, CH 26)

50
ARMSTRONG & UEL.
Chairmakers.
> Cyrus Armstrong and —— Uel; w. -1839, Lawrenceburg, Dearborn Co. Adv. the dissolution of their partnership in the *Political Beacon* 11 December 1839.

51
ARNOLD, DAVID. Cabinetmaker.
> Born 1831, Ohio; w. 1850, Washington Twp., Miami Co. (C)

52
ASHBROOK, J. R. Cabinetmaker.
> Born c. 1825, Ohio; w. 1850, Goshen, Elkhart Co. (C)

53
ASHTON, BENJAMIN.
Cabinetmaker.

Born c. 1824, Kentucky; w. 1850, Sheffield Twp., Tippecanoe Co. (C)

54
ASKINS, THOMAS. Cabinetmaker.
Born c. 1818, Virginia; w. 1850, Rockport, Spencer Co. (C)

55
ATKINSON, ELIJAH. Cabinetmaker.
W. 1820, Washington Co. Annual product listed as "Desks, Bureaus, Cupboards, &c." Prices were "Desks $30; Bureaus $22; Cupboards $18 &c." The census taker noted the firm was "in good order. Little demand." (MC)

56
ATTER, DAVID. Cabinetmaker.
Born c. 1828, Pennsylvania; w. 1850, Monroe Twp., Howard Co. (C)

57
AUSTILL, WILLIAM. Cabinetmaker.
Born c. 1814, Ohio; w. 1850, Rush County. (C)

58
AVERY, FRANCIS M. Cabinetmaker.
Born c. 1824, Tennessee; w. 1850, Deerfield, Randolph Co. In same household, cabinetmakers Francis Simans and Daniel Fenton. (C)

59
AXE, ELIAS. Cabinetmaker.
W. 1835—before 1845, Independence, La Porte Co. Opened a cabinet shop in 1835; disappears from the records by 1845. (CH 13)

60
AXE, SAMUEL. Cabinetmaker.
Born c. 1805, Virginia; w. 1850, Center Twp., Porter Co. (C)

61
AYERS, ——. Cabinetmaker.
Born c. 1825, Indiana; w. 1850, Madison, Jefferson Co. (C)

62
AYLER, AUGUSTUS. Cabinetmaker.
Born c. 1828, Germany; w. 1850, Winchester, Randolph Co. (C)

63
BACHELOR, WILLIAM. Cabinetmaker.
Born c. 1811, Maine; w. 1850, Goshen, Elkhart Co. (C)

64
BACON, ALFRED. Cabinetmaker.
Born c. 1828, New York; w. 1850, Union Twp., Miami Co. (C)

65
BAILEY, ADANIJA M. Chairmaker.
Born c. 1826, Indiana; w. 1850, Taylor Twp., Owen Co. (C)

66
BAILEY, DANIEL. Cabinetmaker.
Born c. 1831, Pennsylvania; w. 1850, Marion, Grant Co. (C)

67
BAILEY, JACOB R. Cabinetmaker.
Born c. 1821, Pennsylvania; w.

1850, Perrysville, Vermillion Co. In same household, Lorenzo B. Hold, cabinetmaker. (C)

68

BAIRD, GEORGE. Cabinetmaker. Born c. 1791, Pennsylvania; w. 1850, Franklin Twp., De Kalb Co. (C)

69

BAKER, DANIEL. Cabinetmaker. Born c. 1810, Pennsylvania; w. 1850, Cotton Twp., Switzerland Co. (C)

70

BAKER, EDWARD.
Cabinetmaker.
Born c. 1827, District of Columbia; w. 1850, Madison, Jefferson Co. (C)

71

BAKER, L. J. Cabinetmaker.
Born c. 1824, Kentucky; w. 1850, Pleasant Mills, Adams Co. (C)

72

BAKER, SAMUEL. Cabinetmaker and house joiner.
Born 14 July 1817, Fayette Co., Pennsylvania; came to North's Landing (near Rising Sun), Ohio Co., c. 1835 with two brothers, one of whom was a cabinetmaker. He was apprenticed to this brother for three years, and c. 1838 set up his own shop in Jefferson Co. (CH 7)

73

BAKER, SAMUEL. Cabinetmaker. Born c. 1818, Pennsylvania; w. 1850, Posey Twp., Switzerland Co. (C)

74

BALDWIN, DAVID.
Cabinetmaker.
W. 1835, Jay County. He was a blacksmith, gunsmith, and cabinetmaker. (CH 38)

75

BALDWIN, LOUIS H.
Cabinetmaker.
Born c. 1824, Ohio; w. 1850, New Frankfort, Scott Co. (C)

76

BALDWIN, MILTON.
Cabinetmaker.
Born c. 1829, Indiana; w. 1850, Greensboro Twp., Henry Co. Lived with Mathew Sanders, cabinetmaker. (C)

77

BALL, BENJAMIN F.
Cabinetmaker.
Born c. 1832, Ohio; w. 1850, Portage Twp., St. Joseph Co. (C)

78

BALL, ISAAC. Cabinetmaker and funeral director.
Born 1826, New Jersey (CH) or Indiana (C); apprenticed in Ohio; moved to Indianapolis in 1845; in 1847 to Terre Haute, Vigo Co. Still alive in 1891. A child's rosewood coffin with glass insert is in the Vigo County Historical Society Museum. An early partner was Charles Triche. (CH 9)

79

BALL, THOMAS. Cabinetmaker. Born c. 1833, Ohio; w. 1850, La Porte, La Porte Co. Lived with Willard N. Ball, cabinetmaker. (C)

80
BALL, WILLARD N.
Cabinetmaker.
Born c. 1813, New York; w. 1850, La Porte, La Porte Co. In same residence, cabinetmakers Thomas Ball and Charles Page. (C)

81
BANTA, TIRAS A. Cabinetmaker.
Born c. 1819, Indiana; w. 1850, Gosport, Owen Co. In 1850 he made furniture worth $550. (C, MC)

82
BARBER, LUCIEN. Cabinetmaker.
Born c. 1832, Ohio; w. 1850, Wayne Twp., Allen Co. Lived with George Carol, cabinetmaker. (C)

83
BARGER, DAVID. Cabinetmaker.
Born c. 1811, Virginia; w. 1850, Milford, Decatur Co. (C)

84
BARKER, HARRY. Cabinetmaker and chairmaker.
Born c. 1807, New York; w. 1850, Eel Twp., Cass Co. Five men in shop, making "25 Bureaus, 100 Tables $950; 80 Bedsteads, Chairs & other work $1,600." (C, MC)

85
BARKER, HENRY W.
Cabinetmaker.
Born c. 1818, Indiana; w. 1850, Bainbridge Twp., Dubois Co. In same household, Daniel McGinney, apprentice. (C)

86
BARKER, JOBE. Cabinetmaker.
Born c. 1825, North Carolina; w. 1850, Raysville, Henry Co. In same household, Benjamin Hacket, cabinetmaker. (C)

87
BARKER, WILLIAM R.
Chairmaker.
Born c. 1814, Kentucky; w. 1850, Franklin Twp., Marion Co. (C)

88
BARLOW, ALLEN. Chairmaker.
Born c. 1812, Kentucky; w. 1850, Boone County. (C)

88a
BARNER, JOHN. Cabinetmaker.
Born 1810, North Carolina; w. 1828-1832, Monroe, Morgan, Marion cos.; 1832-, Frankfort, Clinton Co. (*Memorial Services of the Life and Character of John Barner* [Frankfort, 1882]).

89
BARNES, JOSEPH. Chairmaker.
Born c. 1808, Kentucky; w. 1850, Otter Creek Twp., Ripley Co. (C)

90
BARNES (BARNS), NATHANIEL S. Cabinetmaker.
Born c. 1810, New York; w. 1850, Lauramie Twp., Tippecanoe Co. Two men in shop; they made 250 pieces of furniture in 1850, worth $1,500. Living with Mr. Barnes were Jerome Mozely and Jeremiah Learning, cabinetmakers. (C, MC)

91
BARNES, S. A. Cabinetmaker.
   Born c. 1817, North Carolina; w.
   1850, Spartanburg, Randolph Co.
   (C)

92
BARNETT, WILLIAM.
Cabinet and chair business.
   Born c. 1812, Kentucky; w. 1850,
   Carroll County. Three men in
   shop; in 1850 they made "30
   Bureaus $850; 100 Tables $450;
   50 Bedsteads $250; 200 Chairs
   $250." (C, MC)

93
BARNHART, MAHLON.
Chairmaker.
   Born c. 1825, Ohio; w. 1850,
   Franklin Twp., Montgomery Co.
   (C)

94
BARNHART, SOLOMON.
Cabinetmaker.
   Born c. 1794, Maryland; w. 1850,
   Franklin Twp., Montgomery Co.
   (C)

95
BARNITT, GEORGE.
Cabinetmaker.
   Born c. 1826, Indiana; w. 1850,
   Petersburg, Pike Co. (C)

96
BARRICK, M. Cabinetmaker.
   Born c. 1796, Virginia; w. 1850,
   Lafayette, Tippecanoe Co. (C)

97
BARTLETT, CHARLES.
Apprentice cabinetmaker.
   Born c. 1832; w. 1850, Logan
Twp., Fountain Co. Apprenticed
to Marmaduke Jennings, cabinet-
maker, q.v. (C)

98
BARTLETT, OTIS. Cabinetmaker.
   Born c. 1805, Canada; w. 1850,
   Newville Twp., De Kalb Co. (C)

99
BARTLEY, DANIEL E.
Cabinetmaker.
   Born c. 1810, Connecticut; w.
   1850, Harrison Twp., Bartholo-
   mew Co. (C)

100
BARTLOW, WILLIAM H.
Cabinetmaker.
   Born c. 1814, Indiana; w. 1850,
   Springfield Twp., Franklin Co.
   (C)

101
BASS, BLAKE. Cabinetmaker.
   Born c. 1827; w. 1850, Moores-
   ville, Morgan Co. (C)

102
BASSETT, STEPHEN.
Cabinetmaker.
   Born c. 1818, Indiana; w. 1850,
   Kent, Jefferson Co. (C)

103
BATES, JACOB L. Cabinetmaker.
   Born c. 1817, Pennsylvania; w.
   1850, Jackson Twp., Kosciusko Co.
   (C)

104
BATHEL, ELI. Cabinetmaker.
   Born c. 1832, Ohio; w. 1850, Tip-
   pecanoe Twp., Kosciusko Co.
   Lived with Andrew Nichols,
   cabinetmaker. (C)

105
BATMAN, JOHN C.
Cabinetmaker.
   Born c. 1823, Kentucky; w. 1850,
   Franklin Twp., Putnam Co. (C)

106
BATTERTON, GEORGE W.
Cabinetmaker.
   Born c. 1804, Kentucky; w. 1850,
   Bloomington, Monroe Co. Two
   men in shop; in 1850 they made
   160 pieces of furniture valued at
   $1,000. In same household, Jno.
   Cherry and Christopher M. Mc-
   Callie, cabinetmakers. (C, MC)
   See also BETTERTON, C. W.,
   probably same.

107
BATTERTON, PETER.
Cabinetmaker.
   W. -1824-, Bloomington, Monroe
   Co. Adv. in *Indiana Gazette*, 23
   December 1824: "PETER BAT-
   TERTON, Respectfully informs
   the public, that he still continues
   to occupy his old stand, at the
   corner of main south and east
   streets in Bloomington, as a
   CABINET SHOP. . . . N.B.
   one or two young men of moral
   characters & of industrious habits
   will be taken as apprentices to
   the Cabinet business."

108
BAUGHMAN, IRA J.
Cabinetmaker.
   Born c. 1816, Pennsylvania; w.
   1850, Frankfort, Clinton Co. (C)

109
BAUM, ENOS. Cabinetmaker.
   Born c. 1819, Pennsylvania; w.
   1850, Pleasant Twp., Steuben Co.
   (C)

110
BAXTER, WILLIAM G.
Chairmaker.
   Born c. 1816, Ohio; w. 1850,
   Jackson Twp., Hancock Co. (C)

111
BAYLEY, PALMAN.
Fancy chairmaker.
   Born c. 1821, Illinois; w. 1850,
   Vernon Twp., Jennings Co. (C)

112
BAYLISS, WILLIAM H.
Cabinetmaker.
   Born c. 1811, Kentucky; w. 1850,
   Carter Twp., Spencer Co. (C)

113
BAYLY, C. P. Chairmaker.
   Born c. 1824, Indiana; w. 1850,
   Vernon Twp., Jennings Co. (C)

114
BEALE, JOSHUA. Cabinetmaker.
   Born c. 1819, Pennsylvania; w.
   1850, Peru, Miami Co. (C)

115
BEAM, ADAM. Cabinetmaker.
   Born c. 1812, Bedford Co., Penn-
   sylvania; w. 1850, New Castle,
   Henry Co. In same household,
   two apprentice cabinetmakers,
   Henry Armfield and Jefferson
   Rader. (C) *See also* BRENE-
   MAN & BEAM.

116
BEAM, DAVID. Cabinetmaker;
lumberyard owner.

W. -1832- , Indianapolis, Marion
Co. Six chairs known; ash candle
stand illustrated in *Indianapolis
Star* 28 January 1940, has baluster
stem and three cabriole legs. Day
bed, cherry, illustrated *ibid.*, 7
April 1940, has four arrow-shaped
spindles in back rest.

117
BEARD, THOMAS. Chairmaker.
Born c. 1830, Ohio; w. 1850,
Taylor Twp., Howard Co. (C)

118
BEATTY, WILLIAM.
Cabinetmaker and chairmaker.
Born c. 1815, Ohio; w. 1850,
Oswego, Kosciusko Co. Two men
in shop, using horse power to
produce annually "Bureaus, Tables
Chairs worth $1,000." (C, MC)

119
BEATY, ANDREW R.
Cabinetmaker.
Born c. 1832, Illinois; w. 1850,
Vienna, Scott Co. (C)

120
BEATY, SAMUEL. Cabinetmaker.
Born c. 1805, Kentucky; w. 1850,
Vienna, Scott Co. In same house-
hold, Andrew R. Beaty, cabinet-
maker. (C)

121
BEATY, WILLIAM J.
Cabinetmaker.
Born c. 1828, Kentucky; w. 1850,
Vienna, Scott Co. (C)

122
BEAVER, JACOB [Sr.].
Cabinetmaker.
Born c. 1788, Virginia; w. 1850,

Clay Twp., Miami Co. In same
household, cabinetmakers Lewis,
Jacob [Jr.], and Peter Beaver.
(C)

123
BEAVER, JACOB [Jr.].
Cabinetmaker.
Born c. 1832, Virginia; w. 1850,
Clay Twp., Miami Co. Lived with
Jacob Beaver [Sr.], cabinet-
maker. (C)

124
BEAVER, LEWIS. Cabinetmaker.
Born c. 1829, Virginia; w. 1850,
Clay Twp., Miami Co. Lived with
Jacob Beaver [Sr.], cabinet-
maker. (C)

125
BEAVER, PETER. Cabinetmaker.
Born c. 1835, Indiana; w. 1850,
Clay Twp., Miami Co. Lived with
Jacob Beaver [Sr.], cabinet-
maker. (C)

126
BECKNER, S. H. Chairmaker.
W. -1839-, Lafayette, Tippecanoe
Co. Adv. in *Indiana Eagle* 2
January 1839, his "Windsor Chair-
Making Shop" on Ferry Street
between Ohio and Illinois streets.

127
BEEDY—*see* PAXSON
(PAXON) AND BEEDY.

128
BEKHART, HENRY.
Cabinetmaker.
Born c. 1814, Pennsylvania; w.
1850, Bluffton, Wells Co. Lived
with Thomas Bowden, cabinetmaker. (C)

129
BELL, GEORGE. Chairmaker.
Born c. 1835, Indiana; w. 1850,
Clark Twp., Montgomery Co.
Lived with Samuel N. Bell, chair-
maker. (C)

130
BELL, SAMUEL N. Chairmaker.
Born c. 1801, Virginia; w. 1850,
Clark Twp., Montgomery Co. In
same household, George Bell,
chairmaker. (C)

131
BELLHAMMER, JACOB.
Chairmaker.
Born c. 1818, Virginia; w. 1850,
Dalton Twp., Wayne Co. (C)

132
BELLHAMMER, SOLOMON.
Cabinetmaker.
Born c. 1827, Virginia; w. 1850,
Dalton Twp., Wayne Co. In
same household, Thomas Davis
and Henry Trussell, cabinet-
makers. (C)

133
BELMONT, JAMES B.
Cabinetmaker.
Born c. 1810, London, England;
w. -1844-1850-, Washington Twp.,
Decatur Co. In 1844 was a mem-
ber of the firm of Belmont &
Ricketts. In 1850 there were four
men working in his shop, making
300 pieces of furniture valued at
$2,000. (C, MC, CH 24)

134
BELMONT & RICKETTS.
Cabinetmakers.

James B. Belmont and ——
Ricketts; w. -1844-, Washington
Twp., Decatur Co. (CH 24)

135
BENDER, WILLIAM.
Cabinetmaker.
Born c. 1816, Pennsylvania; w.
1850, Otsego Twp., Steuben Co.
(C)

136
BENEDICT, SAMUEL GOOD-
RICH. Cabinetmaker.
W. -1833-1837-, Muncie area, Del-
aware Co.; Elizabethtown, Bar-
tholomew Co.; and Middletown,
Henry Co. Account book in
Indiana Historical Society Li-
brary. (*See above*, pp. 28-29.)

137
BENNER, ABSALOM.
Cabinetmaker.
Born c. 1827, Ohio; w. 1850, Clay
Twp., Miami Co. (C)

138
BENNETT, JAMES K.
Cabinetmaker.
Born c. 1806, Kentucky; w. 1850,
Franklin Twp., Johnson Co. (C)

139
BENTON, HENRY. Cabinetmaker.
Born c. 1786, Massachusetts; w.
1850, Brownstown Twp., Jackson
Co. (C)

140
BERRY, CHARLES E.
Cabinetmaker.
Born c. 1828, Virginia; w. 1850,
Parke Co. Lived with John B.
Innis, chairmaker. (C)

141
BERRY, PURNEL. Cabinetmaker.
Born c. 1805, Maryland; w. 1850,
Posey Twp., Fayette Co. (C)

141a
BEST, DAVID—*see* EVANS,
CALVIN J.

142
BETTERTON, C. W.—*see* BET-
TERTON & DORSEY.

143
BETTERTON & DORSEY.
Cabinetmakers.
C. W. Betterton and C. A.
Dorsey; w. 1840-, New Albany,
Floyd Co. Adv. in *New-Albany
Argus* 2 January 1840: "C. W.
BETTERTON & C.A. DORSEY
Have associated themselves togeth-
er, and will carry on the *CABI-
NET BUSINESS* at the old
stand of *Devoe & Betterton* in
this city. They are prepared to
execute any order in their line in
the neatest and speediest manner.
The WARE ROOM is well
furnished with most articles in
their line . . . ." (*See also*
BATTERTON, GEORGE W.,
possibly same.)

144
BIER, ERNST. Cabinetmaker.
Born c. 1802, Germany; w. 1850,
Ray Twp., Franklin Co. (C)

145
BIERDS, JAMES. Cabinetmaker.
Born c. 1823, Virginia; w. 1850,
Lawrence Twp., Marion Co. (C)

146
BISHOP, DAVID M.
Cabinetmaker.
Born c. 1823, Indiana; w. 1850,
Knox Co. (C)

147
BISHOP, JAMES. Chairmaker.
Born c. 1826, Kentucky; w. 1850,
Greencastle, Putnam Co. (C)

148
BIXLER, DAVID. Cabinetmaker.
Born c. 1830, Ohio; w. 1850, Van
Buren Twp., Shelby Co. Lived
with George Bixler, cabinetmaker.
(C)

149
BIXLER, GEORGE.
Cabinetmaker.
Born c. 1794, Pennsylvania; w.
1850, Van Buren Twp., Shelby
Co. In same household, also
cabinetmakers, Levi Bixler and
David Bixler. (C)

150
BIXLER, LEVI. Cabinetmaker.
Born c. 1828, Ohio; w. 1850, Van
Buren Twp., Shelby Co. Lived
with George Bixler, cabinetmaker.
(C)

151
BLACK, ALFRED. Chairmaker.
Born c. 1820, Tennessee; w. 1850,
Washington Twp., Greene Co.
(C)

152
BLACK, ELISHA. Chairmaker.
Born c. 1826, Tennessee; w. 1850,
Greene Co. (C)

153
BLACK, PETER S. Chairmaker.
Born c. 1824, Tennessee; w. 1850,
Washington Twp., Greene Co.
(C)

154
BLACK, ROBERT. Cabinetmaker.
Born c. 1818, Kentucky; w. 1850,
Jennings Twp., Scott Co. (C)

155
BLACKBURN, JOHN.
Cabinetmaker.
Born c. 1794, England; w. 1850,
Whitewater Twp., Franklin Co.
(C)

156
BLACKBURN, THOMAS.
Chairmaker.
Born c. 1827, Virginia; w. 1850,
Union Twp., Montgomery Co.
(C)

157
BLACKLEY, CYRUS.
Cabinetmaker.
Born c. 1826, Virginia; w. 1850,
Emmettsville, Randolph Co. (C)

158
BLACKWELL, EZEKIEL.
Cabinetmaker.
Born c. 1787, Kentucky; w. 1850,
Shawswick Twp., Lawrence Co.
(C)

158a
BLAIN, WILLIAM. Chairmaker.
W. -1836-, Richmond, Wayne Co.
Adv. in the *Palladium*, 4 June
1836: "The partnership heretofore
existing under the firm of [James
T.] Layman & Blain is this day

dissolved by mutual consent. . . ."
"The Chair-making will be continued by WILLIAM BLAIN
who respectfully solicits public
patronage."

159
BLAIR, F. J. Cabinetmaker.
Born c. 1831, Maryland; w. 1850,
Muncie, Delaware Co. Lived with
John H. Jamison, cabinetmaker,
q.v. (C)

160
BLAN, JAMES. Cabinetmaker.
Born c. 1825, Indiana; w. 1850,
Franklin Twp., Hendricks Co.
(C)

161
BLAN, MINER. Cabinetmaker.
Born c. 1821, Kentucky; w. 1850,
Franklin Twp., Hendricks Co.
(C)

162
BLESS, GEORGE. Cabinetmaker.
Born c. 1808, Pennsylvania; w.
1850, Liberty Twp., Shelbv Co.
(C)

163
BLYTHE, ROBERT.
Cabinetmaker.
Born c. 1812, Pennsylvania; w.
1850, Brown Twp., Washington
Co. (C)

164
BOBLETT, ISAAC. Cabinetmaker.
Born c. 1806, Virginia; w. 1850,
Rush Co. Two men in shop, mak-
ing furniture and miscellaneous
items worth $500 annually. (C,
MC)

165
BOESE, HENRY (?).
Cabinetmaker.
   Born c. 1812, Germany; w. 1850,
   Lawrenceburg, Dearborn Co. (C)

166
BOGUE, HENRY. Cabinetmaker.
   Born c. 1827, Ohio; w. 1850,
   Posey Twp., Rush Co. (C)

167
BOICOURT, SAMUEL (Rev.).
Cabinetmaker and turner.
   W. 1817-, Princeton, Gibson Co.
   Had a cabinet shop and also made
   spinning wheels. (CH 47) See
   Plate XI.

168
BOLANDER, WILLIAM.
Chairmaker.
   Born c. 1810, Pennsylvania; w.
   1850, Centerville, Wayne Co. (C)

169
BOLDINGER, ALFRED.
Cabinetmaker.
   Born c. 1834, Ohio; w. 1850,
   Brownsville Twp., Union Co.
   Lived with Xavier Boldinger,
   cabinetmaker. (C)

170
BOLDINGER, XAVIER (or
HAVIER). Cabinetmaker.
   Born c. 1811, Switzerland; w.
   1850, Brownsville Twp., Union
   Co. In same household, Alfred
   Boldinger, cabinetmaker. Two
   men working in shop in 1850
   made furniture valued at $1,000.
   (C, MC)

171
BOLEBY, JOHN. Cabinetmaker.
   Born c. 1812, New Jersey; w.
   1850, Brookville, Franklin Co.
   (C)

172
BOLLON, THOMAS—see BOW-
LAND, THOMAS.

173
BOND—see WILSON & BOND.

174
BONEBRAKE, ISAAC.
Cabinetmaker.
   Born c. 1818, Ohio; w. 1850, Van
   Buren Twp., Fountain Co. (C)

175
BONSAL, VINCENT P.
Cabinetmaker.
   Born c. 1825, Delaware; w. 1850,
   Parke Co. Lived with Jacob W.
   Striker, cabinetmaker. B e g a n
   work with Reuben Kendall (q.v.).
   Later had an extensive shop of
   his own. (C, CH 48)

176
BOON, JOHN [Sr.]. Chairmaker.
   Born c. 1798, North Carolina;
   w. 1850, Washington Twp.,
   Hamilton Co. In same household,
   John Boon [Jr.], cabinetmaker.
   (C)

177
BOON, JOHN [Jr.].
Cabinetmaker.
   Born c. 1829, Indiana; w. 1850,
   Washington Twp., Hamilton Co.
   Lived with John Boon [Sr.],
   cabinetmaker. (C)

178
BOONE, JOEL M. Cabinetmaker.
Born c. 1792, North Carolina; w.
1850, Hendricks Twp., Shelby Co.
(C)

179
BORLAND, ANDREW.
Cabinetmaker.
Born c. 1834, Indiana; w. 1850,
Shawswick Twp., Lawrence Co.
Lived with Matthew Borland,
cabinetmaker. (C)

180
BORLAND, MATTHEW.
Cabinetmaker.
Born c. 1794, Pennsylvania; w.
1850, Shawswick Twp., Lawrence
Co. In same household, Andrew
Borland, cabinetmaker. (C)

181
BORLAND, WALTER.
Cabinetmaker.
Born c. 1832, Indiana; w. 1850,
Shawswick Twp., Lawrence Co.
Lived with John B. Buskirk,
cabinetmaker. (C)

182
BOUSE, PETER. Cabinetmaker.
Born c. 1822, Pennsylvania; w.
1850, Concord Twp., Elkhart Co.
(C)

183
BOVINE, DAVID. Cabinetmaker.
Born c. 1819, Switzerland; w.
1850, Harrison Twp., Wells Co.
In same household, cabinetmakers
Henry Schafter, Paul I. Schafter,
and Jacob Entzle. (C)

184
BOWDEN, THOMAS.
Cabinetmaker.
Born c. 1816, England; w. 1850,
Bluffton, Wells Co. In same
household, Henry Bekhart, cabi-
netmaker. (C)

185
BOWEN, ABRAM. Cabinetmaker.
Born c. 1830, Ohio; w. 1850,
Ripley Twp., Rush Co. (C)

186
BOWEN, HUGH. Cabinetmaker.
Born c. 1814, Pennsylvania; w.
1850, Newcastle Twp., Fulton Co.
(C)

187
BOWEN, JAMES W.
Cabinetmaker.
Born c. 1823, Kentucky; w. 1850,
Haddon Twp., Sullivan Co. Lived
with Hosea Buckley, cabinet-
maker. (C)

188
BOWEN, JONATHAN.
Cabinetmaker.
Born c. 1828, Ohio; w. 1850,
Bloomfield Twp., La Grange Co.
(C)

189
BOWERS, GEORGE W.
Cabinetmaker.
Born c. 1818, Ohio; w. 1850, Bear
Creek Twp., Jay Co. (C)

190
BOWLAND (BOLLON),
THOMAS. Cabinetmaker.
Born c. 1811, Indiana; w. 1850,
Montgomery Twp., Jennings Co.
Two men were employed in his
shop making bureaus and bed-
steads valued at $1,000. (C, MC)

191
BOWMAN, DANIEL.
Cabinetmaker.
  Born c. 1814, Pennsylvania; w.
  1850, Jefferson Twp., Noble Co.
  (C)

192
BOWMAN, HENRY J.
Cabinetmaker.
  Born c. 1826, Ohio; w. 1850,
  Knox Twp., Jay Co. (C)

193
BOWMAN, JOHN. Chairmaker.
  Born c. 1796, Pennsylvania; w.
  1850, Richland Twp., Miami Co.
  (C)

194
BOYD, A[BRAHAM?].
Cabinetmaker.
  W. 1839, Mt. Carmel, Franklin
  Co. Adv. in Brookville *Indiana
  American* 6 September 1839,
  "CABINET WAREROOMS . . .
  at Mt. Carmel . . . on hand a
  general assortment of *TABLES,
  BUREAUS, WORK-STANDS
  AND BEDSTEADS. . . .*"

195
BOYD, ELIAS D. Cabinetmaker.
  Born c. 1827, Ohio; w. 1850,
  Vermillion Twp., Vermillion Co.
  (C)

196
BOYD, JAMES P. Cabinetmaker.
  Born c. 1811, District of
  Columbia; w. 1850, La Porte, La
  Porte County. (C)

197
BOYER, JOHN. Cabinetmaker.
  Born c. 1821, Pennsylvania; w.
  1850, Washington Twp., Elkhart
  Co. (C)

198
BOYER, JOSEPH. Cabinetmaker
and chairmaker.
  Born c. 1826, France; w. 1850,
  Noble Twp., Wabash Co. (C)

199
BRACKNEY, JOHN. Chairmaker.
  Born c. 1826, Ohio; w. 1850,
  Carroll Co. (C)

200
BRADFIELD, JAMES M.
Cabinetmaker.
  Born c. 1819, Virginia; w. 1850,
  Liberty Twp., Wabash Co. (C)

201
BRANSON, DAVID—
see SHELTON, SYLVESTER R.,
& DAVID BRANSON.

202
BRANSON, OWEN.
Cabinetmaker.
  Born c. 1825, Indiana; w. 1850,
  Waltz Twp., Wabash Co. Two
  men working in shop, annually
  making furniture worth $700. (C,
  MC)

203
BRASHER, JESSE. Chairmaker.
  Born c. 1778, North Carolina;
  w. 1850, Eel River Twp., Greene
  Co. (C)

204
BRASKET, ISAAC. Chairmaker.
  Born c. 1792, Virginia; w. 1850,
  Independence, Warren Co. (C)

205
BRATTEN, GEORGE.
Chairmaker.
  Born c. 1829, Indiana; w. 1850,

New Albany, Floyd Co. Lived with George W. Porter, cabinetmaker. (C)

206
BRATTON, JAMES.
Cabinetmaker.
Born c. 1817, Kentucky; w. 1850, Wayne Twp., Montgomery Co. (C)

207
BRAULSFORT, ALLEN.
Chairmaker.
Born c. 1831, Ohio; w. 1850, Carroll Co. Lived with John Tutwiler, chairmaker, q.v. (C)

208
BRAZELTON, CHARLES.
Cabinetmaker.
Born c. 1824, Indiana; w. 1850, Princeton, Gibson Co. (C)

209
BRAZINGTON, JOSEPH.
Cabinetmaker.
Born c. 1826, North Carolina; w. 1849, Jackson Twp., Miami Co.; w. 1850, Rush Co. (CH 30, C)

210
BRENEMAN, JACOB.
Cabinetmaker.
Born c. 1810, Westmoreland Co., Pennsylvania; c. 1832, moved to Indiana; 1835, established a log shop in New Castle, Henry Co. After a few years moved his shop to Broadway in New Castle. Later joined Adam Beam to form firm of Breneman & Beam, q.v. Still in business in 1850.
Furniture known: footstool, 18" square at top; table with "two empire curved feet and the third one a heavy six-inch ball turned

from solid mahogany"; a cabinet with "R B" carved in the door; a rocking chair with splat back. (C; *Indianapolis Star,* 29 December 1940; 29 September 1940; 8 December 1940).

211
BRENEMAN & BEAM.
Cabinetmakers.
Jacob Breneman and Adam Beam; w. 1850, New Castle, Henry Co. Seven men worked in shop; in 1850 they produced cabinet ware worth $2,000. George Alspaugh became a member of this firm, and with Hugh Mullin later formed the New Castle Furniture Association. Lyre-pedestal square table, c. 1840, illustrated in *Indianapolis Star,* 7 July 1940. (C, MC)

212
BRICE, HENRY. Cabinetmaker.
Born c. 1823, Ohio; w. 1850, Peru, Miami Co. (C)

213
BRIGGS, A., & Co. Bedstead manufacturers.
W. -1850-, Harrison Twp., Dearborn Co. Ten men employed, using steam power to make annually 4,500 bedsteads worth $13,500. (MC)

214
BRIM, ELMORE. Chairmaker.
Born c. 1834, Indiana; w. 1850, Harrison Twp., Vigo Co. Lived with Henry Jamison, chairmaker. (C)

215
BRIMM, JEFFERSON.
Chairmaker.

Born c. 1832, Indiana; w. 1850, Harrison Twp., Vigo Co. Lived with Henry Buckingham. (C)

216.
BRINDLEY, JOHN.
Cabinetmaker.
Born c. 1823, Indiana; w. 1850, New Albany, Floyd Co. In same household, William Danner and Earnest Prally, cabinetmakers. (C)

217
BRINER, JOHN. Cabinetmaker.
Born c. 1822, Ohio; w. 1850, Van Buren Twp., Fountain Co. In same household, William Briner, cabinetmaker. (C)

218
BRINER, WILLIAM.
Cabinetmaker.
Born c. 1829, Indiana; w. 1850, Van Buren Twp., Fountain Co. Lived with John Briner, cabinetmaker. (C)

219
BRITTS, GEORGE. Cabinet shop. W. 1833-, Montgomery Co. In partnership with a Mr. Dodd. (CH 31)

220
BRITZ, WILLIAM.
Cabinetmaker.
Born c. 1816, Germany; w. 1850, Bainbridge Twp., Dubois Co. (C)

221
BRODRICK, CHARLES S.
Cabinetmaker.
Born c. 1821, Ohio; w. 1850, Concord Twp., Elkhart Co. (C)

222
BRODRICK, MARK A.
Cabinetmaker.
Born c. 1810, Ohio; w. 1850, Concord Twp., Elkhart Co. (C)

223
BROHM, PETER. Cabinetmaker.
Born c. 1796, Stuttgart, Germany; w. 1850, Madison, Jefferson Co. (C)

224
BROIL, CHARLES B.
Cabinetmaker.
Born c. 1820, Pennsylvania; w. 1850, Franklin Twp., Owen Co. (C)

225
BROOKVILLE CHAIR MANU-FACTORY—see H A R T L E Y, WHEAT & CO.

226
BROOMBAUGH, EDWARD.
Cabinetmaker.
Born in Ohio; w. 1850, Concord Twp., Elkhart Co. Lived with Nathan Markle, cabinetmaker. (C)

227
BROWN, EDWARD.
Cabinetmaker.
Born c. 1812, Ohio; w. 1850, Parke Co. (C) See also HESS & BROWN.

228
BROWN, GEORGE—see HUMPHREY, LAWSON F.

229
BROWN, GEORGE W.
Cabinetmaker.
Born c. 1825, Indiana; w. 1850, Russell Twp., Putnam Co. (C)

230
BROWN, HENRY. Carpenter and cabinetmaker.
> W. -1834-, New Carlisle, St. Joseph Co. Built Augustine homestead in New Carlisle in 1834. (FWP)

231
BROWN, JAMES. Cabinetmaker.
> Born c. 1828, Indiana; w. 1850, Curry Twp., Sullivan Co. (C)

232
BROWN, JAMES S. Chairmaker.
> Born c. 1809, New York; w. 1850, Mishawaka, St. Joseph Co. (C)

233
BROWN, THOMPSON. Cabinetmaker.
> Born c. 1828, Indiana; w. 1850, Greencastle, Putnam Co. (C)

234
BROWN, WILLIAM. Cabinetmaker and joiner.
> W.-1836-1842-, Lawrenceburg, Dearborn Co. Adv. in *Indiana Palladium* 28 May 1836: "New Cabinet Shop! The undersigned has commenced the Above business on Short street, in a part of his Joiner shop, where he intends keeping constantly on hand a general assortment of the best kind of ware. Persons wishing to purchase will please call and examine for themselves.

> "He is also having erected a first rate horse power turning lathe, where he will be able to accommodate persons in that line on the shortest notice, and at Cincinnati prices. WILLIAM BROWN. N.B. Thirty five dollars per thousand in cash will be paid for a quantity of Cherry scantling 4½ and 5 in square."

> Listed as a "furniture businessman" in Lawrenceburg *Political Beacon* 11 December 1839.

> Adv. in the *Political Beacon* 4 June 1841: "SPLENDID FURNITURE . . . he still continues to keep his Ware-rooms filled with the best Furniture, consisting in part of *Side-Boards, Secretarys, Ward-Robes, Sophas, Dressing Bureaus,* Common and Fancy four and six Draw Bureaus, Centre tables, End tables, Card tables, Dressing tables, Work tables, Breakfast and Dining tables, Wash stands, Book cases, Cribs and Cradles, Looking Glasses of different sizes, a superior article, also common, French, Fancy and High Post Bedsteads, Cot Bedsteads, Common and Fancy Chairs, Children's Rocking Chairs, Settees of various sizes and patterns, &c. &c. In addition to the above, he will also keep constantly on hand and for sale, Window Sash, Wash Boards, Quilt Frames, Clothe Racks, Auger handles, Rolling Pins, Towel Rollers, and a superior article of Copal Varnish . . . ."

> Adv. in *Political Beacon*, 6 May 1842: "Wm. Brown, Manufacturer of Pattented Right and Left Wood Screw Round Rail Bedsteads."

235
BROWNLEY, JESSE S.
Cabinetmaker.
Born c. 1822, Pennsylvania; w.
1850, Posey Twp., Switzerland
Co. (C)

236
BRUDY (BRUDE), JOHN G.
Cabinetmaker.
Born c. 1825, Germany; w. 1850,
Decatur, Adams Co. (C)

237
BRUNER, JACOB.
Cabinetmaker.
Born c. 1820, Ohio; w. 1850,
Albion, Noble Co. (C, CH 12)

238
BUCHANAN, ALEXANDER.
Cabinetmaker.
Born c. 1818, Trumbull Co., Ohio;
served apprenticeship in Youngs-
town, Ohio; 1838, moved to Grant
Co., Indiana, then to Wabash Co.
W. 1840-1850, Marion, Grant Co.,
where he manufactured furniture
with David Norton as his partner.
This partnership lasted several
years. In 1850, two men working
in this shop made furniture worth
$1,000. Buchanan later opened the
first undertaking establishment in
Marion, while continuing to make
furniture. Business was later sold
to Samuel Whistler; the firm
was still in existence in 1902,
when it was known as Buchanan
and Son, undertakers, marble and
granite dealers. (C, MC, CH 45)

239
BUCKINGHAM, GARROT.
Cabinetmaker.

W. 1850, Carroll Co. Two men
in shop; in 1850 they made furniture worth $1,000. (MC)

240
BUCKINGHAM, HENRY.
Chairmaker.
Born c. 1814, Maryland; w. 1850,
Harrison Twp., Vigo Co. In same
household, Jefferson Brimm,
chairmaker. (C) *See also* JAMI-
SON & BUCKINGHAM.

241
BUCKLEY, HOSEA (HOSIA) C.
Cabinetmaker and turner.
Born c. 1823, Virginia; w. 1850,
Haddon Twp., Sullivan Co. His
shop had four men working, using
"Dogs for turning," and making
miscellaneous products w o r t h
$1,300 annually. In same house-
hold, James W. Bowen, cabinet-
maker. (C, MC)

242
BUCKLEY, SMITH M.
Cabinetmaker.
Born c. 1795, Virginia; w. 1850,
Haddon Twp., Sullivan Co. In
same household, Andrew Curry,
cabinetmaker. (C)

243
BUDLETT, ROBERT F.
Cabinetmaker.
Born c. 1824, New York; w. 1850,
New Albany, Floyd Co. Lived
with S. H. Wills, cabinetmaker.
(C)

244
BUESS, ELIAS. Cabinetmaker.
Born c. 1816, Virginia; w. 1850,
Franklin Twp., Wayne Co. (C)

245
BULLOCK, WILLIAM.
Chairmaker.
  W. -1839-, Lafayette, Tippecanoe
  Co. Adv. in *Indiana Eagle*, 13
  February 1839: *"CHAIR &*
  SPINNING WHEEL MANU-
  FACTORY. . . . will keep con-
  stantly on hand, a supply of Cane,
  Slat-back, and Common Chairs,
  Settees and Sociables, finished
  with gold and bronze, in the best
  manner." Had taken over the shop
  formerly occupied by D. Rhein,
  cabinetmaker. Also offered to do
  house and sign painting, paper
  hanging, and gilding. *See also*
  RHEIN (RHINE), DAN.

246
BUMIN (or BURMIN), LYMAN.
Cabinetmaker.
  Born c. 1815, New York; **w.**
  1850, Lafayette, Tippecanoe Co.
  (C)

247
BUNKER, CHARLES D.
Cabinetmaker.
  Born c. 1818, Ohio; w. 1850,
  Ripley Twp., Montgomery Co.
  (C)

248
BURCH, BERNARD Z.
Cabinetmaker.
  Born c. 1818, Ohio; w. 1850,
  Logansport, Cass Co. Worked
  with Israel Neal. (C) *See also*
  NEAL & BURCH.

249
BURGE, JOHN. Cabinetmaker.
  Born c. 1805, Kentucky; w. 1850,
  Stockton Twp., Greene Co. (C)

250
BURGER, GEORGE H.
Cabinetmaker.
  Born c. 1831, New York; w.
  1850, Danville, Hendricks Co.
  (C)

251
BURGESS, JOB D. Chairmaker.
  Born c. 1823, Ohio; w. 1850,
  Laughery Twp., Ripley Co. (C)

252
BURK, JOHN. Cabinetmaker.
  Born c. 1824, Kentucky; w. 1850,
  Greensburg, Decatur Co. (C)

253
BURK, RICHARD. Cabinetmaker.
  W. -1841-, Richmond, Wayne Co.
  Adv. in *Richmond Palladium* 23
  October 1841: "The undersigned
  having purchased of Stephen Duncan his CABINET ESTAB-
  LISHMENT, and having purchased a quantity of the best
  materials, he is now prepared to
  furnish work of every description
  in the line of CABINET FUR-
  NITURE, at prices suited to the
  times, and on accommodating
  terms. He keeps a good assortment of Tables, Bureaus, Stands,
  &c. on hand. He also keeps on
  hand first rate WHEAT FANS,
  of the best of seasoned lumber
  and good workmanship."

254
BURKART, D. Cabinetmaker.
  Born c. 1828, Indiana; w. 1850,
  Gosport, Owen Co. (C)

255
BURKETT, BENJAMIN.
Chairmaker.

Born c. 1828, Indiana; w. 1850, Franklin Twp., Kosciusko Co. (C)

256
BURLEY—see CALLY & BURLEY.

257
BURNS, JOHN. Chairmaker.
W. -1829-, Marion Co. Child's rocking chair made by him is in the collections of the Children's Museum of Indianapolis. (See Plate XII.)

258
BURNWOOD, JOSEPH.
Cabinetmaker.
Born c. 1811, Pennsylvania; w. 1850, Noble Twp., Wabash Co. (C)

259
BURROWS, WILLIAM F.
Chairmaker.
Born c. 1805, Virginia; w. 1850, St. Omer, Decatur Co. (C)

260
BURT, ALONZO. Cabinetmaker.
Born c. 1815, New York; w. 1850, Laurel Twp., Franklin Co. (C)

261
BUSHAM, MORRIS.
Cabinetmaker.
Born c. 1824, Vermont; w. 1850, Mill Grove Twp., Steuben Co. (C)

262
BUSKIRK—see HOUSTON & BUSKIRK.

263
BUSKIRK, JAMES W.
Cabinetmaker.
Born c. 1826, Indiana; w. 1850, Pierson Twp., Vigo Co. (C)

264
BUSKIRK, JOHN B.
Cabinetmaker.
Born c. 1816, Kentucky; w. 1850, Shawswick Twp., Lawrence Co. In same household, Walter Borland and Fountain C. Crump, cabinetmakers. (C) See also HOUSTON & BUSKIRK.

265
BUSKIRK, PETER Y.
Cabinetmaker.
Born c. 1822, Indiana; w. 1850, Pierson Twp., Vigo Co. (C)

266
BUTCHER, DANIEL.
Cabinetmaker.
Born c. 1826, Indiana; w. 1850, Clear Creek Twp., Monroe Co. (C)

267
BUTLER, JAMES E.
Cabinetmaker.
Born c. 1821, Virginia; w. 1850, Lewisville, Henry Co. (C) See also BUTLER & POLK.

268
BUTLER, JOSEPH.
Cabinetmaker.
Born c. 1825, Virginia; w. 1850, Greensboro Twp., Henry Co. In same household, Lindsay Freeman, cabinetmaker. (C)

269
BUTLER & POLK (POLKE).
Cabinetmakers and chairmakers.

James E. Butler and James W. Polk; w. 1850, Lewisville, Henry Co. Three men working in shop, using horse power. In 1850 their annual product was listed as 200 chairs worth $200; 70 bureaus and tables $495; and other articles worth $50. (C, MC)

270
BUZZARD, SOLOMON.
Cabinetmaker.
> Born c. 1824, Ohio; w. 1850, Carroll Co. (C)

271
BYBEE, WILLIAM.
Cabinetmaker.
> Born c. 1820, Kentucky; came to Belle Union and then to Mount Meridian, Putnam Co. W. -1850-, Mt. Meridian. His father was also a cabinetmaker. Two chairs, one with three scalloped slats, made of hickory, illustrated in *Indianapolis Star* 16 February 1941. (C)

272
BYRAM, T. B. Cabinetmaker.
> Born c. 1813, Ohio; w. 1850, Boone Twp., Warrick Co. (C)

273
CADWELL, JOHN. Chairmaker.
> Born c. 1824, Ireland; w. 1850, Mishawaka, St. Joseph Co. Lived with Seth Clark, chairmaker. (C)

274
CALDRAM, WILLIAM—*see* COLDRAM, WILLIAM.

275
CALDWELL, B. W. S.
Cabinetmaker.
> Born c. 1808, Pennsylvania; w. 1850, Rush Co. Two men worked in the shop; in 1850 they made "furniture & miscellaneous" worth $700. (C, MC)

276
CALDWELL, JAMES G. [Sr.].
Chair manufactory.
> Born c. 1810, Pennsylvania; w. 1850, Jeffersonville, Clark Co. Four men working in shop; their raw materials are listed as "turned lumber" and paint. They made 100 dozen chairs in 1850, valued at $1,700. In the same household were James G. Caldwell [Jr.], chairmaker, and William Caldwell, ornamental painter. James G. Caldwell, Sr., was listed as an ornamental painter by trade. (C, MC)

277
CALDWELL, JAMES G. [Jr].
Chairmaker.
> Born c. 1832, Ohio; w. 1850, Jeffersonville, Clark Co. (C) *See also* CALDWELL, JAMES G. [Sr.].

278
CALDWELL, WILLIAM.
Ornamental painter.
> Born c. 1834, Ohio; w. 1850, Jeffersonville, Clark Co. (C) *See* CALDWELL, JAMES G. [Sr.].

279
CALLOWAY, WILLIAM.
Cabinetmaker.
> Born 1832, Indiana; w. 1850, Harrison Twp., Fayette Co. Lived with Henry Meldrum, cabinet maker. (C)

280
CALLUMBER, JNO.
Cabinetmaker.
Born c. 1824, Virginia; w. 1850,
Rush Co. (C)

281
CALLY & BURLEY.
Cabinetmakers.
W. 1850, Madison Co. Five men
in shop made furniture worth
$2,000 in 1850. (MC) *See* COL-
LIS, ARSEMUS, possibly same.

282
CAMERON, JAMES.
Cabinetmaker.
W. -1835-, Rockville, Parke Co.
Adv. in *Rockville Intelligencer,*
18 July 1835, that he operated a
cabinet business and would provide "FASHIONABLE FURNI-
TURE, which he will sell for
cash, plank, scantling, or on a
liberal *credit . . . .*"

283
CANON, JOHN W.
Cabinetmaker.
Born c. 1820, Pennsylvania; w.
1850-1860, Vincennes, Knox Co.
Four men in shop; their annual
product was listed as "50 Bed-
steads $250; 30 Bureaus $600; 50
Tables $195; 30 Coffins $300;
Sundrys $900." (C, MC, CH 20)

284
CAP, ALBERT. Chairmaker.
Born c. 1815, Canada; w. 1850,
Mishawaka, St. Joseph Co. In
same household, Henry Sherman,
apprentice. (C)

285
CAPP, WILLIAM. Cabinetmaker.
Born c. 1834, Indiana; w. 1850,
Shelbyville, Shelby Co. (C)

286
CARLIN, WILLIAM D.
Cabinetmaker.
Born c. 1814, Pennsylvania; w.
1850, Noblesville, Hamilton Co.
(C)

287
CAROL, GEORGE. Cabinetmaker.
Born c. 1822, Pennsylvania; w.
1850, Wayne Twp., Allen Co. In
same household, Lucien Barber,
cabinetmaker. (C)

288
CARPENTER, ISRAEL.
Cabinetmaker.
Born c. 1825, Indiana; w. 1850,
Posey Twp., Franklin Co. (C)

289
CARPENTER, JOHN.
Cabinetmaker.
Born c. 1821, Indiana; w. 1850,
Washington Twp., Shelby Co.
Three men worked in his shop,
making 300 bedsteads worth $200
and other articles worth $400 in
1850. (C, MC)

290
CARR, JOHN E. Cabinetmaker.
Born c. 1817, Ohio; w. 1850,
Harrison Twp., Fayette Co. (C)

291
CARR, SAMUEL. Cabinetmaker.
Born c. 1822, Indiana; w. 1850,
Jefferson Twp., Henry Co. (C)

292
CARRUTHERS, GEORGE.
Cabinetmaker.

Born c. 1827, Virginia; w. 1850, Shelby Co. Three men worked in this shop; in 1850 they made bedsteads and bureaus worth $1,500. In the same household, James Morris and William Chambers, cabinetmakers. (C, MC)

293
CARSON, ANDREW.
Chairmaker.
Born c. 1827, Ohio; w. 1850, Boone Co. (C)

294
CARSON, ELI. Chairmaker.
Born c. 1826, Ohio; w. 1850, Frankfort, Clinton Co. Lived with Madison Carson, chairmaker. (C)

295
CARSON, ENOS. Chairmaker.
Born c. 1824, Ohio; w. 1850, Boone Co. (C)

296
CARSON, HUSTON. Chairmaker.
Born c. 1822, Ohio; w. 1850, Franklin Twp., Montgomery Co. (C)

297
CARSON, JAMES. Chairmaker.
Born c. 1783, Tennessee; w. 1850, Boone Co. (C)

298
CARSON, JAMES S.
Chairmaker.
Born c. 1819, Ohio; w. 1850, Union Twp., Montgomery Co. Three men working in shop, using machinery powered by horse; raw materials included hickory and oak. Their product was given as "1500 Springback Chairs $1000." (C, MC)

299
CARSON, LEANDER.
Chairmaker.
Born c. 1819, Ohio; w. 1850, Gillam Twp., Jasper Co. (C)

300
CARSON, MADISON.
Chairmaker.
Born c. 1821, North Carolina; w. 1850, Frankfort, Clinton Co. In same household, Eli Carson, chairmaker. (C)

301
CARSON, ROBERT H.
Chairmaker.
Born c. 1811, Tennessee; w. 1850, Boone Co. (C)

302
CARTER, WILLIAM.
Cabinetmaker.
Born c. 1825, Kentucky; w. 1850, Harrison Co. (C)

303
CASHOTT, THOMAS.
Chairmaker.
Born c. 1831, Ireland; w. 1850, Lafayette, Tippecanoe Co. (C)

304
CASSADAY, WILLIAM.
Cabinetmaker.
Born c. 1812, New Jersey; w. 1850, Olive Twp., St. Joseph Co. (C)

305
CASSNER, JOHN. Cabinetmaker.
Born c. 1832, Ohio; w. 1850, Greens Fork Twp., Randolph Co. (C)

306
CASTATOR, ELIJAH.
Cabinetmaker.
Born c. 1812, Pennsylvania; w. 1850, Hagerstown, Wayne Co. In same household, Andrew I. Lucus, cabinetmaker. (C)

307
CHALLUS (CHALICE), EBEN-EZER. Farmer, carpenter, and cabinetmaker.
Born 1808, New York; settled on a farm about a mile northwest of Roseville, Parke Co., in 1830. Made several kinds of furniture. A chest made by him is known. Also made coffins; family has book listing persons for whom he made them; his own name is listed at the end. (C, CH 10)

308
CHAMBERS, JAMES.
Cabinetmaker.
Born c. 1812, Kentucky; w. 1850, Bean Blossom Twp., Monroe Co. In same household, William Chambers, cabinetmaker. (C)

309
CHAMBERS, JESSE. Chairmaker.
Born c. 1807, Virginia; w. 1850, Washington Twp., Putnam Co. (C)

310
CHAMBERS, WILLIAM.
Cabinetmaker.
Born c. 1832, Kentucky; w. 1850, Charlestown Twp., Clark Co. Lived with John Stockwell, cabinetmaker. (C)

311
CHAMBERS, WILLIAM.
Cabinetmaker.
Born c. 1832, Indiana; w. 1850, Bean Blossom Twp., Monroe Co. Lived with James Chambers, cabinetmaker. (C)

312
CHAMBERS, WILLIAM.
Cabinetmaker.
Born c. 1832, Indiana; w. 1850, Shelbyville, Shelby Co. Lived with George Carruthers, cabinetmaker, q.v. (C)

313
CHAMNESS, JOHN.
Cabinetmaker.
Born c. 1826, Indiana; w. 1850, Dalton Twp., Wayne Co. (C)

314
CHAMNESS, OWEN. Cabinet shop.
W. 1850, east half, Hendricks Co. In 1850 he produced furniture worth $500. (MC)

315
CHAPIN, CHARLES C.
Chairmaker.
Born c. 1810, Virginia; w. 1850, North Madison, Jefferson Co. (C)

316
CHAPMAN, JOHN.
Cabinetmaker.
Born c. 1822, Kentucky; w. 1850, Eel River Twp., Hendricks Co. (C). See also CRAIG & CHAPMAN.

317
CHAPMAN, JOHN A.
Cabinetmaker.
Born c. 1822, Kentucky; w. 1850, west half, Hendricks Co. (C) Probably same man as above.

318
CHARLES, ABRAHAM.
Cabinetmaker.
Born c. 1833, Pennsylvania; w.
1850, Indianapolis, Marion Co.
Lived with William W. Weaver,
q.v. (C)

319
CHARLES, ELISHA F.
Cabinetmaker.
Born c. 1820, North Carolina;
w. 1850, Jackson Twp., Washington Co. Two men in shop, using
machinery powered by horse; in
1850 they produced furniture
worth $1,000. (C, MC)

320
CHARLES, JESSE. Chairmaker.
Born c. 1813, Indiana; w. 1850,
Wayne Twp., Henry Co. (C)

321
CHASE, CHESTER. Chairmaker.
Born c. 1829, New York; w.
1850, Benton Twp., Elkhart Co.
Lived with Sulivan Chase, chairmaker. (C)

322
CHASE, SULIVAN. Chairmaker.
Born c. 1800, Connecticut; w.
1850, Benton Twp., Elkhart Co.
In same household, Chester Chase,
chairmaker. (C)

323
CHERRY, JNO. Cabinetmaker.
Born c. 1823, South Carolina; w.
1850, Bloomington, Monroe Co.
Lived with George W. Batterton,
cabinetmaker. (C)

324
CHREVISTON, WILLIAM.
Cabinetmaker.

W. -1831-1832-, South Bend, St.
Joseph Co. Had shop opposite
Union Hall. Adv. in *Northwestern
Pioneer,* 1831 through 21 March
1832.

325
CHRISMAN, JAMES.
Cabinetmaker.
Born c. 1828, Virginia; w. 1850,
Middletown, Henry Co. (C)

326
CHRISTIAN, MARTIN.
Cabinetmaker.
Born c. 1827, Germany; w. 1850,
Lawrenceburg, Dearborn Co. (C)

327
CHRISTIE, SAMUEL F.
Chairmaker.
Born c. 1827, Ohio; w. 1850,
Jennings Twp., Scott Co. Listed
as being blind. (C)

328
CHRISTMAN, JOHN.
Cabinetmaker.
Born c. 1832, Germany; w. 1850,
Eel Twp., Cass Co. Lived with
William T. S. Manly, cabinetmaker, q.v. (C)

329
CHRISTY, BARNY.
Cabinetmaker.
Born c. 1822, Indiana; w. 1850,
Jeffersonville, Clark Co. (C)

330
CHRISTY, BARNEY.
Cabinetmaker.
Born c. 1820; w. 1850, New Albany, Floyd Co. Lived with
George W. Porter, cabinetmaker,
q.v. (C). Probably same man as
above.

331
CHURCH, UZZIEL, and
CHENEY SPEERS. Makers of
beds and wheels.
> W. -1820-, Brownsville, Fayette
> (now Union) Co. Equipment in-
> cluded "Turning Lathe going by
> Water." Annual product was list-
> ed as "Flax wheels 4.00; Clock
> Reels 2.00, Not [Knot] Reels
> 1.50; Quill Wheels 2.00; Bed-
> steads from $15 down to $3.00."
> (MC)

332
CLAPSADDLE, JOHN.
Chairmaker.
> Born c. 1812, Pennsylvania; w.
> 1850, Putnamville, Putnam Co.
> (C)

333
CLARK, A. W. L. Chairmaker.
> Born c. 1830, Ohio; w. 1850,
> Goshen, Elkhart Co. Lived with
> Aaron B. Clark, chairmaker.
> (C)

334
CLARK, AARON B. Chairmaker.
> Born c. 1798, Massachusetts; w.
> -1841-1850, Goshen, Elkhart Co.
> In same household, Columbus B.
> Clark, painter, and A. W. L.
> Clark, chairmaker. (C, CH 14)

335
CLARK, BENJAMIN.
Chairmaker.
> Born c. 1827, Massachusetts; w.
> 1850, Anderson Twp., Madison
> Co. Lived with Randolph Lacy
> (?), cabinetmaker. (C)

336
CLARK, COLUMBUS B. Chair
painter.

Born c. 1828, Ohio; w. 1850,
Goshen, Elkhart Co. Lived with
Aaron B. Clark, chairmaker. (C)

337
CLARK, EPHRAIM.
Cabinetmaker.
> Born c. 1810, Ohio; w. 1850,
> Vernon Twp., Washington Co.
> (C)

338
CLARK, ISAIAH. Apprentice
chairmaker.
> Born c. 1833; w. 1850, Mishawaka,
> St. Joseph Co. Apprenticed to
> Seth Clark, chairmaker. (C)

339
CLARK, JOHN. Cabinetmaker.
> Born c. 1824, Crawford Co.,
> Indiana; w. 1850, Jennings Twp.,
> Crawford Co. (C)

340
CLARK, JOSEPH N. Chairmaker.
> Born c. 1820, Ohio; w. 1850,
> Rockport, Spencer Co. (C)

341
CLARK, SAMUEL A.
Cabinetmaker.
> Born c. 1823, Indiana; w. after
> 1843-1850-, Clark Twp., Johnson
> Co. Listed as an early cabinet-
> maker in Clarksburg, which was
> established in 1843; his shop ran
> for "several years." (C, CH 29)

342
CLARK, SETH. Chairmaker.
> Born c. 1805, Connecticut; w.
> 1850, Mishawaka, St. Joseph Co.
> In same household, two appren-
> tices (Isaiah Clark and William
> Clark) and John Cadwell, chair-
> maker. (C)

343
CLARK, WILLIAM.
Cabinetmaker.
> Born c. 1814, Massachusetts; w. 1850, Perry Twp., Lawrence Co. (C)

344
CLARK, WILLIAM. Apprentice chairmaker.
> Born c. 1835; w. 1850, Mishawaka, St. Joseph Co. Apprenticed to Seth Clark, chairmaker. (C)

345
CLARY, HIRAM. Cabinetmaker.
> Born c. 1810, Ohio; w. 1850, Noble Twp., Wabash Co. (C)

346
CLAYTON, CHARLES. Cabinetmaker.
> Born c. 1823, Kentucky; w. 1850, Harrison Twp., Vigo Co. (C)

347
CLEARWATER, T H E R I A N-THUM. Cabinetmaker.
> Born c. 1832, Indiana; w. 1850, for Elisha L. (or J.) Cunningham, Putnamville, Putnam Co. (C)

348
CLEMENS, JESSE. Chair painter.
> Born c. 1834, Kentucky; w. 1850, Jeffersonville, Clark Co. Lived with William Guy, chairmaker, q.v. (C)

349
CLEMENSEN, ANDREW. Cabinetmaker.
> Born c. 1833, Massachusetts; w. 1850, Utica Twp., Clark Co. (C)

350
CLEMENSON, ANDREW. Cabinetmaker.
> Born c. 1834, Indiana; w. 1850, New Albany, Floyd Co. Lived with Alexander H. D o r s e y, cabinetmaker. (C) Probably same as person above.

351
CLIFTON, WARREN. Cabinetmaker.
> Born c. 1810, North Carolina; w. 1850, Franklin Twp., Washington Co. (C)

352
CLINE, HENRY. Cabinetmaker.
> Born c. 1805, Germany; w. 1850, Shawswick Twp., Lawrence Co. In same household, Adam Ruth, cabinetmaker. (C)

353
CLINE, WILLIAM. Cabinetmaker.
> W. 1823-, Edinburg, Johnson Co. Manufactured chairs, bedsteads, bureaus, etc. Employed one or two men. (CH 29)

354
CLOUD, WILLIAM. Apprentice cabinetmaker.
> Born c. 1833, Indiana; w. 1850, Paoli, Orange Co. Apprentice to William A. Liston, cabinetmaker, q.v. (C)

355
CLOW, ISAAC. Chairmaker.
> Born c. 1815, New York; w. 1850, Noble Twp., Wabash Co. Lived with Oliver Hill, chairmaker and painter. (C)

356
COBB, JOSEPH. Cabinetmaker.
Born c. 1827, Illinois; w. 1850,
Franklin Twp., Johnson Co. (C)
See also PARRISH & COBB.

357
COBB, LEVI. Chairmaker.
W. -1826-, New Albany, Floyd
Co. Adv. in *Indiana Recorder
and Public Advertiser,* 16 December 1826, that he made plain and
fancy Windsor chairs.

358
COBLE, DAVID. Cabinetmaker.
Born c. 1816, Pennsylvania; w.
1850, Ripley Twp., Rush Co. In
same household, Abraham Rowen,
cabinetmaker. (C)

359
COCHRAN, JAMES.
Cabinetmaker.
Born c. 1788, Connecticut; w.
1850, Bloomington, Monroe Co.
(C)

360
COCHRAN, JOHN W.
Cabinetmaker.
Born c. 1812, Indiana; w. 1850,
Jefferson Twp., Switzerland Co.
(C) *See also* ALLEY & COCHRAN.

361
COCKEFAIR, JAMES M.
Cabinetmaker.
Born c. 1821, New Jersey; w.
1850, Jackson Twp., Fayette Co.
Operated a "mechanic shop" where
three men were employed; in
1850 they made "200,000 Laths
$600; Furniture $675; 100 Glass
frames $100." (C, MC)

362
CODZENBAUGH, JOHN.
Cabinetmaker.
Born c. 1825, Germany; w. 1850,
Harrison Twp., Vigo Co. Lived
with Sylvester Williams, cabinetmaker. (C)

363
COEN, JAMES S. Cabinetmaker.
Born c. 1825, Ohio; w. 1850,
Fountain Co. In 1850 he produced
"12 Bureaus $264; 25 Tables
$137; 40 Bedsteads $240; 6 Stands
$18; 6 Coffins $54." (C, MC)

364
COFFMAN, GEORGE.
Cabinetmaker.
Born c. 1827, Ohio; w. 1850,
Whitley Co. In same household,
John Drawbaugh, cabinetmaker.
(C)

365
COLDRAM (or CALDRAM),
WILLIAM. Cabinetmaker.
Born c. 1829, Pennsylvania; w.
1850, Jackson Twp., Randolph Co.
(C)

366
COLE, THOMAS. Cabinetmaker.
Born c. 1802, Maryland; w. 1850,
Cotton Twp., Switzerland Co.(C)

367
COLEMAN, ALEXANDER.
Cabinetmaker.
Born c. 1824, Pennsylvania; w.
1850, Whitley Co. (C)

368
COLEMAN, PETER—*see* KUHLMAN (COLEMAN), PETER.

369
COLEY, ROBERT. Chairmaker.
Born c. 1802, Ohio; w. 1850,
Danville, Hendricks Co. (C)

370
COLLIS, ARSEMUS.
Cabinetmaker.
Born c. 1802, Ohio; w. 1850,
Anderson Twp., Madison Co.
Lived with Randolph Lacy(?),
chairmaker. (C)

371
COLVIN, JAMES. Cabinetmaker.
Born c. 1820, Ireland; w. 1850,
New Frankfort, Scott Co. (C)

372
COLVIN, JOHN. Chairmaker.
Born c. 1825, Ireland; w. 1850,
New Frankfort, Scott Co. In
same household, Joseph Hough,
chairmaker. (C)

373
COMBS, JACOB. Chairmaker.
Born c. 1803, Ohio; w. 1850,
Mooresville, Morgan Co. (C)

374
COMBS, JESSE.
Cabinetmaker and chairmaker.
Arrived in Indianapolis, 1827;
died 1857. Made chairs for the
legislature that met in the old
courthouse. Worked on a farm at
Ben Davis, Marion Co., until
1835-36, when he moved to his
own farm west of Indianapolis.
(*Indianapolis Star*, 24 December
1967)

375
COMBS, JOHN. Cabinetmaker.
Born c. 1823, Indiana; w. 1850,
Washington Twp., Shelby Co.
(C)

376
COMINS, ROBERT.
Cabinetmaker.
Born c. 1824, Ohio; w. 1850,
White Co. (C)

377
COMPTON, JOSEPH.
Chairmaker.
Born c. 1820, Kentucky; w. 1850,
Perry Twp., Martin Co. (C)

378
CONE, FRANCIS. Cabinetmaker.
Born c. 1828, Indiana; w. 1850,
Harrison Twp., Vigo Co. (C)
See also CONE & WEATHER-
WAX.

379
CONE & WEATHERWAX
(WETHERWAX). Cabinetmakers.
Francis Cone and William Weath-
erwax; w. 1850, Harrison Twp.,
Vigo Co. Three men in shop made
in 1850 "25 Bureaus $500; 50 Bed-
steads $250; 4 Sofas $140; 50
Tables $400; Other Articles $500."
(C, MC)

380
CONKLIN, AMOS. Chairmaker.
W. c. 1830, Connersville, Fayette
Co. (CH 27) *See also* CONK-
LIN & COOMBS.

381
CONKLIN, FREEMAN.
Cabinetmaker.
Born c. 1814, Ohio; w. 1850, Con-
nersville, Fayette Co. (C)

382
CONKLIN & COOMBS. Chair
Factory.

Amos Conklin and W.H. Coombs;
w. c. 1830, Connersville, Fayette
Co. (CH 27)

383
CONNELLY, ARTHUR G.
Cabinetmaker.
Born c. 1799, Kentucky; w. 1850,
Carroll Co. Two men worked in
the shop, and in 1850 they pro-
duced "20 Bureaus $280; 50
Tables $200; 30 Bedsteads $120,"
and other articles valued at $150.
(C, MC)

384
CONOOTA, JULIUS.
Cabinetmaker.
Born c. 1817, Germany; w. 1850,
Wayne Twp., Allen Co. (C)

385
CONRAD, CHARLES P.
Cabinetmaker.
Born c. 1835, Kentucky; w. 1850,
Rush Co. Listed twice in county
census, once in household of
Marcus L. Johnson, cabinetmaker.
May indicate either an apprentice-
ship or journeyman status. (C)

386
COOK, FERDINAND G.
Cabinetmaker.
Born c. 1812, Germany; w. 1850,
Harrison Twp., Vigo Co. (C)
See also GANNEAR & COOK.

387
COOK, GUADALOUPE.
Cabinetmaker.
Born c. 1813, Germany; w. 1850,
Harrison Twp., Vigo Co. Lived
with Joseph Dewolph, cabinet-
maker. (C)

388
COOK, HENRY. Cabinetmaker.
Born c. 1822, France; w. 1850,
Milford, Decatur Co. (C)

389
COOK, JAMES S. Cabinetmaker.
Born c. 1803, North Carolina; w.
1850, Franklin Twp., Wayne Co.
(C)

390
COOK, JOHN. Cabinetmaker.
Born c. 1827, Indiana; w. 1850,
Harrison Twp., Vigo Co.

391
COOK, WILLIAM. Chairmaker.
Born c. 1830, Indiana; w. 1850,
Marion, Grant Co. Lived with
Lemuel Turner, chairmaker. (C)

392
COOLEY [COOLY], ABRAM C.
Cabinetmaker.
Born c. 1813, New York; w.
-1850-1885-, Connersville, Fayette
Co. In 1850 he reported that he
had made "30 Bedsteads $180;
20 Tables $100; 12 Bureaus $200;
other articles $200." In May 1865
he joined Warren Wanee, a carpenter, in a furniture-making
firm. From the autumn of 1866
to 1869, the firm included Abram
C. Cooley, George W. Gregg, and
William Newkirk. In 1870 it became Cooley, Morrison & Co.,
and later the Indiana Furniture
Company. This company continued in business until 1908, when
it became the Krell Auto Grand
Piano Company. The last date
that Mr. Cooley is known to have
been associated with the firm is
1885. (C, MC, CH 1, 27)

393
COOMBS, JOEL. Cabinetmaker.
Born c. 1813, Pennsylvania; w.
1850, Liberty, Union Co. (C)

394
COOMBS, W. H. Chairmaker.
W. c. 1830-, Connersville, Fayette
Co. (CH 27) *See also* CONK-
LIN & COOMBS.

395
COOMER, JONATHAN.
Cabinetmaker.
Born c. 1808, New York; w.
1850, Bloomfield Twp., La Grange
Co. (C)

396
COOMER, SEYMOR.
Cabinetmaker.
Born c. 1813, New York; w.
1850, Richland Twp., Steuben Co.
(C)

397
COON, WILLIAM. Cabinetmaker.
W. -1840-, Anderson, Madison Co.
Chest of drawers made by him,
illustrated in *Indianapolis Star*, 30
May 1943: "cherry with back and
end panels of sycamore; height
47." Written beneath the top
board: "Made by William Coon.
May 6, 1840. Andersontown,
Madison County, Indiana."

398
COOPER, THOMAS.
Cabinetmaker.
Born c. 1830, Ohio; w. 1850,
Harrison Twp., Bartholomew Co.
(C)

399
CORDER, AARON.
Cabinetmaker.
Born c. 1825, Ohio; w. 1850, Pipe
Creek Twp., Madison Co. (C)

400
CORLIN, ROBERT L.
Cabinetmaker.
Born c. 1832, Indiana; w. 1850,
Noblesville, Hamilton Co. (C)

401
CORN, JOHN. Chairmaker.
Born c. 1802, North Carolina; w.
1850, Van Buren Twp., Kosciusko
Co. (C)

402
CORNEL, J. L. Chairmaker.
Born c. 1828, Ireland; w. 1850,
Jeffersonville, Clark Co. (C)

403
COSSART, HENRY.
Cabinetmaker.
Born c. 1773, New York; w. 1850,
Utica Twp., Clark Co. (C)

404
COTNER, ALFRED.
Cabinetmaker.
Born c. 1829, Indiana; w. 1850,
Charlestown Twp., Clark Co. (C)

405
COULING, JOHN. Cabinetmaker.
Born c. 1821, England; w. 1850,
Mt. Etna, Huntington Co. (C)

406
COULTER, JOSEPH.
Cabinetmaker.
Born c. 1831, Ohio; w. 1850, Mt.
Etna, Huntington Co. Lived with
Thomas Mahoney, cabinetmaker.
(C)

407
COURTNEY, JOSEPH H.
Chairmaker.
> Born c. 1818, Kentucky; w. 1850,
> Henry Twp., Henry Co. (C)

408
COWAN, SAMUEL. Chairmaker.
> Born c. 1824, Ohio; w. 1850, Jackson Twp., Elkhart Co. (C)

409
COWING, JOHN. Chairmaker.
> Born c. 1825, Virginia; w. 1850,
> Posey Twp., Franklin Co. (C)

410
COX, EDWIN. Cabinetmaker.
> Born c. 1829, Ohio; w. 1850,
> Madison, Jefferson Co. (C)

411
COX, WILLIAM. Cabinetmaker.
> Born c. 1803, New York; w.
> 1850, Madison, Jefferson Co. (C)

412
CRAIG, JAMES H. Cabinetmaker.
> Born c. 1825, Ohio; w. 1850, Eel
> River Twp., Hendricks Co. (C)
> *See also* CRAIG & CHAPMAN.

413
CRAIG & CHAPMAN. Cabinet
shop.
> James H. Craig and John Chapman; w. 1850, Eel River Twp.,
> Hendricks Co. (MC)

414
CRAIGMILES, A. Cabinetmaker.
> Born c. 1798, Kentucky; w. 1850,
> Clinton Twp., Decatur Co. (C)

415
CRAMER, MARTIN.
Cabinetmaker.
> Born c. 1807, Pennsylvania; w.
> 1850, Scott Twp., Montgomery
> Co. In same household, Washington Cramer, cabinetmaker. (C)

416
CRAMER, WASHINGTON.
Cabinetmaker.
> Born c. 1830, Pennsylvania; w.
> 1850, Scott Twp., Montgomery
> Co. Lived with Martin Cramer,
> cabinetmaker. (C)

417
CRAWFORD, STEPHEN C.
Furniture shop.
> W. 1850, west half, Hendricks
> Co. In 1850 the products of this
> shop were valued at $2,000. (MC)

418
CRAWFORD, WILLIAM.
Chairmaker.
> Born c. 1805, Ireland; w. 1850,
> Parke Co. Lived with James S.
> Laman, chairmaker, q.v. (C)

419
CRAWFORD, WILLIAM.
Chairmaker.
> Born c. 1805, Ireland; w. 1850,
> Harrison Twp., Vigo Co. (C)

420
CREPPS, GEORGE.
Cabinetmaker.
> Born c. 1828, Ohio; w. 1850,
> Jefferson Twp., Noble Co. (C)

421
CRESS, HENRY. Cabinetmaker.
> Born c. 1827, Indiana; w. 1850,
> Clay Twp., Decatur Co. (C)

422
CRISMAN, BENJAMIN.
Chairmaker.
> Born c. 1809, Pennsylvania; w. 1850, Gosport, Owen Co. (C)

423
CRITTENDEN, SAMUEL.
Cabinet and chair shop.
> Born c. 1799, Kentucky; in Indiana by 1829; w. 1850, Columbus, Bartholomew Co. Four men working in shop, using horse power to move machinery which produced cabinet furniture valued at $2,250 and 60 dozen chairs worth $750. (C, MC)

424
CROOK, ANDERSON B.
Cabinetmaker.
> Born c. 1831, Illinois; w. 1850, Greene Co. Two men worked in the shop, which in 1850 produced "cabinetware worth $500." (C, MC)

425
CROPPER, JONATHAN.
Cabinetmaker.
> Born c. 1806, Kentucky; w. 1850, Pike Twp., Marion Co. (C)

426
CROPPER, MORDECAI.
Cabinetmaker.
> W. 1830s in Marion Co.; moved west in 1838. (TH 49)

427
CROSBY, DAVID. Cabinetmaker.
> Born c. 1831, Illinois; w. 1850, Fairbanks Twp., Sullivan Co. Lived with William D. Weir, cabinetmaker. (C)

428
CROSBY, J. H. Cabinetmaker.
> **Born c. 1819, Maine; w. 1850,** Concord Twp., Elkhart Co. (C)

429
CROSE, M. Cabinetmaker.
> Born c. 1831, New York; w. 1850, Indianapolis, Marion Co. (C)

430
CROWPER, E. S. Cabinetmaker.
> Born c. 1822, Kentucky; w. 1850, Decatur Co. Two men worked in the shop, which produced 150 pieces of cabinet ware valued at $600 in 1850. (C, MC)

431
CRUMP, FOUNTAIN C.
Cabinetmaker.
> Born c. 1831; w. 1850, Shawswick Twp., Lawrence Co. Lived with John B. Buskirk, cabinetmaker. (C)

432
CUIN, JOHN S. Cabinetmaker.
> Born c. 1823, Indiana; w. 1850, Greenville Twp., Floyd Co. (C)

433
CULBERSON, JOSEPH.
Cabinetmaker.
> W. 1820, Lawrence Co. Prices given for his products were "Desks $35; Bureaus $18; Tables $7 & $10; Cupboards $20, &c." (MC)

434
CULMER, GEORGE F.
Chairmaker.
> Born c. 1824, Pennsylvania; w. 1850, Perry Twp., Lawrence Co. (C)

435
CUMMINGS, *see also* CUMMINS.

436
CUMMINGS, JAMES.
Cabinetmaker.
　Born c. 1808, Kentucky; w. 1850,
　Aurora, Dearborn Co. (C)

437
CUMMINGS (CUMMINS),
JOSEPH. Cabinetmaker.
　Born c. 1816, Pennsylvania; w.
　1850, Jennings Twp., Fayette Co.
　(C)

438
CUMMINGS, THOMAS.
Cabinetmaker.
　W. -1840-, Leavenworth, Craw-
　ford Co. Adv. in *Leavenworth
　Arena,* 30 July 1840: "CABI-
　NET MAKI N G / T H O M A S
　CUMMINGS."

439
CUMMINS, JOSEPH.
Cabinetmaker.
　Born c. 1820, Ohio; w. 1850,
　Shelbyville, Shelby Co. Two men
　worked in this shop, and in 1850
　produced "Bureaus, Tables &c"
　valued at $800. The other man
　was probably Thomas F. Kirk, a
　cabinetmaker who lived in the
　same household. (C, MC)

440
CUNNINGHAM, ELISHA L. (or
J.). Cabinetmaker.
　Born c. 1817, Ohio; w. 1850, Put-
　namville, Putnam Co. The annual
　product of his shop was valued
　at $1,600. Living in the same

household were Therianthum
Clearwater and John W. Peck,
cabinetmakers. (C, MC)

441
CURNUTT, WILLIAM.
Cabinetmaker.
　Born c. 1814, Tennessee; w. 1850,
　Jennings Twp., Fayette Co. (C)

442
CURRY, ALEXANDER.
Chairmaker.
　Born c. 1815, Pennsylvania; w.
　1850, New Garden Twp., Wayne
　Co. (C)

443
CURRY, ANDREW.
Cabinetmaker.
　Born c. 1795, Kentucky; w. 1850,
　Haddon Twp., Sullivan Co. Lived
　with Smith M. Buckley, cabinet-
　maker. (C)

444
CURRY, JOHN. Cabinetmaker.
　Born c. 1832, Indiana; w. 1850,
　Salem, Washington Co. (C)

445
CURTIS, GILBERT.
Cabinetmaker.
　Born c. 1825, Illinois; w. 1850,
　Hamilton Twp., Sullivan Co. (C)

446
CURTIS, ROBERT.
Cabinetmaker.
　Born c. 1813, Ohio; w. 1850, New
　Garden Twp., Wayne Co. In same
　household, Alberson Lamb, cabi-
　netmaker. (C)

447
CUTTER (CUTTON, COTTON),
JAMES. Cabinetmaker.
　W. 1820-1824-, Paoli, Orange Co.

The equipment listed for his shop included cabinet machinery and "3 Benches and Tools for them." Under "Remarks," he stated, "Good sale and you gess at the rest." (MC) Probate records of Orange County list him several times as having made coffins for deceased persons in 1823 and 1824.

448
CUTTER, JOHN [Sr.].
Chairmaker and wheelmaker.
> Born c. 1803, Maryland; w. 1850, Carroll Co. In 1850 his shop produced 500 chairs valued at $500, and 6 wool wheels worth $25. Living in the same household were John Cutter [Jr.] and John Urey, chairmakers. (C, MC)

449
CUTTER, JOHN [Jr.].
Chairmaker.
> Born c. 1830, Pennsylvania; w. 1850, Carroll County. Lived with John Cutter [Sr.], chairmaker and wheelmaker, q.v. (C)

450
DAGGET, SIMEON. Chairmaker.
> Born c. 1819, Indiana; w. 1850, Madison Twp., Jefferson Co. (C)

451
DALE, SYDNOR. Cabinetmaker.
> W. 1820, Connersville, Fayette Co. Three men worked in his shop; their raw materials were given as cherry, walnut, and poplar. The prices of their products were as follows: "Side Boards Average $100; Secretaries Average $75; Bureaus Dto $32; Desks Dto $32; Cupboards Dto $18; Tables Best per set $45; Tables Dining & Breakfast $8; Clock Cases Each $25; Bedsteads Best quality $18; Dto Common $3.50; Coffins Raised lids $10; Candle Stands $4; Book Cases $7." (MC)

452
DALZIELL, ROBERT.
Cabinetmaker.
> Born c. 1802, Scotland; w. 1850, Versailles, Ripley Co. (C)

453
DAMART, JOHN I.
Cabinetmaker.
> Born c. 1816, Indiana; w. 1850, Jefferson Twp., Switzerland Co. (C)

454
DAMON (?), SILAS.
Cabinetmaker and chairmaker.
> Born c. 1802, Massachusetts; w. 1850, Pleasant Twp., Steuben Co. (C)

455
DANAHOO, THOMAS.
Cabinetmaker.
> Born c. 1833, Ohio; w. 1850, Anderson Twp., Madison Co. Lived with Randolph Lacy(?), cabinetmaker. (C)

456
DANE, ROBERT. Chairmaker.
> Born c. 1835, Ohio; w. 1850, Noble Twp., Wabash Co. Lived with Oliver Hill, chairmaker and painter. (C)

457
DANNER, WILLIAM.
Cabinetmaker.
> Born c. 1830, Kentucky; w. 1850,

New Albany, Floyd Co. Lived with John Brindley, cabinetmaker. (C)

458
DARBY, JOHN H. Cabinetmaker. Born c. 1828, Indiana; w. 1850, Newburgh, Warrick Co. Lived with John V. Darby, cabinetmaker. (C)

459
DARBY, JOHN V. Cabinetmaker. Born c. 1800, Vermont; w. 1850, Newburgh, Warrick Co. In same household, John H. Darby, cabinetmaker. (C)

459a
DAVEY, JOHN. Cabinetmaker. W. 1826, Terre Haute, Vigo Co. *See* TAYLOR & DAVEY; DAVEY & EAST.

460
DAVEY & EAST. Cabinetmakers and chairmakers.
John Davey and Joseph East; w. 1826, Terre Haute, Vigo Co. Adv. in *Western Register & Terre-Haute Advertiser,* 28 October 1826: "Co-partnership/Davy & East, Respectfully inform the public that they have entered into Copartnership for the purpose of carrying on the CABINET & CHAIR *MAKING BUSINESS/* HOUSE and SIGN *PAINT-ING/*GILDING & GLAZING In Terre-Haute, in the shop recently occupied by Taylor and Davey [q.v.] Cabinet makers, on market street, two squares North of the Court House, where they have and intend keeping on hand,

an assortment of *Chairs and Furniture* of the best quality, which they will sell low for cash or good trade. JOHN DAVEY/ JOSEPH EAST."

461
DAVIDSON, DANIEL. Cabinetmaker.
Born c. 1829, Indiana; w. 1850, Haddon Twp., Sullivan Co. Lived with Benson Riggs [Sr.], cabinetmaker. (C)

462
DAVIDSON, ENOS. Cabinetmaker.
Born c. 1833, Indiana; w. 1850, Williamsburg, Wayne Co. (C)

463
DAVIDSON, GEORGE. Cabinetmaker.
Born c. 1825, Indiana; w. 1850, Haddon Twp., Sullivan Co. (C)

464
DAVIDSON, WILLIAM H. Chairmaker.
W. -1835-1836-, Lawrenceburg, Dearborn Co. Prior to April 1835, worked with Thomas M. Duffy; adv. 9 April 1835 announced dissolution of partnership (see Fig. 2). Adv. in *Indiana Palladium* 26 March 1836: "CHAIR factory . . . on Walnut Street, opposite Jesse Hunt's Hotel, and having on hand a quantity of the best materials for manufacturing Fancy and Windsor Chairs, Arm Chairs and Settees. He also attends to house painting . . . ."

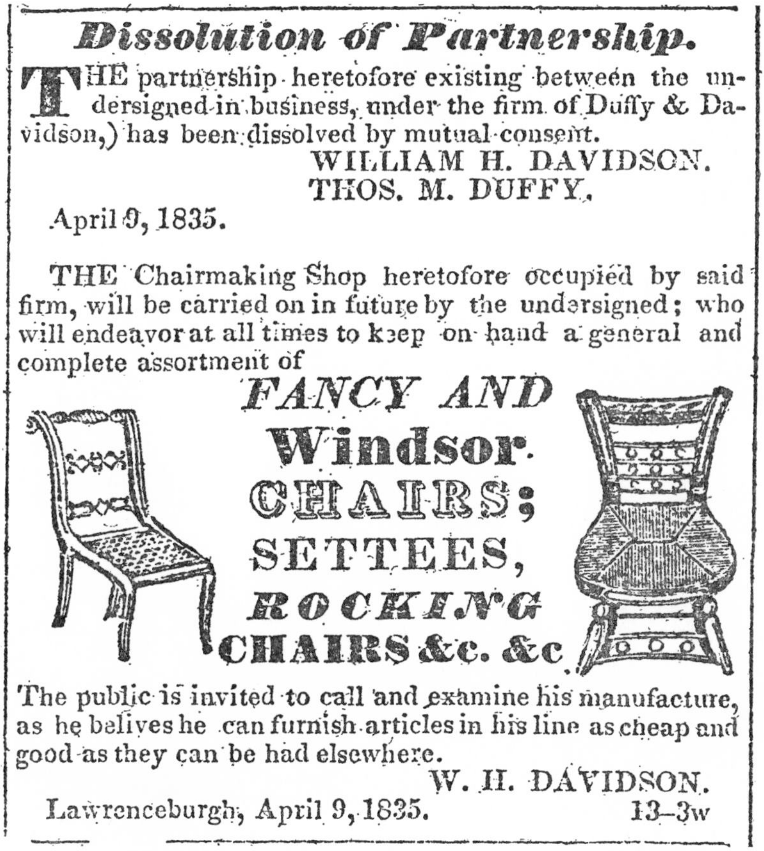

Dissolution of Partnership.

THE partnership heretofore existing between the undersigned in business, under the firm of Duffy & Davidson,) has been dissolved by mutual consent.

WILLIAM H. DAVIDSON.
THOS. M. DUFFY.

April 9, 1835.

THE Chairmaking Shop heretofore occupied by said firm, will be carried on in future by the undersigned; who will endeavor at all times to keep on hand a general and complete assortment of

FANCY AND
Windsor.
CHAIRS;
SETTEES,
ROCKING
CHAIRS &c. &c.

The public is invited to call and examine his manufacture, as he belives he can furnish articles in his line as cheap and good as they can be had elsewhere.

W. H. DAVIDSON.

Lawrenceburgh, April 9, 1835.   13–3w

Fig. 2. From Lawrenceburg *Indiana Palladium*

465
DAVIES, LEWIS. Chairmaker.
  Born c. 1828, Pennsylvania; w. 1850, Chester Twp., Wabash Co. (C)

466
DAVIS, COLTNEY J.
Cabinetmaker.
  Born c. 1820, England; w. 1850, New Albany, Floyd Co. (C)

467
DAVIS, ELIJAH. Chairmaker.
  Born c. 1822, Indiana; w. 1850, Campbell Twp., Jennings Co. (C)

468
DAVIS, ENOS. Cabinetmaker.
  Born c. 1821, North Carolina; w. 1850, Washington Twp., Hamilton Co. In same household, Joseph Davis, cabinetmaker. (C)

469
DAVIS, HARVEY. Cabinetmaker.
Born 15 November 1806, North Carolina; 1824, moved to Wayne County. He was apprenticed to Solomon Thomas, Fountain City, for two and a half years after which he was a journeyman for two years. Then he bought a shop and was in business for sixty years. In 1850, James Thomas and Hezakiah Vanhuis, both cabinetmakers, lived in his household. In 1884 it was said that "He is probably the oldest cabinetmaker and undertaker in the State of Indiana." (C, CH 34)

470
DAVIS, HENRY. Cabinet shop.
W. 1850, New Garden Twp., Wayne Co. The four men in this shop used machinery powered by horses. In 1850 they produced furniture worth $1,500. (MC)

471
DAVIS, HENRY & SAMUEL. Chairmakers.
1820, arrived in Indianapolis, Marion Co. (Indianapolis Star 12 July 1942; Fine Furniture in Indiana [Indianapolis: Public Service Company, n.d.])

472
DAVIS, JAMES. Cabinetmaker.
Born c. 1820, Ireland; w. 1850, Lafayette Twp., Owen Co. (C)

473
DAVIS, JAMES. Cabinetmaker.
Born c. 1805, North Carolina; w. 1850, Cambridge City, Wayne Co. (C)

474
DAVIS, JOHN. Chairmaker.
Born c. 1821, Pennsylvania; w. 1850, Pittsburg, Carroll Co. (C)

475
DAVIS, JOHN. Cabinetmaker.
Born c. 1833, Indiana; w. 1850, Washington Twp., Daviess Co. (C)

476
DAVIS, JOHN M. Cabinetmaker.
Born c. 1817, Kentucky; w. 1850, Morristown, Shelby Co. (C)

477
DAVIS, JOHN P. Cabinetmaker.
Born c. 1780, Pennsylvania; w. 1850, Black Twp., Posey Co. (C)

478
DAVIS, JOSEPH. Cabinetmaker.
Born c. 1830, North Carolina; w. 1850, Washington Twp., Hamilton Co. Lived with Enos Davis, cabinetmaker. (C)

479
DAVIS, JOSEPH B. Chairmaker.
Born c. 1826, North Carolina; w. 1850, Jackson Twp., Wayne Co. He worked alone, using paints and gold leaf among other raw materials; his product in 1850 was 600 chairs and settees valued at $900. (C, MC)

480
DAVIS, NATHAN. Cabinetmaker.
Born c. 1808, Virginia; w. 1850, Noble Twp., Wabash Co. (C)

481
DAVIS, RICE J. Cabinetmaker.
Born c. 1806, Illinois; w. 1850, Haddon Twp., Sullivan Co. (C)

482
DAVIS, SAMUEL—*see* DAVIS, HENRY & SAMUEL.

483
DAVIS, THOMAS. Cabinetmaker.
Born c. 1831, Ohio; w. 1850, Dalton Twp., Wayne Co. Lived with Solomon Bellhammer, cabinetmaker. (C)

484
DAVIS, WILLIAM W. Chairmaker.
Born c. 1817, Pennsylvania; w. 1850, Green Twp., Parke Co. (C)

485
DAVISON, JOHN. Cabinetmaker. W. 1820, Columbia Twp., Fayette Co. He worked alone and in 1820 produced cupboards, bureaus, dining tables, square tables, sugar desks, and two types of coffins. He listed cherry wood as his raw material. (MC)

486
DAY, JNO. Cabinetmaker.
Born c. 1817, Ohio; w. 1850, Wayne Twp., Marion Co. (C)

487
DAY, WILLIAM H. H. Wheelmaker and chairmaker.
Born c. 1821, Ohio; w. 1850, Steuben Co. He worked alone and in 1850 his annual product was valued at $500. (C, MC)

488
DEBOLT, GEORGE. Cabinetmaker.
Born c. 1804, Ohio; w. 1850, Hagerstown, Wayne Co. (C)

489
DECKER, JOHN. Cabinetmaker.
Born c. 1823, Germany; w. 1850, Indianapolis, Marion Co. (C)

490
DEEDS, JOHN. Cabinetmaker.
Born c. 1831, Virginia; w. 1850, Harrison Twp., Miami Co. Lived with William Deeds, cabinetmaker. (C)

491
DEEDS, WILLIAM. Cabinetmaker.
Born c. 1808, Virginia; w. 1850, Harrison Twp., Miami Co. In same household, John Deeds, cabinetmaker. (C)

492
DEFFLER, GEORGE. Cabinetmaker.
Born c. 1830, Germany; w. 1850, Wayne Twp., Allen Co. Lived with William Paul, chairmaker. (C)

493
DEHART, GIDEON M. Cabinetmaker.
Born c. 1830, Ohio; w. 1850, Blue River Twp., Johnson Co. Lived with Harvey Allen, cabinetmaker. (C)

494
DEMICK, JOHN J. Cabinetmaker.
Born c. 1822, Indiana; w. 1850, Princeton, Gibson Co. (C)

495
DEMICK, WILLIAM G. Chairmaker.
Born c. 1819, Pennsylvania; w. 1850, Harrison Twp., Vigo Co. (C)

496
DEMING, FRANKLIN.
Cabinetmaker.
Born c. 1823, New York; w. 1850, Bloomington, Monroe Co. (C)

497
DENAVEN, THOMAS.
Cabinetmaker.
Born c. 1807, North Carolina; w. 1850, Monroe Twp., Madison Co. (C)

498
DENNETT — see OSGOOD & DENNETT.

499
DENNIS, JACOB. Cabinetmaker.
Born c. 1822, Ohio; w. 1850, Jeffersonville, Clark Co. (C)

500
DENNY, HENRY. Cabinetmaker.
Born c. 1834, France; w. 1850, New Albany, Floyd Co. (C)

501
DENNY, JOHN. Cabinetmaker.
Born c. 1789, Pennsylvania; w. 1850, Charlestown, Clark Co. An early and prominent citizen of Charlestown. (C, CH 33)

502
DENTON, THOMAS.
Cabinetmaker.
Born c. 1796, Virginia; w. 1850, Marion Twp., Jasper Co. (C)

503
DENWIDDIE, DAVID.
Chairmaker and undertaker.
W. -1835-1850-, Centre Twp., Wayne Co. Adv. in Centerville *The People's Advocate* 9 October 1835, as chairmaker. Later worked with Robert Denwiddie making chairs and doing house, sign, and ornamental painting. In 1850 two men working in his shop made 115 sets of chairs and 40 settees worth $815. Later he was an undertaker. (MC, TH 46)

504
DENWIDDIE, ROBERT — see DENWIDDIE, DAVID.

505
DEPUE, G. W. Cabinetmaker.
Born c. 1818, Ohio; w. 1850, Boone Twp., Warrick Co. (C)

506
DERRINGTON, MATTHIAS.
Cabinetmaker.
W. 1830s, Williamsburg, Johnson Co. His partner was John Gosney. "Derrington is remembered as a skillful mechanic [craftsman], and numerous specimens of his handiwork are still to be seen. . . ." (CH 29)

507
DEUSTERBERG, H. B., AND SONS. Cabinetmakers and undertakers.
Est. 1830, Vincennes, Knox Co. (Robert W. Habenstein and William M. Lamers, *The History of American Funeral Directing* [Milwaukee: Bulfin Printers, 1962], p. 229.)

508
DEVOE & BETTERTON.
Cabinetmakers.
—— Devoe and C. W. Betterton; w. -1840, New Albany, Floyd Co. Succeeded by Betterton & Dorsey, q.v.

509
DEVOL, BENJAMIN F.
Cabinetmaker.
    Born c. 1809, Ohio; w. 1850,
    Prairie Creek Twp., Vigo Co.
    (C)

510
DEW, JOHN L. Cabinetmaker.
    Born c. 1812, Virginia; w. 1850,
    Washington Twp., Brown Co.
    (C)

511
DEWEES, MARTIN.
Cabinetmaker.
    Born c. 1811, Kentucky; w. 1850,
    Luce Twp., Spencer Co. (C)

512
DEWITT, EPHRAIM.
Cabinetmaker.
    Born c. 1829, Ohio; w. 1850,
    Clinton, Vermillion Co. In same
    household, Elexas Wellman,
    cabinetmaker. (C)

513
DeWOLF, JAMES. Cabinetmaker.
    Born c. 1829, New York; w. 1850,
    Eel Twp., Cass Co. Lived with
    William T. S. Manly, cabinet-
    maker, q.v. (C)

514
DEWOLPH, JOSEPH.
Cabinetmaker.
    Born c. 1816, France; w. 1850,
    Harrison Twp., Vigo Co. In same
    household, Guadaloupe Cook,
    cabinetmaker. (C)

515
DICKERSON, STEPHEN L.
Chairmaker.
    Born c. 1817, Ohio; w. 1850,
    Washington Twp., Owen Co.
    (C)

516
DICKEY, JEROME. Chairmaker.
    Born c. 1833, Indiana; w. 1850,
    Lexington Twp., Scott Co. (C)

517
DICKSON, BENONI.
Chairmaker.
    Born c. 1774, South Carolina; w.
    1850, Cotton Twp., Switzerland
    Co. (C)

518
DIERDUFF, ANDREW.
Cabinetmaker.
    Born c. 1811, Pennsylvania; w.
    1850, Clinton Twp., Putnam Co.
    (C)

519
DILKS, ELIJAH. Chairmaker.
    Born c. 1827, Indiana; w. 1850,
    Salt Creek Twp., Decatur Co.
    (C)

520
DILKS, HENRY. Chairmaker.
    Born c. 1833, Indiana; w. 1850,
    Salt Creek Twp., Decatur Co.
    Lived with Joseph Dilks, chair-
    maker. (C)

521
DILKS, JOSEPH. Chairmaker.
    Born c. 1805, Pennsylvania; w.
    1850, Salt Creek Twp., Decatur
    Co. In same household, Henry
    Dilks and Leonard Dilks, chair-
    makers. (C)

522
DILKS, LEONARD. Chairmaker.
    Born c. 1834, Indiana; w. 1850,

Salt Creek Twp., Decatur Co.
Lived with Joseph Dilks, chairmaker. (C)

523
DILL, A. C., & J. H. JEMISON.
Cabinetmakers.
W. 1845, Centerville, Wayne Co.
Adv. in *Wayne County Record*,
19 November 1845: "A. C. DILL
and J. H. JEMISON, Having
entered into partnership in the
CABINET - MAKING BUSINESS in CENTREVILLE, are
prepared to manufacture, and expect to keep constantly on hand,
MAHOGANY, MAPLE AND
CHERRY BUREAUS, TABLES, BEDSTEADS,
STANDS. . . ."

523a
DILL, ALEXANDER C.
Cabinetmaker.
W. 1835-1850, Centerville, Wayne
Co. Had shop on Main Street a
few doors south of Widup's store;
also listed as being located three
doors west of American House.
In 1850 three men were working
in his cabinet shop and made 75
bedsteads, 30 bureaus, 30 tables,
etc., valued at $1,000. He was
also an undertaker, and in 1835
was a partner in the firm of
West & Dill, q.v. (MC, CH 46)

524
DILLE, STEPHEN. Chairmaker.
Born c. 1825, Ohio; w. 1850,
Centre Twp., Porter Co. (C)

525
DILRA, JOHN. Cabinetmaker.
Born c. 1806, Pennsylvania; w.
1850, Independence, Warren Co.
(C)

526
DINWIDDIE, JAMES B.
Chairmaker.
Born c. 1810, Pennsylvania; w.
1850, Greencastle, Putnam Co. In
same household, David Dix (?),
chairmaker. (C)

527
DIPPLE, JOHN. Cabinetmaker.
Born c. 1818, Germany; w. 1850,
Evansville, Vanderburgh Co. (C)
See also GREAN & DIPPLE.

528
DIX (?), DAVID. Chairmaker.
Born c. 1831, Indiana; w. 1850,
Greencastle, Putnam Co. Lived
with James B. Dinwiddie, chairmaker. (C)

529
DIXON, WILLIAM A. C.
Cabinetmaker.
Born c. 1817, Ohio; w. 1850,
Wayne Twp., Randolph Co. (C)

530
DOANE, EBENEZER.
Cabinetmaker.
Born c. 1832, Indiana; w. 1850,
Paoli, Orange Co. Lived with
Henry Miller, cabinetmaker. (C)

531
DOASH (?), JOHN.
Cabinetmaker.
Born c. 1818, Bavaria; w. 1850,
Madison, Jefferson Co. (C)

532
DODD—*see* BRITTS, GEORGE.

533
DODD, TASWELL A.
Cabinetmaker and chairmaker.
Born c. 1825, Virginia; w. 1850,
Noble Twp., Wabash Co. (C)

534
DOHERTY, ISAAC.
Cabinetmaker.
> Born c. 1829, North Carolina; w.
> 1850, Rush Co. (C)

535
DOLE, ENOCH. Chair factory.
> W. 1826, Terre Haute, Vigo Co.
> Adv. in *Western Register &
> Terre-Haute Advertiser,* 8 July
> 1826: "Chair Factory. The Sub-
> scriber hereby informs the public
> that he manufactures *Fancy
> Chairs, Windsor do., Settees,* and
> every other article in this line of
> business . . . ENOCH DOLE."
> In 1829, Mr. Dole was issued a
> license to keep a tavern in Terre
> Haute, valid until 1830. (Vigo
> Co. Commissioners Record)

536
DONAVAN, EPHRAIM.
Cabinetmaker.
> Born c. 1825, Indiana; w. 1850,
> Blue River Twp., Johnson Co.
> (C)

537
DONNELLEN (DONNOLLAN,
DONNALAND), THOMAS.
Cabinetmaker.
> Born c. 1804, Scotland; w. -1837-
> 1850-, Indianapolis, Marion Co.
> Adv. in *Indiana Democrat* in
> July 1831, and on 20 January
> 1837, for an apprentice to the
> cabinetmaking business. On 18
> October 1837 he was awarded a
> seven dollar prize for the best
> cabinet work exhibited at the
> Marion County Fair (*Indiana
> Democrat*). In 1850 four men
> were listed as working in his shop,
> using horses to power machinery,

and had made 175 bedsteads valued at $875 and 100 desks worth
$300 that year. (C, MC)

538
DOOLITTLE, CHARLES.
Cabinetmaker.
> Born c. 1813, New York; w. c.
> 1847-1850-, East Lima, La Grange
> Co. Two men worked in his shop;
> their machinery was powered by
> water. Their annual product was
> cabinet ware valued at $1,000.
> They made bureaus, chairs, tables,
> and bedsteads and also had a
> turning lathe. (C, MC, CH 12)

539
DORAN, M. W. E. Cabinetmaker.
> Born c. 1821, Ireland; w. 1850,
> Blue River Twp., Johnson Co.
> (C)

540
DORSEY, ALEXANDER H.
Cabinetmaker.
> Born c. 1819, Maryland; w. 1850,
> New Albany, Floyd Co. In same
> household, Andrew Clemenson,
> cabinetmaker. (C) *See also* DOR-
> SEY & BROTHER.

541
DORSEY, C. A. Cabinetmaker.
> Born c. 1817, Kentucky; w. -1840-
> 1850-, New Albany, Floyd Co.
> In 1840 he was a partner in the
> firm of Betterton & Dorsey, q.v.
> In 1850 he was probably in the
> firm of Dorsey & Brother. Also
> in 1850, living in his household
> was Allen W. Shook, cabinet-
> maker. (C)

542
DORSEY & BROTHER.
Cabinetmakers.

Probably Alexander H. and C. A. Dorsey, but this is not verified. W. 1850, New Albany, Floyd Co. Four men worked in the shop; their raw materials were listed as cherry, poplar, walnut, and gum. In 1850 they produced 130 bedsteads, 36 tables, and 24 bureaus valued at $2,000. (MC)

543
DOUGHERTY, JOHN.
Cabinetmaker.
Born c. 1811, Kentucky; w. 1850, Columbus, Bartholomew Co. In same household Samuel L. Dougherty, cabinetmaker. (C)

544
DOUGHERTY, SAMUEL L.
Cabinetmaker.
Born c. 1835, Indiana; w. 1850, Columbus, Bartholomew Co. Lived with John Dougherty, cabinetmaker. (C)

545
DOUGLAS, LEANDER F.
Chairmaker.
Born c. 1805, Kentucky; w. 1850, Clay Twp., Decatur Co. (C)

546
DOUGLASS, JOHN B.
Cabinetmaker.
Born c. 1816, Ohio; w. 1850, Jackson Twp., Clinton Co. He worked alone and listed his raw materials as cherry and walnut lumber. His annual product was valued at $600. (C, MC)

547
DOUGLASS, L. C.
Chair ornamenter.
Born c. 1822; w. 1850, Jeffersonville, Clark Co. (C)

548
DOUGLASS, THOMAS.
Cabinetmaker.
W. 1841-, Franklin, Johnson Co. (CH 29)

549
DOWENS, JOSEPH W.
Cabinetmaker.
Born c. 1828, Indiana; w. 1850, Blue River Twp., Johnson Co. (C)

550
DRAKE, McLAJAH(?).
Cabinetmaker.
Born c. 1821, New Jersey; w. 1850, Orange Twp., Noble Co. (C)

551
DRAKING, FREDERICK.
Cabinetmaker.
Born c. 1824, Indiana; w. 1850, Lawrenceburg, Dearborn Co. (C)

552
DRAPER, EDWARD.
Cabinetmaker.
Born c. 1819, Pennsylvania; w. 1850, New Albany, Floyd Co. (C)

553
DRAPER, JESSE. Cabinetmaker.
Born c. 1804, North Carolina; w. 1850, Bloomington, Monroe Co. (C)

554
DRAPER, JOHN H.
Cabinetmaker.
Born c. 1822, Indiana; w. 1850, Plainfield, Hendricks Co. (C)

555
DRAPER, JOSEPH.
Cabinetmaker.

Born c. 1820, Pennsylvania; w. 1850, Mooresville, Morgan Co. (C)

556
DRAWBAUGH, JOHN. Cabinetmaker.
Born c. 1828, Ohio; w. 1850, Whitley Co. Lived with George Coffman, cabinetmaker. (C)

557
DRENEN, SAMUEL. Chairmaker.
Born c. 1775, Pennsylvania; w. 1850, Harrison Twp., Fayette Co. (C)

558
DREYER (DRYER), FREDERICK. Cabinetmaker.
Born c. 1812, Germany; w. 1841-, 1850, Cambridge City, Wayne Co. Adv. in Centerville *Wayne County Record*, 20 October 1841: "CABINET MAKING. The subscriber begs leave to inform the Public that he still continues to carry on the above business in CAMBRIDGE CITY. . . ." (C)

559
DRIVER, ISAAC. Cabinetmaker.
Born c. 1824, Ohio; w. 1850, Elkhart Twp., Noble Co. (C)

560
DRIVER, THOMAS. Cabinetmaker.
Born c. 1788, Pennsylvania; w. 1850, Elkhart Twp., Noble Co. (C)

561
DRYER, LOUIS. Chairmaker.
Born c. 1828, Ohio; w. 1850, Sheffield Twp., Tippecanoe Co. (C)

562
DUBBS, JACOB. Cabinetmaker.
Born c. 1819, Germany; w. 1850, Mishawaka, St. Joseph Co. (C)

563
DUBOIS, RICHMOND. Cabinetmaker.
Born c. 1814, Indiana; w. 1850, Harmony Twp., Union Co. (C)

564
DUBOIS, WILLIAM. Cabinetmaker.
Born c. 1812, Ohio; w. 1850, Covington, Fountain Co. (C)

565
DUEESE, CHARLES. Chairmaker.
Born c. 1827, Kentucky; w. 1850, Harrison Co. (C)

566
DUFFY, ALEXANDER M. Chairmaker.
W. -1841-, North Madison, Jefferson Co. Adv. in *Republican Banner*, 12 May 1841:
"CHAIRS, CHAIRS. The undersigned has removed his chair ware-room to the second story of the large building on the corner of Main Cross & Mulberry street, where he intends to keep on hand a large assortment of Fancy and Windsor Chairs, Settees, &c., . . . A. M. DUFFY."

567
DUFFY, THOMAS M.—*see* DAVIDSON, WILLIAM H.

568
DUKE, ANDREW J. Cabinetmaker.
Born c. 1833, Indiana; w. 1850,

Indianapolis, Marion Co. Lived with Samuel Duke, cabinetmaker. (C)

569
DUKE, BURTON. Cabinetmaker. Born c. 1831, Indiana; w. 1850, Indianapolis, Marion Co. Lived with Samuel Duke, cabinetmaker. (C)

570
DUKE, SAMUEL. Cabinetmaker. Born c. 1793, Ireland; est. 1833, Indianapolis, Marion Co. Still working in 1850. Adv. in *Indiana Democrat* 1 February 1833: "CABINET MAKING . . . From long experience in the practice of his trade in New-York, Philadelphia, Pittsburgh and Cincinnati he thinks himself able to do work in the most fashionable and approved style . . . ." Burton Duke and Andrew J. Duke, cabinetmakers, lived in the same household in 1850. (C)

571
DUNCAN, MICHAEL. Chairmaker. Born c. 1823, Indiana; w. 1850, Stony Creek Twp., Randolph Co. (C)

572
DUNCAN, STEPHEN. Cabinetmaker. W. 1840, Richmond, Wayne Co. Adv. in the *Palladium*, 11 January 1840: "The subscriber has just finished, and offers for sale, some handsome articles of FUR-NITURE, and good assortment of plain work. . . ." *See also* BURK, RICHARD.

573
DUNCLE, JACOB. Chairmaker. Born c. 1816, Pennsylvania; w. 1850, Knox Co. Two men in shop; in 1850 they made 1,000 chairs valued at $1,000. (C, MC)

574
DUNFEE, WILLIAM H. Cabinetmaker. Born c. 1822, Pennsylvania; w. 1850, Whitley Co. (C)

575
DUNHAM, E. LIVINGSTON. Fancy painter. Born c. 1830, Ohio; w. 1850, Vernon Twp., Jennings Co. (C)

576
DUNHAM, WILLIAM. Fancy chairmaker. Born c. 1790, Kentucky; w. 1850, Union Twp., Jennings Co. Two men in shop; their raw materials included poplar lumber. In 1850 they produced chairs, settees, etc., worth $700. (C, MC)

577
DUNKLE, JONATHAN. Chairmaker. Born c. 1825, Pennsylvania; w. 1850, Carroll Co. (C) *See also* TUTWILER & DUNKLE.

578
DUNNEGAN, ELIJAH. Cabinetmaker. Born c. 1827; w. 1850, Gosport, Owen Co. (C)

579

DURLIN, ANDREW. Chairmaker.
Born c. 1809, Pennsylvania; w.
1850, Lynn Twp., Posey Co. (C)

580

DUZAN, WILLIAM.
Cabinetmaker.
Born c. 1810, Kentucky; w. 1850,
Indianapolis, Marion Co. (C)

581

EGAN, D. R. Cabinetmaker.
Born c. 1828, Indiana; w. 1850,
Princeton, Gibson Co. (C)

582

EAST, JOSEPH. Chairmaker.
Born c. 1796, Pennsylvania; w.
1826, Terre Haute, Vigo Co., in
firm of Davey & East, q.v. Still
working in 1850, when there were
two men in his shop; they made
500 chairs that year, valued at
$650. (C, MC)

583

EATON, CHARLES G.
Chairmaker.
Born c. 1829, Illinois; w. 1850,
Parke Co. Lived with John B.
Innis, chairmaker. (C)

584

EATON, ROBERT. Cabinetmaker.
Born c. 1827, Ohio; w. 1850,
Rising Sun, Ohio Co. (C)

585

EDWARDS, JOHN.
Cabinetmaker.
Born c. 1825, Ohio; w. 1850, Jef-
ferson Twp., Miami Co. (C)

586

EDWARDS, THO. W.
Cabinetmaker.
Born c. 1811, Ohio; w. 1850,
Shelbyville, Shelby Co. (C)

587

EDWARDS, TOM. Cabinetmaker.
Born c. 1835, Ohio; w. 1850,
Sugar Creek Twp., Shelby Co.
(C)

588

EDWARDS, WILLIAM.
Chairmaker.
Born c. 1828, Indiana; w. 1850,
Winchester, Randolph Co. Lived
with Lewis Walker, chairmaker.
(C)

589

EGBERT, GEORGE. Chairmaker.
Born c. 1822, Ohio; w. 1850,
Pleasant Twp., Grant Co. (C)

590

EICKHOFF, FRANCIS.
Cabinetmaker.
Born c. 1811, Germany; w. 1850,
Wayne Twp., Allen Co. (C)

591

ELDRIDGE, SOLOMON.
Chairmaker.
Born c. 1813, North Carolina; w.
1850, Shawswick Twp., Lawrence
Co. (C)

592

ELEMAN, JAMES. Chairmaker.
Born c. 1823, Indiana; w. 1850,
Jefferson Twp., Miami Co. (C)

593

ELLER, MOSES. Cabinetmaker.
Born c. 1809, Pennsylvania; w.
1850, Mishawaka, St. Joseph Co.
(C)

594
ELLIOTT, AUGUSTINE.
Cabinetmaker.
    Born c. 1832, Kentucky; w. 1850,
    Greencastle, Putnam Co. Lived
    with Greenup Lee, cabinetmaker.
    (C)

595
ELLISON, ALEXANDER.
Chairmaker.
    Born c. 1818, New York; w.
    1850, York Twp., Elkhart Co.
    (C)

596
ELTZROTH, JOHN. Chairmaker.
    Born c. 1829, Ohio; w. 1850, Mt.
    Pleasant Twp., Delaware Co. (C)

597
EMBREE, THOMAS B.
Cabinetmaker.
    Born c. 1823, Illinois; w. 1850,
    Patoka, Gibson Co. (C)

598
EMERICK, ELIAS. Chairmaker.
    Born c. 1821, Ohio; w. 1850,
    Portage Twp., St. Joseph Co.
    (C)

599
EMERY, WILLIAM.
Cabinetmaker.
    Born c. 1832, Indiana; w. 1850,
    Salem, Washington Co. Lived
    with Westley Smith, cabinet-
    maker, q.v. (C)

600
EMINGER, ANDREW.
Chairmaker.
    Born c. 1818, Pennsylvania; w.
    1844-1850, Bloomfield Twp., La
    Grange Co. (C, CH 12)

601
ENGLE, ALLEN. Cabinetmaker.
    Born c. 1831, Illinois; w. 1850,
    Washington Twp., Parke Co. (C)

602
ENGLE, JAMES. Cabinetmaker.
    Born c. 1814, Ohio; w. 1850,
    Washington Twp., Parke Co. (C)

603
ENGLERTH, GEORGE D.
Cabinetmaker.
    Born c. 1825, Pennsylvania; w.
    1850, Greensboro Twp., Henry Co.
    (C)

604
ENGLISH, CHARLES.
Cabinetmaker.
    Born c. 1821, New Jersey; w.
    1850, Vernon Twp., Hancock Co.
    (C)

605
ENTZLE, JACOB. Cabinetmaker.
    Born c. 1821, Germany; w. 1850,
    Harrison Twp., Wells Co. Lived
    with David Bovine, cabinetmaker.
    (C)

606
EPAERY, REASON.
Cabinetmaker.
    Born c. 1816, Kentucky; w. 1850,
    Harrison Co. (C)

607
ESHELMAN, JACOB.
Cabinetmaker.
    Born c. 1786, Pennsylvania; w.
    1850, Jackson Twp., Hamilton Co.
    (C)

608
ESHLIMAN, HENRY F.
Cabinetmaker.

Born c. 1822, Pennsylvania; w. 1850, Jackson Twp., Wayne Co. (C)

609
ESPY, GEORGE. Cabinetmaker.
Born c. 1799, Pennsylvania; w. -1837-1850-, Indianapolis, Marion Co. Partner in firm of Espy & Sloan, q.v. (C)

610
ESPY & SLOAN.
Cabinet- and chairmakers.
George Espy and John(?) Sloan; w. -1837-1850-, Indianapolis, Marion Co. Awarded second prize for cabinet work at the Marion County Fair in 1837 (*Indiana Democrat* 18 October 1837). Adv. in *Indiana State Gazette* 3 November 1838: "ESPY & SLOAN CABINET AND CHAIR MAKERS . . . Coffins made to order." In 1850 there were four men working in this shop, using horse power to make 100 pairs of bedsteads, 75 tables, 50 bureaus and "Other Articles of Work." Child's chair made by this firm in 1847 is in the collection of the Children's Museum, Indianapolis (Plate XIII). William W. Weaver, q.v., also worked for this firm at one time. *See also* SLOAN, JOHN; STONE, JOHN.

611
ESTAL, THOMAS.
Cabinetmaker.
Born c. 1820, Kentucky; w. 1850, Wayne Twp., Henry Co. (C)

612
ETHELL, WILLIAM G. Printer, glazier, and chairmaker.
Born 1821; w. -1848-, Muncie, Delaware Co. (CH 36)

613
EVANS, CALVIN J.
Cabinetmaker.
Born c. 1816, North Carolina; w. 1850, Parke Co. In same household, John M. Wadding, cabinetmaker. Prior to 1860, Calvin Evans and a David Best conducted a cabinet shop at Annapolis, Parke Co. (C, CH 10)

614
EVANS, FRANK. Cabinetmaker.
Born c. 1828, Indiana; w. 1850, Charlestown Twp., Clark Co. (C)

615
EVERHART, JAMES.
Cabinetmaker.
Born c. 1804, Pennsylvania; w. 1850, Richland Twp., Steuben Co. In same household, Albert Morley, cabinetmaker. (C)

616
EWING, JOHN. Chairmaker.
Born c. 1831, Indiana; w. 1850, Lafayette, Tippecanoe Co. (C)

617
FADELY, MICHAEL.
Cabinetmaker.
Born c. 1822, Virginia; w. 1850, Jefferson Twp., Henry Co. (C)

618
FAIRFIELD, HARISON.
Cabinetmaker.
Born c. 1832, New York; w. 1850, Wayne Twp., Wayne Co. (C)

619
FAIRFIELD, HARRISON.
Cabinetmaker.
  Born c. 1830, Pennsylvania; w.
  1850, Wayne Twp., Wayne Co.
  (C)

620
FANVELT, ANTHONY.
Cabinetmaker.
  Born c. 1804, Germany; w. 1850,
  Ray Twp., Franklin Co. (C)

621
.FARGHER, THOMAS.
Cabinetmaker.
  Born c. 1832, Isle of Man; w.
  1850, La Porte, La Porte Co.
  Father was a carpenter and
  joiner. (C)

622
FARRIS, WASHINGTON.
Cabinetmaker.
  Born c. 1823, Ohio; w. 1850,
  Highland Twp., Franklin Co. (C)

623
FAY, EZRA. Cabinetmaker.
  Born c. 1817, Maine; w. 1850,
  Bluffton, Wells Co. (C)

624
FENKLE, CONRAD.
Cabinetmaker.
  Born c. 1819, Pennsylvania; w.
  1850, Columbus, Bartholomew Co.
  (C)

625
FENTON, DANIEL.
Cabinetmaker.
  Born c. 1829, Indiana; w. 1850,
  Deerfield, Randolph Co. Lived
  with Francis M. Avery, cabinet-
  maker. (C)

626
FENTON, DANIEL.
Cabinetmaker.
  , Born c. 1831, Indiana; w. 1850,
  Pine Twp., Warren Co. (C)

627
FERGUS (FURGUS), ROBERT.
Cabinetmaker.
  Born c. 1811, England; w. 1850,
  Evansville, Vanderburgh Co. Five
  men worked in his shop and in
  1850 produced cabinet furniture
  worth $3,600. (C, MC)

628
FERMER, WYATT.
,Cabinetmaker.
  Born c. 1831, Ohio; w. 1850,
  Brookville, Franklin Co. (C)

629
FERRIS, EZRA. "Furniture businessman."
  W. -1839-, Lawrenceburg, Dearborn Co. Listed as a "furniture
  businessman" in the *Political Beacon* 11 December 1839. Ferris, a
  Baptist preacher and physician,
  , was also a territorial and state
  legislator, and member of the 1816
  Constitutional Convention.

630
FIELD, DAVID. Cabinetmaker.
  Born c. 1800, Vermont; w. 1850,
  Orange Twp., Noble Co. (C)

631
FILO, EDWARD S.
Cabinetmaker.
  Born c. 1821, Pennsylvania; w.
  1850, Michigan Twp., La Porte
  Co. (C)

632
FINK, CHARLES.
Cabinetmaker.
> Born c. 1813, Pennsylvania; w.
> 1850, Wayne Twp., Allen Co.,
> when there were six men in his
> shop who made furniture valued
> at $2,500. He was a member of
> the board of aldermen of the city
> of Fort Wayne, 1846-47, and
> he died prior to 1875. Cabinet-
> makers William Keefer and Ed-
> ward Rowe lived in his house-
> hold in 1850. (C, MC, CH 21)

633
FINNELL, BENJAMIN.
Cabinetmaker.
> Born c. 1823, Virginia; w. 1850,
> Liberty Twp., Union Co. (C)

634
FISHER, ANTHONY.
Cabinetmaker.
> Born c. 1812, Germany; w. 1850,
> Wayne Twp., Allen Co. (C)

635
FISHER, JOHN P.
Cabinetmaker.
> Born c. 1828, Indiana; w. 1850,
> Shawswick Twp., Lawrence Co.
> Lived with Michael W. Houston,
> cabinetmaker, q.v. (C)

636
FISHER, MICHAEL.
Cabinetmaker.
> Born c. 1817, Germany; w. 1850,
> Wayne Twp., Allen Co. (C)

637
FISHER, SAMUEL. Chairmaker.
> Born c. 1821, Indiana; w. 1850,
> Haddon Twp., Sullivan Co. (C)

638
FITLER, JACOB B. Cabinetmaker
and chairmaker.
> Born c. 1810, Pennsylvania; w.
> 1850, Indianapolis, Marion Co.
> Listed as a chairmaker in the
> population census, he was listed
> as a cabinetmaker and chairmaker
> in the industrial census. Twelve
> men worked in his shop with
> machinery powered by steam. In
> 1850 they produced 800 dozen
> chairs, 500 bedsteads, 200 tables
> and $5,000 worth of other work.
> (C, MC)

639
FITZPATRICK, HENRY.
Cabinetmaker.
> Born c. 1799, Kentucky; w. 1850,
> Bono Twp., Lawrence Co. (C)

640
FLAIR, FRANCIS. Cabinetmaker.
> Born c. 1822, Germany; w. 1850,
> Shelbyville, Shelby Co. (C)

641
FLEHART, AZARIAH.
Cabinetmaker.
> Born c. 1809, Kentucky; w. 1850,
> Harrison Twp., Vigo Co. In same
> household, William Flehart,
> cabinetmaker. (C)

642
FLEHART, WILLIAM.
Cabinetmaker.
> Born c. 1827, Ohio; w. 1850,
> Harrison Twp., Vigo Co. Lived
> with Azariah Flehart, cabinet-
> maker. (C)

643
FLEMING, SAMUEL.
Chairmaker.
> Born c. 1823, Ohio; w. 1850,

Huntington, Huntington Co. Lived with John Hoover, chairmaker. (C)

644
FLEMING, SAMUEL G. Cabinetmaker.
> Born c. 1827, Ohio; w. 1850, Warren, Huntington Co. Lived with Michael Oats, cabinetmaker. (C)

645
FLETCHER, E. H. Cabinetmaker.
> Born c. 1800, Virginia; w. 1850, Parke Co. In same household, Gran(?) Fletcher, cabinetmaker. (C)

646
FLETCHER, GRAN(?). Cabinetmaker.
> Born c. 1830, Virginia; w. 1850, Parke Co. Lived with E. H. Fletcher, cabinetmaker. (C)

647
FLETCHER, ZACHARIAH. Cabinetmaker.
> Born c. 1799, North Carolina; w. 1850, Cambridge City, Wayne Co. (C)

647a
FLOYD, JOHN, *see* RICE, JOHN.

648
FOGEL, C. G. FERDINAND. Cabinetmaker.
> Born c. 1826, Prussia; w. 1850, Portage Twp., St. Joseph Co. Lived with John E. Mason, cabinetmaker. (C)

649
FORD, JAMES. Cabinetmaker.
> Born c. 1817, Maryland; w. 1850, **Wayne Twp., Hamilton Co. (C)**

650
FORD, WILLIAM. Cabinetmaker.
> Born c. 1815, Maryland; w. 1850, Wayne Twp., Hamilton Co. (C)

651
FOSTER, JOHN. Cabinetmaker.
> Born c. 1801, Pennsylvania; w. 1850, Lima, La Grange Co. (C)

652
FOSTER, LEWIS. Cabinetmaker.
> Born c. 1815, Ohio; w. 1850, Marion, Grant Co. (C)

653
FOSTER, RILEY (RELEY). Cabinetmaker.
> Born c. 1811, New York; w. 1850, Vernon, Jennings Co. Two men in shop; in 1850 they made "160 Bureaus, bedsteads &c." valued at $1,000. William Foster, cabinetmaker, lived in same household, as did R. Levit, a wheat fan maker. (C, MC)

654
FOSTER, WILLIAM. Cabinetmaker.
> Born c. 1832, Indiana; w. 1850, Vernon, Jennings Co. Lived with Riley Foster, cabinetmaker. (C)

655
FOUST, PHILLIP. Cabinetmaker.
> Born c. 1830, Ohio; w. 1850, Ripley Twp., Rush Co. (C)

656
FOY, PHINEAS H. Cabinetmaker.
> Born c. 1815, Connecticut; w. -1845-1850-, Greenfield, Hancock Co. In 1850 there were four men working in his shop, who made

50 bureaus, 200 bedsteads, and 100 tables worth $2,250. (C, CH 44, MC)

657
FRANKENBARGER, DARIUS. Cabinetmaker.
Born c. 1828, Pennsylvania; w. 1850, Randolph Twp., Tippecanoe Co. (C)

658
FRANKIN, MATTHIAS. Cabinetmaker.
Born c. 1820, Germany; w. 1850, Peru, Miami Co. (C)

659
FRAZER (FRAZEE), JOSHUA. Cabinetmaker.
Born c. 1826, Ohio; w. 1850, Jefferson Twp., Miami Co. Four men worked in his shop using 100,000 feet of lumber. Their cabinet furniture was valued at $2,000. (C, MC)

660
FREDLIN, JOHN. Cabinetmaker.
Born c. 1827, Germany; w. 1850, Evansville, Vanderburgh Co. (C)

661
FREEMAN, FLETCHER. Cabinetmaker.
Born c. 1827, Indiana; w. 1848-1850, Sullivan, Sullivan Co. In Sullivan Freeman lived on the south side of the city square. (C, CH 52)

662
FREEMAN, LINDSAY. Cabinetmaker.
Born c. 1833, North Carolina; w.

1850, Greensboro Twp., Henry Co. Lived with Joseph Butler, cabinetmaker. (C)

663
FRENCH, LEWIS. Cabinetmaker.
Born c. 1806, Connecticut; w. 1850, Jefferson Twp., Switzerland Co. (C)

664
FRENCH, SIMON. Chairmaker.
Born c. 1801, New Jersey; w. 1850, Union Twp., Montgomery Co. (C)

665
FRITZ, JOHN. Cabinetmaker.
Born c. 1829, Indiana; w. 1850, Greencastle, Putnam Co. (C)

666
FRY, RANDALL S. Chairmaker.
Born c. 1810, Pennsylvania; w. 1850, Noblesville, Hamilton Co. (C)

667
FULLER, AARON. Cabinetmaker.
Born c. 1820, Ohio; w. 1850, Cedar Creek Twp., Lake Co. In same household, James Allen, cabinetmaker. (C)

668
FULLERTON, WILLIAM H. Upholsterer.
Born c. 1834, Pennsylvania; w. 1850, Utica Twp., Clark Co. Lived with William T. Fullerton. (C)

669
FULLERTON, WILLIAM T. Upholsterer.
Born c. 1804, Pennsylvania; w. 1850, Utica Twp., Clark Co. In

the same household, also an upholsterer, William H. Fullerton. (C)

670
FURGENSON, ALEX. U. Cabinetmaker.
Born c. 1834, Scotland; w. 1850, Madison, Jefferson Co. (C)

670a
GAAR, JONAS. Cabinetmaker.
Born 1792, Virginia; died 1875, Richmond, Wayne Co.; w. Richmond 1820-. (CH 53)

671
GABLE, CHARLES. Cabinetmaker.
Born 1805, Hesse Darmstadt, Germany, where he served a seven-year apprenticeship to the cabinetmaking trade. Served as a journeyman until 1830 when he sailed from Lyons, France, to Baltimore, Maryland. He began making chairs and pianos and moved to Louisville, Kentucky, where he operated a chair factory and had an undertaking establishment. He moved to Charlestown, Clark Co., where he was recorded in the 1850 census and where he died in 1859. (C, CH 45)

672
GABRIEL, JOHN. Cabinetmaker.
Born c. 1825, Ohio; w. 1850, Van Buren Twp., Fountain Co. (C)

673
GABRIEL, JOHN S. Cabinetmaker.
Born c. 1823, Ohio; w. 1850, Covington, Fountain Co. (C) *See also* UHLER & GABRIEL.

674
GAGEBY, JAMES. Cabinetmaker.
Born c. 1805, Pennsylvania; w. -1850 to late 1880s, Decatur Co. In 1850 there were three men working in his shop; they produced that year "282 pieces Furniture &c.," valued at $1,500. In 1852 Gageby was a member of the firm of Gageby and Siling, who were using steam-powered machinery to produce furniture; by 1857, fifteen men were working in this establishment, which was destroyed by fire in the late 1880s. (C, MC, CH 24)

675
GAGEBY, JAMES A. Cabinetmaker.
Born c. 1834, Indiana; w. 1850, Greensburg, Decatur Co. (C)

676
GAINEY, WILLIAM WILSHIRE. Cabinetmaker, merchant, and civil servant.
Born 5 June 1831, Monroe Co.; w. 1850, Perry Twp., Lawrence Co. Later was a clerk in Bloomfield and a merchant there prior to 1862; from 1862 to 1869 he was in the civil service; and from 1869 to 1890 he operated a general store in Bloomfield. (C, CH 8)

677
GALLOWAY, JOHN E. Cabinetmaker.
Born c. 1820, Kentucky; w. 1850, Haw Creek Twp., Bartholomew Co. (C)

678

GANDY, WILLIAM H.
Cabinetmaker.
  Born c. 1829, Virginia; w. 1850,
  Whitley Co. (C)

679

GANIER, JOHN. Cabinetmaker.
  Born c. 1826, Pennsylvania; w.
  1850, Harrison Twp., Vigo Co.
  (C) *See also* GANNEAR &
  COOK.

680

GANNEAR & COOK.
Cabinetmakers.
  John Ganier (Gannear) and Ferdinand G. Cook; w. 1850, Harrison Twp., Vigo Co. Six men
  employed in this shop; in 1850
  they produced 37 bureaus worth
  $750, 200 bedsteads for $1,000,
  150 tables valued at $800, and
  "Safes & Other Articles" worth
  $1,000. (MC)

681

GAPEN, ZACHARIAH.
Cabinetmaker and undertaker.
  W. 1835, Centerville, Wayne Co.
  Manufactured bureaus, secretaries,
  bedsteads, sideboards, tables, pillar
  and claw stands, common tables,
  and coffins. There was a potter
  of the same name working in
  Jacksonburg. (CH 46)

682

GARDNER, ANDREW.
Cabinetmaker and undertaker.
  Born c. 1796, Boston, Mass.; w.
  1814-1860, Vincennes, Knox Co.
  He arrived in Vincennes in 1814
  and died in the spring of 1860.
  He was succeeded by his son
  Dexter Gardner, whose son

George Gardner took over in 1901.
Since 1902 the firm which is still
in business has been known as
Dexter Gardner & Son. In 1850
its products were 60 bedsteads
worth $360, 40 tables $200, 13
bureaus $223, and 60 coffins $480.
By 1853 Andrew Gardner had
turned largely to the undertaking
business.
  Furniture known: chest and
cradle owned by Francis Vigo
Chapter, D.A.R.; secretary, chairs,
clock case, desk, and chest or bonnet box privately owned. See
Plates VI and IX.
  Others involved in the firm included Elbridge G. Gardner, who
joined about 1840 and was still
living in 1902 (a corner cupboard
made by him is extant). In 1850
Andrew Gardner's sons James
(age 23) and George (age 15)
were also listed in the same household as cabinetmakers. *See above,*
pp. 24-28; Account book (microfilm in Indiana State Library, C,
MC, CH 11)

683

GARDNER, BENJAMIN.
Cabinetmaker.
  Born c. 1822, Indiana; w. 1850,
  Noblesville, Hamilton Co. (C)

684

GARDNER, DEXTER—*see*
GARDNER, ANDREW.

685

GARDNER, ELBRIDGE—*see*
GARDNER, ANDREW.

686

GARDNER, GEORGE.
Cabinetmaker.

Born c. 1835, Indiana; w. 1850,
Vincennes, Knox Co. (C) *See
also* GARDNER, ANDREW.

687
GARDNER, JAMES. Cabinet-
maker.
Born c. 1827, Indiana; w. 1850,
Vincennes, Knox Co. (C) *See
also* GARDNER, ANDREW.

688
GARDNER, JOHN. Chairmaker.
Born c. 1821, Pennsylvania; w.
1850, Madison, Jefferson Co. (C)

689
GARMIRE, JOHN.
Cabinetmaker.
Born c. 1816, Pennsylvania; w.
1850, La Grange Co. Four men in
shop; in 1850 they produced
cabinet ware worth $2,000. (C,
MC)

690
GARRETT, MADISON.
Chairmaker.
Born c. 1830, North Carolina;
w. 1850, Washington Twp., Ham-
ilton Co. Lived with William
Garrett, turner. (C)

691
GARRETT, WILLIAM. Turner.
Born c. 1800, North Carolina; w.
1850, Washington Twp., Hamilton
Co. In same household, Madison
Garrett, chairmaker. (C)

692
GASEWAY, WILLIAM.
Cabinetmaker.
Born c. 1816, Kentucky; w. 1850,
Washington Twp., Gibson Co.
(C)

693
GASKILL, JOHN. Chairmaker.
Born c. 1817, Ohio; w. 1850,
Franklin Twp., Montgomery Co.
(C)

694
GAY, ZEBULEN. Chairmaker.
Born c. 1776, Vermont; w. 1850,
Huntington Co. (C)

695
GEARING, JOHN. Cabinetmaker.
Born c. 1822, Germany; w. 1850,
St. Johns Twp., Lake Co. (C)

696
GEBHART, JACOB.
Cabinetmaker.
Born c. 1822, Germany; w. 1850,
Kelso Twp., Dearborn Co. (C)

697
GEISELMAN (GUYSELMAN),
JOHN. Wheelwright and chair-
maker.
Born c. 1816, Pennsylvania; w.
1836-1850-, Warsaw, Kosciusko
Co. (C, CH 6)

698
GELLESPIE, ALEXANDER J.
Cabinetmaker.
Born c. 1815, Ohio; w. 1850,
Prairie Twp., Kosciusko Co. (C)

699
GETTYS, JOHN. Cabinetmaker.
Born c. 1818, Pennsylvania; w.
1850, Waltz Twp., Wabash Co.
(C)

700
GHARKEY, DAVID.
Cabinetmaker.
Born c. 1774, Germany; w. 1850,
Muncie, Delaware Co. (C)

701
GIFFORD, SAMUEL.
Cabinetmaker.
 Born c. 1829, Indiana; w. 1850,
 Madison, Jefferson Co. (C)

702
GIFT, LEWIS. Cabinetmaker.
 Born c. 1814, Indiana; w. 1850.
 Lagro Twp., Wabash Co. (C)

703
GILBERT, B. P.
Painter and chairmaker.
 Born c. 1807, Vermont; w. 1850,
 Michigan City, La Porte Co. (C)

704
GILES, FRANCIS M.
Cabinetmaker.
 Born c. 1829, Indiana; w. 1850,
 Posey Twp., Franklin Co. (C)

705
GILL, JAMES. Cabinetmaker.
 Born c. 1821, Pennsylvania; w.
 1850, Monroe Twp., Pulaski Co.
 (C)

706
GILLMORE, THOMAS S.
Cabinetmaker.
 Born c. 1816, Kentucky; w. 1850,
 Harrison Co. (C)

707
GILLS—see KRANELE
(KRAENLE) & GILLS.

708
GILSON, JAMES W. Chairmaker.
 Born c. 1817, Ohio; w. 1850,
 Marshall Co. (C)

709
GIPSON, ARCHIBALD.
Chairmaker.
 Born c. 1783, New Jersey; w.
 1850, Warren Twp., Marion Co.
 (C)

710
GIPSON, JASPER M.
Chairmaker.
 Born c. 1825, Ohio; w. 1850,
 Warren Twp., Marion Co. (C)

711
GITHEN (GITHENS), ELIJAH.
Chairmaker.
 Born in New Jersey; w. 1833-c.
 1847, Richmond, Wayne Co.
 Later was a grocer. He and his
 brother Griffith D. Githen(s),
 q.v., adv. in the *Palladium,* 18
 January 1834, that they "have
 permanently established themselves
 in this town in the CHAIR
 MAKING BUSINESS. . .
 [and] have on hand a large and
 general assortment of Fancy and
 Winsor chairs, settees, &c, which
 they will sell low for cash or
 approved country produce." (CH
 34)

712
GITHEN (GITHENS),
GRIFFITH D. Chairmaker.
 Born c. 1810, New Jersey; w.
 1850-1869, Wayne Twp., Wayne
 Co. He was the brother of Elijah
 Githen, q.v. In 1850 he produced
 100 sets of chairs valued at $500;
 25 settees worth $125, and other
 articles worth $150. In 1860 his
 shop made 800 chairs. (C, MC,
 CH 34)

713
GIVENS, BENJAMIN. Cabinet-
maker.
 Born c. 1825, Indiana; w. 1850,
 Danville, Hendricks Co. (C)

714
GIVINS, JAMES P.
Cabinetmaker.
 Born c. 1817, Illinois; w. 1850,
 Van Buren Twp., Monroe Co.
 Two men working in shop; in
 1850 they produced furniture
 valued at $1,000. (C, MC)

715
GIVINS, JOHN B. Cabinetmaker.
 Born c. 1822, Indiana; w. 1850,
 Van Buren Twp., Monroe Co. In
 same household, Shelton Hazel-
 wood, cabinetmaker. (C)

716
GLAZIER, EDWIN.
Cabinetmaker.
 Born c. 1816, Massachusetts; w.
 1850, Harrison Twp., Vigo Co.
 (C)

717
GLEASON, JOHN. Cabinetmaker.
 Born c. 1827, New York; w.
 1850, Harrison Twp., Morgan Co.
 (C)

718
GLISNER, R. A. Cabinetmaker.
 Born c. 1826, Ohio; w. 1850,
 Union Twp., Montgomery Co.
 (C)

719
GLOVER, WILLIAM.
Cabinetmaker.
 Born c. 1829, Indiana; w. 1850,
 Vernon Twp., Washington Co.
 (C)

720
GLUTSBACHER, FRED.
Cabinetmaker.
 Born c. 1807, Saxony; w. 1850,
 Madison, Jefferson Co. (C)

721
GOBEN, ANDREW J.
Chairmaker.
 Born c. 1831, Indiana; w. 1850,
 Lexington, Scott Co. (C)

722
GOLD, JOHN JACOB.
Cabinetmaker.
 Born c. 1826, Germany; w. 1850,
 Indianapolis, Marion Co. (C)

723
GOOD, ASHAM. Chairmaker.
 Born c. 1780, North Carolina; w.
 1850, Washington Twp., Randolph
 Co. (C)

724
GOODWIN, MOSES.
Cabinetmaker.
 Born c. 1824, Indiana; w. 1850,
 Lawrenceburg, Dearborn Co. (C)

725
GOODWIN, SIDNEY B.
Cabinetmaker.
 W. -1827-1856-, Terre Haute,
 Vigo Co. Account book is in the
 library of the Indiana Historical
 Society. *See above,* pp. 29-30.

726
GOODYEAR, GEORGE H.
Cabinetmaker.
 Born c. 1819, Pennsylvania; w.
 1850, Princeton, Gibson Co. Francis A. Hoskins worked with him,
 and in 1850 they produced 100
 tables and bedsteads in addition
 to other unspecified articles, the
 whole valued at $1,200. (C, MC)

727
GORDON—*see*
LIFE & GORDON.

728
GORDON, SILAS. Cabinetmaker.
Born c. 1793, Virginia; w. 1850,
Emmettsville, Randolph Co. (C)
See LIFE & GORDON.

729
GORDON, WILLIAM.
Cabinetmaker.
Born c. 1828, Ohio; w. 1850,
Wayne Twp., Henry Co. (C)

730
GOSNEY, JOHN—*see* GOSNEY
& DERRINGTON.

731
GOSNEY & DERRINGTON.
Cabinetmakers.
John Gosney and Matthias Derrington; w. 1830s, Williamsburg,
Johnson Co. "Derrington is remembered as a skillful mechanic,
and numerous specimens of his
handiwork are still to be seen
. . . . [1888]." (CH 29)

732
GOSSETT, ELIJAH.
Cabinetmaker.
Born c. 1818, Tennessee; w. 1850,
Salem, Washington Co. Three
men in shop; in 1850 they produced furniture worth $2,500. In
same household, Bartlett Young,
cabinetmaker. (C, MC)

733
GOULD, INGRAHAM. Turner.
Arrived in Springville, La Porte
Co., in 1834; in 1845 he erected
a turning lathe and "did large
business in manufacture of bedsteads and other furniture requir-
ing turned work." (CH 13)

734
GOVER, JOHN B. Cabinetmaker.
Born c. 1796, Virginia; w. 1850,
Jeffersonville, Clark Co. (C)

735
GRABLE (GRAEBLE), LEWIS.
Cabinetmaker.
Born c. 1816, Germany; w. 1850,
Wayne Twp., Allen Co. (C)

736
GRACE, JESSE. Chairmaker.
W. 1830, Indianapolis, Marion Co.
Adv. in *Indiana Journal* 10 February 1830: "House and Sign
Painting and CHAIR MAKING.
Jesse Grace still continues to
carry on the above business on
Meridian street, a few doors south
of Washington street, where the
public can be accommodated with
any kind of work in his line, of
the best materials, and made in
the best style. Persons wishing
any description of Windsor
Chairs, Settees, Cradle Settees,
&c. &c. can be accommodated by
an application." He also wanted
an apprentice and a journeyman.

737
GRAFFE, FREDERICK.
Cabinetmaker.
Born c. 1810, Germany; w. 1850,
Wayne Twp., Allen Co. (C) *See
also* MUHLER & GRAFFE.

738
GRAHAM, HUGH. Cabinetmaker.
Born c. 1831; w. 1850, Indiana-
polis, Marion Co. Lived with
George Espy, cabinetmaker, q.v.
(C)

739
GRAHAM, STILWELL.
Cabinetmaker.
Born c. 1813, Kentucky; w. 1850,
Pleasant Twp., Switzerland Co.
(C)

740
GRAMLY, ISAAC. Cabinetmaker.
Born c. 1822, Pennsylvania; w.
1850, Muncie, Delaware Co.
George Myers listed as his apprentice. (C)

741
GRAMPUS, DANIEL.
Cabinetmaker.
Born c. 1825, Germany; w. 1850,
Eel Twp., Cass Co. (C)

742
GRAY, ENOS. Cabinetmaker.
Born c. 1825, Indiana; w. 1850,
Rising Sun, Ohio Co. Lived with
John T. Whitlock, cabinetmaker.
(C)

743
GRAY, JAMES. Upholsterer.
Born c. 1830, Ohio; w. 1850,
Pleasant Twp., Switzerland Co.
(C)

744
GREAN & DIPPLE.
Cabinetmakers.
—— Grean and John Dipple; w.
1850, Evansville, Vanderburgh Co.
Three men worked in this shop,
and in 1850 they produced cabinet
furniture valued at $1,000. (MC)
William Grese, q.v., was living
next door to John Dipple according to census record.

745
GREEN, CHARLES. Chairmaker.
Born c. 1834, Ohio; w. 1850,
Greensburg, Decatur Co. Lived
with Eli Green, chairmaker. (C)

746
GREEN, ELI. Chairmaker.
Born c. 1802, New Jersey; w.
1850, Greensburg, Decatur Co.
Three men worked in his shop
(probably William and Charles
Green were the other two, for
they lived in his household); in
1850 they produced 1,500 chairs
valued at $1,500. (C, MC)

747
GREEN, JOB. Chairmaker.
Born c. 1795, New Jersey; w.
1850, Wayne Twp., Wayne Co.
In same household, Thomas I.
Green, chairmaker. (C)

748
GREEN, MASON F.
Cabinetmaker.
Born c. 1802, Kentucky; w. 1850,
Marrs Twp., Posey Co. (C)

749
GREEN, SAMUEL. Chairmaker.
Born c. 1794, Pennsylvania; w.
1850, Jackson Twp., Jackson Co.
(C)

750
GREEN, THOMAS I.
Chairmaker.
Born c. 1830, New Jersey; w.
1850-1860-, Richmond, Wayne Co.
In 1850 he was living with Job
Green, chairmaker. In 1860 Thomas Green listed his raw materials
as "walnut, backs, slats, glue etc."
and he produced 60 dozen chairs
that year. (C, MC)

751
GREEN, WILLIAM. Chairmaker.
Born c. 1828, Ohio; w. 1850,
Greensburg, Decatur Co. Lived
with Eli Green, chairmaker, q.v.
(C)

752
GREER, JAMES. Cabinetmaker.
Born c. 1815, Pennsylvania; w.
1838-1870-, Indianapolis, Marion
Co. *See* RAMSEY & GREER.
In the 1860 industrial census
Greer listed his raw materials as
"poplar, cherry, walnut, etc." and
his product was furniture worth
$400. (C, CD, MC)

753
GREGG, JOHN. Cabinetmaker.
Born c. 1813, North Carolina; w.
1850, Centerville, Wayne Co. (C)

754
GREGG & CO. Cabinetmaker.
W. 1850, Centre Twp., Wayne
Co. Five men worked in this shop,
using horse and hand power. In
1850 they produced 100 bedsteads,
40 bureaus, and other articles
valued at $1,600. (MC)

755
GRESE, WILLIAM.
Cabinetmaker.
Born c. 1818, Germany; w. 1850,
Evansville, Vanderburgh Co. (C)
See also GREAN & DIPPLE,
possibly same.

756
GRIEBLE, LEWIS. Cabinetmaker.
Born c. 1816, Germany; w. 1850,
Wayne Twp., Allen Co. (C)

757
GRIFFIN, WILLIAM.
Cabinetmaker.
Born c. 1833, Virginia; w. 1850,
Lawrenceburg, Dearborn Co. (C)

758
GRIFFITH, AMOS.
Cabinetmaker.
W. Indianapolis, 1824. **Adv. in**
Indianapolis Gazette, 16 March
1824, "a complete variety of Cabinet Work," also "a large quantity
of IRISH POTATOES. The
terms of sale will be cash in
hand." However, he said that he
would "continue to exchange cabinet work for merchantable cherry,
walnut, ash and poplar plank and
scantling."

759
GRIFFITH, JOHN WESLEY.
Cabinetmaker.
Born c. 1833, Indiana; w. 1850,
Versailles, Ripley Co. Lived with
William Griffith, cabinetmaker.
(C)

760
GRIFFITH, WILLIAM.
Cabinetmaker.
Born c. 1833, Ohio; w. 1850,
Lawrenceburg, Dearborn Co.
Lived with Cyrus Armstrong,
furniture merchant and manufac-
turer, q.v. (C)

761
GRIFFITH, WILLIAM.
Cabinetmaker.
Born c. 1809, Kentucky; w. 1850,

Versailles, Ripley Co. In same household, John Wesley Griffith, cabinetmaker. (C)

762
GRIMBLY, GEORGE.
Cabinetmaker.
Born c. 1812, Connecticut; w. 1850, Rising Sun, Ohio Co. (C)

763
GRIMES, GEORGE J.
Cabinetmaker.
Born c. 1818, Ohio; w. 1850, Washington Twp., Owen Co. (C)

764
GROSEMAN, GEORGE.
Cabinetmaker.
Born c. 1802, Germany; w. 1850, Vanderburgh Co. (C)

765
GROVE, JAMES. Chairmaker.
Born c. 1826, Ohio; w. 1850, Auburn, De Kalb Co. (C)

766
GROW, JOHN. Cabinetmaker.
Born c. 1817, Virginia; w. 1850, Pleasant Twp., Grant Co. (C)

767
GUY, WILLIAM. Chairmaker.
Born c. 1823, New York; w. 1850, Jeffersonville, Clark Co. In his household were Elisha Stevens, chairmaker; a Mr. Lane, cabinetmaker; and Jesse Clemens, chair painter. (C)

768
GUYMON, PRESTLEY.
Cabinetmaker.
Born c. 1821, North Carolina; w. 1848-1850-, Greenfield, Hancock Co. (C, CH 44)

769
HACKET, BENJAMIN.
Cabinetmaker.
Born c. 1824, North Carolina; w. 1850, Raysville, Henry Co. Lived with Jobe Barker, cabinetmaker. (C)

770
HACKLEMAN, CYRUS.
Cabinetmaker.
Born c. 1810, Indiana; w. 1850, Jackson Twp., Hamilton Co. (C)

771
HAFF (?), WILLIAM.
Cabinetmaker.
Born c. 1829, Ohio; w. 1850, Richland Twp., Miami Co. (C)

772
HAFFNER, JOSEPH—see
HARDMAN & HAFFNER.

773
HAGER, ANDREW.
Cabinetmaker.
Born c. 1821, Germany; w. 1850, Ferdinand Twp., Dubois Co. (C)

774
HAIN, LEONARD—see
HAINES, LENARD; STOVER, MATHIAS.

775
HAINES, JAMES. Chairmaker.
Born c. 1830, Ohio; w. 1850, Portage Twp., St. Joseph Co. Lived with Lenard Haines, chairmaker. (C)

776
HAINES, LENARD. Chairmaker.
Born c. 1798, North Carolina; w. 1850, Portage Twp., St. Joseph

Co. In same household, James Haines, chairmaker. (C) *See also* STOVER, MATHIAS.

777
HALE, ELIAS. Cabinetmaker.
Born c. 1805, Kentucky; w. 1850, Hamilton Twp., Sullivan Co. (C)

778
HALE, WILLIAM P. Cabinetmaker.
Born c. 1825, Kentucky; w. 1850, Hamilton Twp., Sullivan Co. (C)

779
HALL, DAVID W. Cabinetmaker.
Born c. 1820, Boone Co.; w. 1850, Boone Co. Three men were working in this shop in 1850, and they produced 30 bureaus valued at $360; 50 bedsteads at $250; 25 tables for $125; and other furniture worth $100. (C, MC)

780
HALL, HARRISON H. Cabinetmaker.
Born c. 1823, Kentucky; w. 1850, Centre Twp., Rush Co. (C)

781
HALL, JAMES. Cabinetmaker.
Born c. 1808, Indiana; w. 1850, Shelby Twp., Jefferson Co. (C)

782
HALL, JAMES A. Cabinetmaker.
Born c. 1806, Virginia; w. 1850, Centre Twp., Rush Co. (C)

783
HALL, THOMAS C. Cabinetmaker.
W. 1838, Rising Sun, Ohio Co. Adv. in *Rising Sun Journal* 30 October 1838 (*see* Fig. 3):

". . . his old stand on the South side of Main Street, near the Corner of Walnut, where he will keep constantly on hand and make to order, all articles in his line of business, such as Sideboards, Bureaus, Breakfast, Dining and Sidetables, Plain and Fancy Bedsteads, Stands, &c. &c."

784
HALL, THOMAS I. Cabinetmaker.
Born c. 1835, Indiana; w. 1850, Madison, Jefferson Co. Lived with William I. Hall, cabinetmaker, q.v. (C)

785
HALL, WILLIAM I. Cabinetmaker.
Born c. 1809, Maryland; w. -1841-1850, Madison, Jefferson Co. Adv. in *Republican Banner* 12 May 1841: "CABINET WARE-ROOM /WILLIAM HALL/ Respectfully informs the citizens of Madison and its vicinity that he has removed his WARE-ROOM about one square above the Court House, on Main-cross street, where he is prepared to manufacture every article in the above business with neatness and despatch." In the same household in 1850 was Thomas I. Hall, cabinetmaker. (C)

786
HALLER, PHILLIP. Cabinetmaker.
Born c. 1822, Germany; w. 1850, Indianapolis, Marion Co. (C)

787
HALLGARTH, NIMROD. Cabinetmaker.

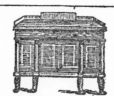

CABINET FURNITURE.
THOMAS C. HALL

TAKES this method of returning his sincere thanks to his friends and former customers, for the very liberal patronage he has heretofore received, and at the same time would inform the public in general, that he continues the Cabinet Making business at his old stand on the South side of Main Street, near the Corner of Walnut, where he will keep constantly on hand and make to order, all articles in his line of business, such as Sideboards, Bureaus, Breakfast, Dining and Sidetables, Plain and Fancy Bedsteads, Stands, &c. &c.

His Stock of Lumber is of the first quality, and from his long experience in the business, and his full determination to employ none but the best of workmen, and to be prompt in fulfilling all his contracts, he confidently anticipates a continuance of past favors.

☞ ALL orders from town or country, will be most thankfully received, and attended to with punctuality and despatch.

Rising Sun, Sept. 12, 1838.—1-tf.

Fig. 3.   From *Rising Sun Journal*

Born c. 1822, Indiana; w. 1850, Pleasant Twp., Switzerland Co. (C)

788
HALSEY, DANIEL.
Cabinetmaker.
Born c. 1791, New York; w. 1850, Olive Twp., St. Joseph Co. (C)

789
HALSTEAD, SAMUEL.
Cabinetmaker.
Born c. 1810, Ohio; w. 1850, Charlestown Twp., Clark Co. (C)

790
HAM, LAWSON. Chairmaker.
Born c. 1820, Kentucky; w. 1850, Pike Twp., Marion Co. (C)

791
HAMAL, GEORGE D.
Cabinetmaker.
Born c. 1810, Germany; w. 1850, Posey Twp., Rush Co. (C)

792
HAMILTON, JAMES.
Cabinetmaker.
Born c. 1809, Ohio; w. 1850, Madison, Jefferson Co. (C)

793
HAMLIN, ALVIN.
Cabinetmaker.
> Born c. 1792, New York; w.
> 1850, Johnson Twp., La Grange
> Co. (C)

794
HAMMER, JOSEPH.
Cabinetmaker.
> Born c. 1810, Tennessee; w. 1850,
> Perry Twp., Wayne Co. (C)

795
HAMMOND, JACOB.
Cabinetmaker.
> Born c. 1810, Germany; w. 1850,
> Evansville, Vanderburgh Co. (C)
> See also HERMON, JACOB, pos-
> sibly same.

796
HANEY, ROBERT.
Apprentice cabinetmaker.
> Born c. 1833, Indiana; w. 1850,
> Brown Twp., Hancock Co. Lived
> with William Smith, cabinet-
> maker. (C)

797
HANKINS, WILLIAM S.
Cabinetmaker.
> Born c. 1830, Kentucky; w. 1850,
> Indianapolis, Marion Co. (C)

798
HANMAN, ABEL. Cabinetmaker.
> Born c. 1817, Virginia; w. 1850,
> Pike Twp., Marion Co. (C)

799
HANN, JAMES. Cabinetmaker.
> Born c. 1834, Indiana; w. 1850,
> Greensburg, Decatur Co. (C)

800
HANNAH, HENRY.
Cabinetmaker.
> Born c. 1791, Virginia; w. 1850,
> Whitley Co. (C)

801
HANS, ALBERT. Cabinetmaker.
> Born c. 1800, Germany; w. 1850,
> New Albany, Floyd Co. (C)

802
HANVILLE, JAMES.
Chairmaker.
> Born c. 1811, New York; w.
> 1850, Galena Twp., La Porte Co.
> In 1850 the average number of
> employees in this shop was one
> and one half. That year the pro-
> ducts of his shop were 1,000
> chairs, 40 settees, 150 small chairs,
> 4 dozen cane seat chairs, and
> other work totaling $612. (C,
> MC)

803
HARBAUGH, H. Cabinet shop.
> W. 1850, Bono Twp., Lawrence
> Co. In 1850 he produced furni-
> ture valued at $800. (MC)

804
HARDMAN, HENRY.
Cabinetmaker.
> W. 1829, Salem, Washington Co.
> See HARDMAN & HAFFNER.

805
HARDMAN & HAFFNER.
Cabinetmakers.
> Henry Hardman and Joseph Haff-
> ner. W. 1829, Salem, Washington
> Co. Notices in the Western An-
> notator, 4 July 1829 (dissolving
> late firm of Henry Hardman and
> Joseph Haffner, cabinetmakers)
> and 11 July 1829 (partnership

denied by Haffner, who states they had intended to be partners when a new shop was completed, but it was never built).

806
HARGROVE, BENJAMIN.
Chairmaker.
Born c. 1788, Kentucky; w. 1850, Hanover Twp., Shelby Co. (C)

807
HARLAN, GEORGE W.
Chairmaker.
Born c. 1812, Kentucky; w. 1850, Montgomery Twp., Jennings Co. He worked alone in his shop and in 1850 made 250 chairs valued at $600. (C, MC)

808
HARLAN, JOSEPH. Chairmaker.
Born c. 1807, Kentucky; w. 1850, Lexington, Scott Co. Three men worked in this shop; their raw materials included o a k a n d hickory. In 1850 they produced 1,000 chairs valued at $750. (C, MC)

809
HARLOW, JOHN. Chairmaker.
Born c. 1804, Ohio; w. 1850, Brown Twp., Montgomery Co. (C)

810
HARNED, ROBERT.
Cabinetmaker.
Born c. 1823, Indiana; w. 1850, Washington Twp., Washington Co. In same household, John Taylor, cabinetmaker. (C)

811
HARPER, ASA.
Cabinetmaker and carpenter.

Born in North Carolina; 1833, arrived in La Porte, La Porte Co.; 1835, moved to Cool Spring Twp. and Michigan Twp.; 1836, moved to Michigan City where he continued in business and also worked as a ship carpenter until 1856. He died about 1884. (CH 13)

812
HARPER, J.W.D. Cabinetmaker.
Born c. 1819, Indiana; w. 1850, Whitewater Twp., Franklin Co. (C)

813
HARRELL, JACOB.
Cabinetmaker.
Born c. 1811, Indiana; w. 1850, Lagro Twp., Wabash Co. (C)

814
HARRIS, J. D.
"Cabinet Ware-house."
W. 1835, Indianapolis, Marion Co. Adv. in *Indiana Aurora* (Indianapolis), 26 December 1835, illustrating a piano: "New Cabinet Ware-house . . . . he intends keeping on hand, and making to order all articles of furniture in his line, plain and fancy . . . . J. D. HARRIS."

815
HARRIS, McCLARY. Chairmaker.
Born c. 1822, New York; w. 1850, Perrysville, Vermillion Co. Lived with Benjamin Lacy, chairmaker. (C)

816
HARRISON, ROBSON.
Cabinetmaker.
Born c. 1830, Ohio; w. 1850,

Indianapolis, Marion Co. Lived with Charles W. Williams, cabinetmaker. (C)

817
HARROD, ISAAC. Cabinetmaker.
Born c. 1819, Indiana; w. 1850, Jennings Twp., Scott Co. (C)

818
HARSHBURGER, JACOB. Cabinetmaker.
W. c. 1833, Montgomery Co. Had six to eight workmen. (CH 31)

819
HARSHMAN, WILLIAM. Cabinetmaker.
Born c. 1830, Ohio; w. 1850, Jackson Twp., Randolph Co. (C)

820
HART, HETH J. Cabinetmaker.
Born c. 1819, Ohio; w. 1850, Middletown, Henry Co. (C)

821
HART, JAMES. Cabinetmaker.
Born c. 1817, Ireland; w. 1850, Bloomfield, Greene Co. In 1850 he produced furniture worth $700. (C, MC)

822
HARTER, HENRY R. Cabinetmaker.
Born c. 1820, Ohio; w. 1850, Orange Twp., Noble Co. (C)

823
HARTER, RANDOLPH. Cabinetmaker.
Born c. 1830, Germany; w. 1850, Bainbridge Twp., Dubois Co. (C)

824
HARTLEY, WILLIAM—*see* HARTLEY, WHEAT & Co.

825
HARTLEY, WHEAT & Co. Chair manufactory.
William Hartley and James E. Wheat; w. 1838, Brookville, Franklin Co. Adv. in *Indiana American* 14 September 1838, "BROOKVILLE C H A I R *MANUFACTORY*. THE subscribers respectfully inform the citizens of Brookville and the surrounding country, that they have established themselves in the Chair Manufacturing Business, in all its various branches. They will be at all times ready to accommodate persons with Cane Seat, Fancy and Windsor Chairs; Settees, &c. of every description, and of the latest Cincinnati fashions. ALSO; House and Sign Painting; doors, counters, &c. painted in imitation of Mahogany, Curled Maple, Oak and all other imitations of Wood or Marble. Their shop is in the bottom part of Brookville, northeast of the court-house, and opposite Mr. Clarkson's residence. HARTLEY, WHEAT & Co." On 25 January 1839 the same advertisement was repeated for Wheat & Longe. On 26 July 1839 James E. Wheat advertised alone. *See* WHEAT, JAMES E.

826
HARTMAN, NOAH J. Cabinetmaker.
Born c. 1823, Virginia; w. 1850, Clark Twp., Montgomery Co.(C)

827
HARVEY, BENJAMIN. Cabinetmaker.
Born c. 1826, Virginia; w. 1850, Fall Creek Twp., Henry Co. (C)

828
HASCALL, ISAAC.
Cabinetmaker.
    Born c. 1824, Massachusetts; w.
    1850, Troy Twp., Perry Co. (C)

829
HASE, ELIAS H. Chairmaker.
    Born c. 1782, "on the Ocean;"
    w. 1850, Centre Twp., Lake Co.
    (C)

830
HASEN, AMASA. Cabinetmaker.
    Born c. 1820, Pennsylvania; w.
    1850, Adams Twp., Ripley Co.
    (C)

831
HASTLINE, GEORGE.
Cabinetmaker.
    Born c. 1815, Pennsylvania; w.
    1850, Lawrenceburg, Dearborn Co.
    (C)

832
HATCH, JULIAN. Cabinetmaker
and chairmaker.
    Born c. 1834, Ohio; w. 1850,
    Centre Twp., Porter Co. Lived
    with N. R. Strong, cabinetmaker
    and chairmaker. (C)

833
HATFIELD, GEORGE C.
Cabinetmaker.
    Born c. 1817, Pennsylvania; w.
    1850, Mill Twp., Grant Co. (C)

834
HATFIELD, JOHN.
Carpenter and cabinetmaker.
    Born c. 1820, Indiana; w. 1850,
    Washington, Wayne Co. Listed as
    cabinetmaker in 1850 census; still
    living in 1884. (C, CH 34)

835
HATFIELD, JONAS.
Cabinetmaker.
    Born c. 1811, Ohio; w. 1850,
    Washington, Wayne Co. Operated
    cabinet shop employing 2 men us-
    ing hand and horse power. An-
    nual product listed as "15 Bu-
    reaus $210; 20 Tables $80; 100
    Bedsteads $300." (MC, C)

836
HATFIELD, THOMAS.
Chairmaker.
    Born c. 1790, Pennsylvania; w.
    1850,Washington, Wayne Co. (C)

837
HAVENS, H. H. Cabinetmaker.
    Born c. 1829, New York; w.
    1850, Marshall Co. (C) *See*
    SUTPHEN & HAVENS.

838
HAWK, JOHN. Cabinetmaker.
    Born c. 1800, Pennsylvania; w.
    1850, Stony Creek Twp., Henry
    Co. (C)

839
HAWKINS, ISAAC.
Cabinetmaker.
    Born c. 1823; w. 1850, Bethlehem
    Twp., Hamilton Co. (C)

840
HAWKINS, SAMUEL L.
Wheelwright and chairmaker.
    Born c. 1821, Kentucky; 1836,
    arrived in Danville, Hendricks
    Co., where he worked first as a
    wheelwright and then as a chair-
    maker until 1863. After 1865 he
    was a house painter and was
    still living in 1885. The 1850
    industrial census reported his
    chair shop made chairs worth

$500. James Peters, a journeyman musical instrument maker, made dulcimers in this shop, date unknown. (C, MC, CH 22)

841
HAY, MICHAEL. Cabinetmaker.
Born c. 1812, Pennsylvania; w. 1850, Randolph Co. (C)

842
HAYHS, ———. Chairmaker.
Born c. 1835, Maryland; w. 1850, Lawrenceburg, Dearborn Co. Lived with Cyrus Armstrong, furniture merchant and manufacturer, q.v. (C)

843
HAZELTINE, OSCAR. Cabinetmaker.
Born c. 1829, Indiana; w. 1850, Indianapolis, Marion Co. (C)

844
HAZELWOOD, SHELTON. Cabinetmaker.
Born c. 1829, Indiana; w. 1850, Van Buren Twp., Monroe Co. Lived with John B. Givens, cabinetmaker. (C)

845
HEACOCK, MILES. Cabinetmaker.
Born c. 1813, Pennsylvania; w. 1850, Dudley Twp., Henry Co. (C)

846
HEALLY, ———. Cabinetmaker.
Born c. 1818; w. 1850, Lafayette, Tippecanoe Co. (C) *See* SMITH & HEATLY, possibly same.

847
HEATLY—*see* SMITH & HEATLY.

848
HEATON, DAVID. Chairmaker.
Born c. 1771, Virginia; w. 1850, Campbell Twp., Jennings Co. (C)

849
HECKENDORN, ROBERT G. Cabinetmaker.
Born c. 1834, Pennsylvania; w. 1850, White Co. Lived with Samuel Heckendorn, cabinetmaker. (C)

850
HECKENDORN, SAMUEL. Cabinetmaker.
Born c. 1809, Pennsylvania; w. 1850, White Co. In same household, Robert G. Heckendorn, cabinetmaker. (C)

851
HEDGES, I. (or J.) B. Cabinetmaker.
Born c. 1820, Georgetown, D.C.; w. 1850, Bluffton, Wells Co. (C)

852
HEFFERMAN, MICHAEL. Cabinetmaker.
Born c. 1826; w. 1850, Lafayette, Tippecanoe Co. (C)

853
HEIN, DANIEL. Cabinetmaker.
Born c. 1820, Ohio; w. 1850, Lafayette, Tippecanoe Co. (C)

854
HELMS, GEORGE. Cabinetmaker.
Born c. 1809, Pennsylvania; w. 1850, Monroe Twp., Putnam Co. (C)

855
HEMPHILL, WILLIAM—*see* RECTOR, W. H.

856
HENDERSON, CHARLES.
Cabinetmaker.
  Born c. 1795, Kentucky; w. 1850,
Jefferson Twp., Switzerland Co.
(C)

857
HENDERSON, JOHN G.
Cabinetmaker.
  W. 1820-1831-, Salem, Washington Co. The 1820 industrial census
noted two men working in this
shop; their raw materials were
cherry, walnut, and poplar. The
equipment used consisted of 58
planes, 4 screw gauges, 2 dozen
screw clamps, 6 iron screw clamps,
a brace and 30 bits, 30 chisels and
gouges, 9 saws of various kinds,
a turning lathe, and 3 benches.
In 1820 they produced clock cases,
secretaries, desks, circular and
plain bureaus, "Column Bureaus,
Cupboards, &c &c" valued at
$1,200.
  Adv. in *Western Annotator* 3
February 1831: "John G. Henderson Cabinet-making . . . he
wishes to exchange furniture for
fifteen or twenty thousand feet
of cherry and poplar lumber."
Joseph M. Tilford was his apprentice 1829-1832. (CH 39)

858
HENDERSON, THOMAS K.
Cabinetmaker.
  Born c. 1827, Indiana; w. 1850,
Haddon Twp., Sullivan Co. Lived
with   Benson   Riggs   [Sr.],
cabinetmaker. (C)

859
HENDRICKSON, HENRY.
Cabinetmaker.
  Born c. 1815, Delaware; w. 1850,
Parke Co. (C)

860
HENNING, A. H. Cabinetmaker.
  Born c. 1823, Germany; w. 1850,
Martinsville, Morgan Co. (C)

861
HENRICKS, JOHN.
Chairmaker.
  Born c. 1824, Indiana; w. 1850,
Jackson Twp., Rush Co. (C)

862
HENRY, JAMES. Cabinetmaker.
  Born c. 1804, Tennessee; w. from
early 1840s through 1850-, Eel
Township, Cass Co. Reported to
have had a turning lathe; cherry
furniture mentioned. (C, CH 25)

863
HERMON, JACOB. Cabinetmaker.
  W. 1850, Evansville, Vanderburgh
Co. Two men worked in this
shop and in 1850 they produced
cabinet furniture valued at $900.
(MC) *See also* HAMMOND,
JACOB, possibly same.

864
HERVEY, CHARLES M.
Cabinet shop.
  Born c. 1817, New Jersey; w.
1850, Economy, Wayne Co. He
worked alone, using steam powered machinery, and in 1850 produced 75 bedsteads, 12 bureaus,
and 60 coffins. (C, MC)

865
HESS, HARVY H. Cabinetmaker. Born c. 1812, Kentucky; w. 1850, Parke Co. (C) *See* HESS & BROWN.

866
HESS & BROWN. Cabinetmakers. Harvy H. Hess and Edward Brown; w. 1850, Parke Co. Six men in this shop using horse power; they produced furniture valued at $3,000 in 1850. (MC)

867
HIATT, ASHER. Cabinetmaker. Born c. 1815, North Carolina; w. 1850, Greensboro Twp., Henry Co. (C)

868
HIATT, ASHER. Cabinetmaker. Born c. 1814, Indiana; w. 1850, Wayne Twp., Henry Co. (C)

869
HIATT, T. J. Cabinetmaker. W. 1829, Centerville, Wayne Co. (CH 46)

870
HICKMAN, ALBERT. Chairmaker. Born c. 1818, Ohio; w. 1850, Dublin, Wayne Co. (C)

871
HICKMAN, JAMES. Chairmaker. Born c. 1809, Ohio; w. 1850, Sugar Creek Twp., Hancock Co. (C)

872
HIGBEE, H. Furniture manufacturer. W. 1837-, Warsaw, Kosciusko Co. (CH 6)

873
HIGHFILL, SAMUEL. Cabinetmaker. Born c. 1819, Harrison Co.; w. 1850, Patoka Twp., Crawford Co. (C)

874
HILL, CHARLES W. Chairmaker. Born c. 1799, Kentucky; w. 1850, Taylor Twp., Greene Co. In the same household, Joseph Hill, chairmaker. (C)

875
HILL, E. B. Cabinetmaker. Born c. 1805, New York; w. 1850, La Porte, La Porte Co. In same residence, Orlando Hill, cabinetmaker. (C)

876
HILL, ENOCH E. Painter and chairmaker. Born c. 1817, Kentucky; w. 1850, Montgomery Twp., Gibson Co. (C)

877
HILL, HENRY J. Chairmaker. Born c. 1834, Ohio; w. 1850, Princeton, Gibson Co. (C)

878
HILL, JOSEPH. Chairmaker. Born c. 1833, Indiana; w. 1850, Taylor Twp., Greene Co. Lived with Charles W. Hill, chairmaker. (C)

879
HILL, OLIVER. Chairmaker and painter. Born c. 1813, Pennsylvania; w.

1850, Noble Twp., Wabash Co. In same household, Robert Dane and Isaac Clow, chairmakers. (C)

880
HILL, ORLANDO. Cabinetmaker. Born c. 1833, New York; w. 1850, La Porte, La Porte Co. Lived with E. B. Hill, cabinetmaker. (C)

881
HINDS, ALFRED. Cabinetmaker. Born c. 1822, Kentucky; w. 1850, Madison, Jefferson Co. (C)

882
HINES, WILLIAM. Cabinetmaker.
Born c. 1821, Ohio; w. 1850, Clinton, Vermillion Co. (C)

883
HINSON, JOHN. Undertaker. Born c. 1796, England; w. 1850, Evansville, Vanderburgh Co. (C)

884
HISINGER, JACOB. Cabinetmaker.
Born c. 1824, Germany; w. 1850, New Albany, Floyd Co. (C)

885
HITTON, JOHN. Cabinetmaker. Born c. 1830, Indiana; w. 1850, Centerville, Wayne Co. (C)

886
HOBSON, JAMES. Chairmaker. Born c. 1830, Indiana; w. 1850, Vienna Twp., Scott Co. (C)

887
HODENS, VINCENT. Chairmaker.
Born c. 1820, Tennessee; w. 1850, Ward Twp., Randolph Co. (C)

887a
HODGE, JAMES—see MEEKS, ROBERT; SWAIN, JOB.

888
HODGE, WILLIAM B. Cabinetmaker.
Born c. 1817, Pennsylvania; w. 1850, Washington Twp., Grant Co. (C)

889
HOFFMAN, ——. Cabinetmaker. Born c. 1820, Germany; w. 1850, Evansville, Vanderburgh Co. (C)

890
HOFFMAN, ——. Cabinetmaker. Born c. 1815, Germany; w. 1850, Evansville, Vanderburgh Co. (C)

891
HOLD, LORENZO B. Cabinetmaker.
Born c. 1828, Ohio; w. 1850, Perrysville, Vermillion Co. (C)

892
HOLEMAN, HARDIN. Cabinetmaker.
Born c. 1820, Kentucky; w. 1850, North Madison, Jefferson Co. (C)

893
HOLEMAN, TANDY. Cabinetmaker.
Born c. 1784, Indiana; w. 1850, Greene Co. (C)

894
HOLLAND, THOMAS. Cabinetmaker.
Born c. 1787, North Carolina; w. 1850, Haw Creek Twp., Bartholomew Co. (C)

895
HOLLOWAY, GEORGE W.
Apprentice cabinetmaker.
Born c. 1835, Indiana; w. 1850,
Union Twp., Montgomery Co.
Apprentice of Washington Hollo-
way. (C)

896
HOLLOWAY, JOHN.
Cabinetmaker.
Born c. 1826, Kentucky; w. 1850,
Union Twp., Montgomery Co.
(C)

897
HOLLOWAY, WASHINGTON.
Cabinetmaker.
Born c. 1803, Kentucky; w. 1850,
Union Twp., Montgomery Co.
Three men worked in his furniture shop; included in their raw
materials was paint. In 1850 they
produced $2,000 worth of furni-
ture. George W. Holloway was
an apprentice who lived in Washington Holloway's household. (C,
MC)

898
HOLMAN, WILLIAM.
Cabinetmaker.
Born c. 1823, Indiana; w. 1850,
Indian Creek Twp., Monroe Co.
(C)

899
HOLMS, E. Cabinetmaker.
Born c. 1831, Ohio; w. 1850,
Mount Auburn, Shelby Co. (C)

900
HOLMS, ERASTUS. Chairmaker.
Born c. 1832, Ohio; w. 1850,
Clark Twp., Johnson Co. Lived
with Giles Holms, chairmaker.
(C)

901
HOLMS (HOLMES), GILES.
Chairmaker.
Born c. 1810, New York; w.
1849-1859, Clark Twp., Johnson
Co. He employed three or four
men, one of whom was Erastus
Holms, chairmaker, who lived in
the same household. (C, MC, CH
29)

902
HOLOWAY, ELIJAH.
Chairmaker.
Born c. 1796, Delaware; w. 1850,
Medina Twp., Warren Co. (C)

903
HOLSCLAW, NATHANIEL.
Chairmaker.
Born c. 1814, Kentucky; w. 1850,
New Albany, Floyd Co. (C)

904
HOLT, ADAM. Cabinetmaker.
Born c. 1796, Kentucky; w. 1850,
Jeffersonville, Clark Co. (C)

905
HOMER, JOHN. Cabinetmaker.
Born c. 1822, France; w. 1850,
Madison, Jefferson Co. (C)

906
HOOFNAGEL, ——.
Cabinetmaker.
Born c. 1820, Germany; w. 1850,
Madison, Jefferson Co. (C)

906a
HOOK, DAVID. Cabinetmaker.
W. 1823-, Richmond, Wayne Co.
(CH 53)

907
HOOK, JAMES, & CO.
Cabinetmakers.
W. 1850, Harrison Twp., Vigo

Co. Four men worked in this shop; in 1850 they made 15 bureaus, 180 coffins, 35 bedsteads, 12 tables, 4 sofas, and other articles. (MC)

908
HOOLE, JOSEPH.
Cabinetmaker.
  Born c. 1816, England; w. 1850, Rising Sun, Ohio Co. (C) *See* HOOLE & MARBLE.

909
HOOLE, WILLIAM E.
Cabinetmaker.
  Born c. 1808, England; w. 1841, Rising Sun, Ohio Co.; w. 1850, Madison, Jefferson Co. Adv. in Wilmington *Dearborn County Register* 27 March 1841 (see Fig. 4): ". . . CABINET FURNITURE such as Mahogany and Cherry Bureaus, Cherry

Cabinet Making.

Main, between Front and Market s

The subscriber keeps constantly on hand, a general assortment of

CABINET FURNITURE,

such as Mahogany and Cherry Bureaus, Cherry Dining, Breakfast tables, Cherry and Sycamore high post French fancy and Trundle Bedsteads, Mahogany and Cherry work stands, Corner Cupboards, Cribs, Cradles, &c. &c. All of which he will warrant to be as good and as cheap, as can be purchased in this part of the country. He will make to order any article of Furniture that may be called for. Also coffins made on the shortest notice.

N. B. Lumber will be taken in exchange for Furniture.

All persons indebted would confer a great favor, by making immediate settlement.

WM. E. HOOLE.
Rising Sun, Jan. 16, 1841.   14-tf.

Library of Congress

Fig. 4. From Wilmington
Dearborn County Register

Dining, Breakfast tables, Cherry and Sycamore high post French fancy and Trundle Bedsteads, Mahogany and Cherry work stands, Corner Cupboards, Cribs, Cradles, &c. &c." His shop was located on the west side of Main Street near the river in Rising Sun. (C, MC, CH 26)

910
HOOLE & MARBLE.
Furniture establishment.
Joseph Hoole and Jonathon Marble; w. 1850, Rising Sun, Ohio Co. Two men worked in this shop, using machinery powered by horse. In 1850 they made 500 bedsteads valued at $1,500. (MC)

911
HOOVER, JOHN. Painter.
Born c. 1833, Indiana; w. 1850, New Castle, Henry Co. Lived with John Shroyer, painter and chairmaker. (C)

912
HOOVER, JOHN. Chairmaker.
Born c. 1821, Pennsylvania; w. 1850, Huntington, Huntington Co. In same household, Samuel Fleming, chairmaker. (C)

913
HOPE, JOSEPH.
Cabinetmaker and carpenter.
Born c. 1809, Virginia; w. 1850, Howard Co. In 1850 his product was given as "furniture and houses worth $650." (C, MC)

914
HOPKINS, GEORGE N.
Cabinetmaker.

Born c. 1817, New Jersey; w. 1850, Whitewater Twp., Franklin Co. (C)

915
HOPKINS, JOHN. Chairmaker.
Born c. 1808, Kentucky; w. 1850, Boone Co. (C)

916
HORN, SAMUEL. Chairmaker.
Born c. 1801, Pennsylvania; w. 1850, Wayne Twp., Allen Co. (C)

917
HORTON, DAVID.
Cabinetmaker.
Born c. 1816, Pennsylvania; w. 1850, Marion, Grant Co. (C)

918
HORTON, DAVID E. Chairmaker.
Born c. 1815, Ohio; w. 1850, Centre Twp., Grant Co. (C)

919
HORTON, JOSEPH.
Cabinetmaker.
Born c. 1823, Ohio; w. 1850, Marion, Grant Co. (C)

920
HORTON, LEVI. Cabinetmaker.
Born c. 1824, Ohio; w. 1850, Marion, Grant Co. (C)

921
HOSFORD, MILO.
Cabinetmaker.
Born c. 1811, New York; w. 1850, Eugene Twp., Vermillion Co. (C)

922
HOSKINS, FRANCIS A.
Cabinetmaker.
Born c. 1827, Illinois; w. 1850,

Owensville, Gibson Co. Lived with George H. Goodyear, cabinet-maker. (C)

923
HOUGH, ALFRED.
Cabinetmaker.
> Born c. 1810, North Carolina; w. 1850, Middlebury Twp., Elkhart Co. In same household, William Hough, cabinetmaker. (C)

924
HOUGH, JOSEPH. Chairmaker.
> Born c. 1830, Indiana; w. 1850, New Frankfort, Scott Co. Lived with John Colvin, chairmaker. (C)

925
HOUGH, WILLIAM.
Cabinetmaker.
> Born c. 1834, North Carolina; w. 1850, Middlebury Twp., Elkhart Co. Lived with Alfred Hough, cabinetmaker. (C)

926
HOUSTON, MICHAEL W.
Cabinetmaker.
> Born c. 1809, Indiana; w. 1850, Shawswick Twp., Lawrence Co. In same household, John P. Fisher, cabinetmaker. (C) *See also* HOUSTON & BUSKIRK.

927
HOUSTON & BUSKIRK.
"Cabinet Workmen."
> Michael W. Houston and John B. Buskirk; w. 1850, Bono Twp., Lawrence Co. Five men worked in this shop and in 1850 they produced "Cabinet work & other articles" valued at $2,112. The other men in the shop were John P. Fisher, Walter Borland, and Fountain C. Crump. (C, MC)

928
HOUTS, THOMAS F.
Cabinetmaker.
> Born c. 1827, Indiana; w. 1850, Haddon Twp., Sullivan Co. (C)

929
HOWARD, GEORGE W.
Chairmaker.
> Born c. 1806, Kentucky; w. 1850, Hammond Twp., Spencer Co. (C)

930
HOWE, J. R. Cabinetmaker.
> Born c. 1826, Indiana; w. 1850, Perrysville, Vermillion Co. (C)

931
HUBBARD, CALEB.
Cabinetmaker.
> Born c. 1821, North Carolina; w. 1850, Monroe Twp., Howard Co. (C)

932
HUBBARD, R[ICHARD J.].
Cabinetmaker.
> Born c. 1813, North Carolina; w. 1850, Milton, Wayne Co. Three men worked in this shop, and in 1850 they produced bureaus, bedsteads and other items valued at $2,000. (C, MC)

933
HUDSON, EDWARD H.
Chairmaker.
> W. 1815-1822, Brookville, Franklin Co.; -1835-, Centerville, Wayne Co. He arrived in Brookville in 1815. Adv. in *Brookville Enquirer* 23 May 1820: "REMOVAL. Edward H. Hudson

Windsor Chair Manufacturer and Plain & Ornamental S I G N PAINTER . . ." [moved his shop to the public square].

Adv. in same paper, 13 August 1822: "Chair and Wheel MANU-FACTORY. The subscriber respectfully informs his customers and the public in general, that he has added to his Chair Manu-factory, and now carries on the spinning wheel making business . . . including the celebrated PATENT S P I N N I N G WHEEL. He continues to keep at his shop in B r o o k v i l l e CHAIRS of various kinds, executed in a neat and workman-like manner . . . ." Adv. in Centerville *The People's Advocate,* 5 June 1835: "Windsor Chair Making, and *House* and *Sign Painting.* . . . He will keep constantly on hand an assortment of WINDSOR CHAIRS. And all orders for *SIGNS and ORNA-MENTAL PAINTING* will be attended to on the shortest notice, and in good style." Later, Edward Hudson was a shipper of produce on the river and to the West Indies; he is said to have died in a shipwreck. (CH 43)

934
HUFF, ALLEN R. Cabinetmaker.
W. 1839, Rockville, Parke Co. Adv. in *Indiana Register,* 8 June 1839.

935
HUFFMAN, LAMAR. Cabinetmaker.
Born c. 1820, Virginia; w. 1850, Noble Twp., Wabash Co. (C)

936
HUFFORD, JNO. H. Chairmaker.
Born c. 1829, Kentucky; w. 1850, Rush Co. In same household, H. C. Nicholas, cabinetmaker. (C)

937
HUGAL, LEWIS. Cabinetmaker.
Born c. 1810, Germany; w. 1850, Madison, Jefferson Co. (C)

938
HULICK (HULICH), DAVID. Cabinetmaker.
Born c. 1814, Pennsylvania; w. 1850, Highland Twp., Vermillion Co. Four men working in shop; in 1850 they produced furniture worth $2,500. (C, MC)

939
HULIT (HEULET), SAMUEL G. Cabinetmaker.
Born c. 1809, New Jersey; w. 1850, Wayne Twp., Henry Co. In 1850 he produced 150 bed-steads and 35 bureaus. (C, MC)

940
HULL, JOHN. Cabinetmaker.
Born c. 1803, Virginia; w. 1850, Carroll Co. (C)

941
HUMPHREY (HUMPHREYS), LAWSON F. Cabinetmaker.
Born c. 1826, Ohio; w. 1850, Richland Twp., Miami Co. George Brown was his partner at one time. (C, CH 30)

942
HUNBARGER, HENRY. Cabinetmaker.
Born c. 1768, Pennsylvania; w. 1850, Marrs Twp., Posey Co. (C)

943
HUNLEY, CHARLES W.
Cabinetmaker.
 Born c. 1822, Indiana; w. 1850,
 Haddon Twp., Sullivan Co. In
 same household, Samuel Hunley,
 cabinetmaker. (C)

944
HUNLEY, SAMUEL.
Cabinetmaker.
 Born c. 1830, Indiana; w. 1850,
 Haddon Twp., Sullivan Co. Lived
 with Charles W. Hunley, cabinet-
 maker. (C)

945
HUNTER, ROBERT C.
Chairmaker.
 Born c. 1815, Ohio; w. 1850,
 Boone Co. (C)

945a
HURLBUT, HIRAM E.
Cabinetmaker.
 W. 1820, Centerville, Wayne Co.
 (CH 53)

946
HURST, WILLIAM.
Cabinetmaker.
 Born c. 1810, New Jersey; w.
 1850, Jackson Twp., De Kalb Co.
 (C)

947
HUTCHENS, THOMAS A.
Cabinetmaker.
 Born c. 1832, Indiana; w. 1850,
 Williamsburg, Wayne Co. (C)

948
HUTCHISON, JOHN.
Cabinetmaker.
 Born c. 1824, Indiana; w. 1850,
 Petersburg, Pike Co. (C)

949
HYDE, DANIEL. Cabinetmaker.
 Born c. 1816, Ohio; w. 1850,
 Madison Twp., Jay Co. (C)

950
HYDEN, JOHN W. Cabinetmaker.
 Born c. 1824, Kentucky; w. 1850,
 Troy Twp., Perry Co. (C)

951
HYER, BENJAMIN.
Cabinetmaker.
 Born c. 1818; w. 1850, Newbury
 Twp., La Grange Co. (C)

952
HYMON, JOHN. Cabinetmaker.
 Born c. 1824, Kentucky; w. 1850,
 Washington Twp., Daviess Co.
 Lived with Samuel A. Rodarmel,
 cabinetmaker, q.v. (C)

953
IDE, REUBEN P. Chairmaker.
 Born c. 1796, Vermont; w. 1850,
 Monroe Twp., Howard Co. (C)

954
INGERSOLL, HENRY.
Cabinetmaker.
 Born c. 1814, New York; w.
 1850, Indianapolis, Marion Co.
 (C) See SLOAN & INGER-
 SOLL, possibly the same.

955
INMAN—see PRICE, BENJA-
MIN F.

956
INNIS, JOHN B. Chairmaker.
 Born c. 1800, Pennsylvania; w.
 1850, Parke Co. Two men worked
 in his shop; in 1850 they produced "Chairs & sundrys" worth
 $1,000. Living in the same house-

hold were Charles G. Eaton, chairmaker, and Charles E. Berry, cabinetmaker. (C, MC)

957
IRISH, CHARLES.
Cabinetmaker.
> Born c. 1825, Louisiana; w. 1850, Harrison Twp., Vigo Co. (C)

958
ISRAEL, CHARLES.
Cabinetmaker.
> Born c. 1820, Germany; w. 1850, Lawrenceburg, Dearborn Co. (C)

959
JACKSON, ANDREW.
Cabinetmaker.
> Born c. 1828, Ohio; w. 1850, Marshall Co. (C)

960
JACKSON, FRANKLIN B.
Cabinetmaker.
> Born c. 1830, Ohio; w. 1850, Muncie, Delaware Co. Lived with Eli J. Jamison, cabinetmaker. (C)

961
JACKSON, HARVEY.
Chairmaker.
> Born c. 1825, North Carolina; w. 1850, Washington Twp., Hamilton Co. (C)

962
JACKSON, J. Cabinetmaker.
> W. 1850, Washington Twp., Hamilton Co. In 1850 he produced "Cabinetware worth $1200." (MC)

963
JACKSON, JOHN. Cabinetmaker.
> W. 1841-, Franklin, Johnson Co. (CH 29)

964
JACKSON, JOHN W.
Chairmaker.
> Born c. 1816, Ohio; w. 1850, Howard Twp., Howard Co. (C)

965
JACKSON, WILLIAM.
Cabinetmaker.
> Born c. 1816, Tennessee; w. 1850, Washington Twp., Hamilton Co. (C)

966
JACKSON, WILLIAM A.
Chairmaker.
> Born c. 1828, Kentucky; w. 1850, Mount Pleasant Twp., Delaware Co. (C)

967
JACKSON, WILLIAM N.
Cabinetmaker.
> Born c. 1804, North Carolina; w. 1850, Spartanburg, Randolph Co. (C)

968
JAMES, DANIEL H.
Cabinetmaker.
> Born c. 1813, Virginia; w. 1850, Jefferson Twp., Jay Co. (C)

969
JAMES, JOHN. Cabinetmaker.
> Born in Ohio; w. 1850, Concord Twp., Elkhart Co. Lived with Nathan Markle, cabinetmaker. (C)

970
JAMISON, ELI J. Cabinetmaker.
> Born c. 1821, Maryland; w. 1850, Muncie, Delaware Co. In same household, Franklin B. Jackson, cabinetmaker. (C)

971
JAMISON, HENRY. Chairmaker.
Born c. 1816, Pennsylvania; 1842,
probably member of firm of Jami-
son & Lawrence, q.v., Terre
Haute, Vigo Co.; 1850, member
of firm of Jamison & Bucking-
ham, q.v., Harrison Twp., Vigo
Co. In same household in 1850,
Elmore Brim, chairmaker. (C)

972
JAMISON (JEMISON),
JOHN H.
Cabinetmaker and undertaker.
Born c. 1823, Maryland; w. 1845-
1847, Centerville, Wayne Co.; w.
1850-, Muncie, Delaware Co. In
same household, F. J. Blair, cabi-
netmaker. (C, CH 46) *See also*
DILL, A. C., & J. H. JEMISON.

973
JAMISON & BUCKINGHAM.
Chairmakers.
Henry Jamison and Henry Buckingham; w. 1850, Harrison Twp.,
Vigo Co. In 1850 four men were
employed in this establishment;
they made 1,200 chairs worth
$2,400. Raw materials included
paint. (MC)

974
JAMISON & LAWRENCE.
Chairmakers.
Probably Henry Jamison and —
Lawrence; w. 1842, Terre Haute,
Vigo Co. Adv. in *Wabash Ex-
press* 2 November 1842: "CHAIR
FACTORY/J A M I S O N &
L A W R E N C E/C H A I R
MAKERS, have opened a Fac-
tory on Third Street, Terre-
Haute, where they are prepared

to furnish all kinds of Windsor,
Fancy and Plain CHAIRS, at
reasonable prices. . . ."

975
JARETT, THOMAS B.
Cabinetmaker.
Born c. 1806, Virginia; w. 1850,
Clark Twp., Montgomery Co. (C)

976
JARRARD, ISAAC. Cabinetmaker.
Born c. 1820, Ohio; w. 1850,
Tippecanoe Twp., Kosciusko Co.
Lived with Andrew Nichols,
cabinetmaker. (C)

977
JEAN, NELSON. Cabinetmaker.
Born c. 1820, Indiana; w. 1850,
Eel River Twp., Greene Co. (C)

978
JEFFORDS, DAVID.
Cabinetmaker.
Born c. 1810, Vermont; w. 1850,
Concord Twp., De Kalb Co. (C)

978a
JEMISON, J. H.—*see* DILL, A. C.,
AND J. H. JEMISON.

979
JENKINS, JOHN L.
Cabinetmaker.
Born c. 1813, Crawford Co.; w.
1850, Liberty Twp., Crawford Co.
(C)

980
JENNINGS, DAVID.
Cabinetmaker.
Born c. 1816, Virginia; w. 1850,
Connersville, Fayette Co. (C)

981
JENNINGS, MARMADUKE.
Cabinetmaker.

Born c. 1814, New Jersey; w. 1850, Fountain Co. In 1850 he produced 15 bureaus, 15 tables, 30 bedsteads, 12 coffins, 12 stands, and other work totaling in value $565. Charles Bartlett was his apprentice at that time. (C, MC)

982
JETMORE, NATHAN.
Cabinetmaker.
Born c. 1830, Ohio; w. 1850, Lagro Twp., Wabash Co. (C)

983
JEWEL, JAMES. Cabinetmaker.
Born c. 1825, Ohio; w. 1850, Harrison Twp., Vigo Co. (C)

984
JOB, CHARLES W. Cabinetmaker.
Born c. 1833, Kentucky; w. 1850, Harrison Twp., Morgan Co. (C)

985
JOHNSON, ALBERT. Cabinetmaker.
Born c. 1830, Indiana; w. 1850, Paoli, Orange Co. (C)

986
JOHNSON, BENJAMIN.
Chairmaker.
Born c. 1828, Ohio; w. 1850, Jonesboro, Grant Co. (C)

987
JOHNSON, HARVEY.
Chairmaker.
Born c. 1827, Indiana; w. 1850, New Albany Twp., Floyd Co. (C)

988
JOHNSON, JAMES.
Carpenter and cabinetmaker.
Born c. 1800, Pennsylvania; w. 1850, Adams Twp., Ripley Co. (C)

989
JOHNSON, JOHN.
Cabinetmaker.
Born c. 1816, Pennsylvania; w. 1850, Auburn, De Kalb Co. (C)

990
JOHNSON, JOHN E.
Cabinetmaker.
Born c. 1825, Indiana; w. 1850, Belleville, Hendricks Co. (C)

991
JOHNSON, JOHN W.
Cabinetmaker.
Born c. 1829, Indiana; w. 1850, Moores Hill, Dearborn Co. Lived with William Justis, cabinetmaker. (C)

992
JOHNSON, MARCUS L.
Cabinetmaker.
Born c. 1828, Kentucky; w. 1850, Rush Co. In same household, Charles P. Conrad, apprentice (?). (C)

993
JOHNSON, PETER.
Cabinetmaker.
W. -1832-, South Bend, St. Joseph Co. Was also a builder and ship builder; built the first courthouse and started the first keelboat and steamboat line on the St. Joseph River. He was a prominent local citizen. Adv. in *St.*

Joseph Beacon, June 20, 1832. (Information from Northern Indiana Historical Society)

994
JOHNSON, THOMAS H.
Chairmaker.
>Born c. 1820, Pennsylvania; w. 1850, Shelby Twp., Tippecanoe Co. (C)

995
JOHNSON, WILLIAM.
Cabinetmaker.
>Born c. 1826, Indiana; w. 1850, Madison, Jefferson Co. (C)

995a
JOHNSTON, I. L.—*see* MATTHEWS, W., & I. L. JOHNSTON.

996
JOICE, JACOB. Chairmaker.
>Born c. 1817, Ohio; w. 1850, Sheffield Twp., Tippecanoe Co. (C)

997
JOLLIFFE, WILLIAM.
Cabinetmaker.
>Born c. 1820, Ohio; w. 1850, Hensley Twp., Johnson Co. (C)

998
JONES, ANDREW V. (or M.).
Cabinetmaker.
>Born c. 1817, Indiana; w. 1850, Washington Twp., Gibson Co. (C)

999
JONES, BENJAMIN.
Cabinetmaker.
>Born c. 1818, Indiana; w. 1850, Washington Twp., Washington Co. Three men worked in this shop, using machinery powered by horse. In 1850 they produced furniture worth $1,500. In the same household with Mr. Jones were Thomas Newby and William Mount, cabinetmakers. (C, MC)

1000
JONES, ELISHA. Cabinetmaker.
>Born c. 1820, Indiana; w. 1850, Smith Twp., Posey Co. (C)

1001
JONES, HIRAM. Cabinetmaker.
>Born c. 1818, North Carolina; w. 1850, Washington Twp., Rush Co. (C)

1002
JONES, ISRAEL. Chairmaker.
>Born c. 1806, Ohio; w. 1850, Parke Co. (C)

1003
JONES, J. Chairmaker.
>W. 1829-, Vincennes, Knox Co. Adv. in *Western Sun* 20 June 1829: "WINDSOR CHAIRS. J. JONES would inform the public in general, that he has established himself in the house owned by John Pitcher, on the corner of Vigo and Second Streets, where he will have on hand a good assortment of *Chairs and Settees,* of all sizes, and of the best quality, and finished in the neatest manner, at short notice, and which he will sell unusually low for cash, or such articles of produce as may suit."

1004
JONES, JAMES. Cabinetmaker.
>Born 1811, Kentucky; 1833, learned trade from Andrew Reed in Franklin, Johnson Co., Indiana. Died November 1838. (CH 40)

1005
JONES, JOSEPH. Cabinetmaker.
Born c. 1812, Maryland; w. 1850,
New Albany, Floyd Co. (C)

1006
JONES, L. F. Cabinetmaker.
Born c. 1823, Virginia; w. 1850,
Washington Twp., Shelby Co.(C)

1007
JONES, MARSHALL.
Cabinetmaker.
Born c. 1794, Ohio; w. 1850,
Liberty Twp., Union Co. (C)

1008
JONES, OWEN. Cabinetmaker.
Born c. 1821, Ohio; w. 1850,
Owensville, Gibson Co. (C)

1009
JONES, THOMAS A., & CO.
Chair factory.
W. 1850, Union Twp., Jennings
Co. Four men worked in this
establishment; in 1850 they made
2,000 chairs valued at $3,000.
(MC)

1010
JONES, THOMAS D.
Cabinetmaker.
Born c. 1817, Indiana; w. 1850,
Stony Creek Twp., Henry Co.
Two men worked in this shop;
in 1850 they made 50 bureaus
and bedsteads valued at $540.
(MC)

1011
JONES, WILLIAM.
Cabinetmaker.
Born c. 1829, Indiana; w. 1850,
Salem, Washington Co. Lived with
Westley Smith, cabinetmaker, q.v.
(C)

1012
JONSMON, WILLIAM W.
Cabinetmaker.
Born c. 1825; w. 1850, Covington,
Fountain Co. (C)

1013
JORDAN, WILLIAM.
Cabinetmaker.
Born c. 1818, Germany; w. 1850,
Wayne Twp., Noble Co. (C)

1014
JUMPER, JACOB. Cabinetmaker.
Born c. 1815, Ohio; w. 1850,
Sugar Creek Twp., Vigo Co. (C)

1015
JUSTIS, WILLIAM.
Cabinetmaker.
Born c. 1819, Ohio; w. 1850,
Moores Hill, Dearborn Co. In
same household, John W. Johnson,
cabinetmaker. (C)

1016
KARSCH, ADAM. Cabinetmaker.
Born c. 1828, Germany; w. 1850,
Evansville, Vanderburgh Co. (C)

1017
KAUFMAN, ELIAS.
Cabinetmaker.
Born c. 1816, Pennsylvania; w.
Liberty Twp. and Brownsville
Twp., Union Co. In 1850 he pro-
duced $500 worth of furniture.
(C, MC)

1018
KAUSLER, CHRISTIAN.
Cabinetmaker.
Born c. 1825, Germany; w. 1850,
Evansville, Vanderburgh Co. (C)

1019
KEEFER, WILLIAM.
Cabinetmaker.

Born c. 1832, Ohio; w. 1850,
Wayne Twp., Allen Co. Lived
with Charles Fink, cabinetmaker.
(C)

1020
KEIGER, LEWIS G.
Cabinetmaker.
Born c. 1815, Germany; w. 1850,
Vanderburgh Co. (C)

1021
KEIGLER (?), CHARLES.
Cabinetmaker.
Born c. 1808, New Jersey; w.
1850, Vincennes, Knox Co. (C)

1022
KEIPER, CHRISTIAN.
Cabinetmaker.
W. -1841-, Rockville, Parke Co.
Adv. in *Olive Branch* 9 January
1841: "CHEAP! CHEAP!
CHEAP! CABINET MAKING/
CHRISTIAN KEIPER . . .
will sell Bureaus (projecting block
front, and made of the best cherry
materials) from 14 to $16; half
columns from 16 to $18; Cup-
boards from 13 to $15; Bead-
steads from 6 to $8; Breakfast
Tables, and all other work in
proportion. Oh do call, and see
before purchasing elsewhere; he
will not charge for looking at his
work."

1023
KEISER, EARNEST.
Cabinetmaker.
Born c. 1817, Germany; w. 1850,
Columbus, Bartholomew Co. (C)

1024
KEITH, AARON V.
Cabinetmaker.
Born c. 1815, Kentucky; w. 1850,

Pittsboro and/or Brownsburg,
Hendricks Co. In 1850 he produced furniture valued at $500.
He was listed in a county history
as the first man in Pittsboro to
make furniture. (C, MC, CH 22)

1025
KELLEY—*see* SMITH &
KELLEY.

1026
KELLEY, JAMES.
Cabinetmaker.
Born c. 1814; w. 1850, Perrys-
ville, Vermillion Co. (C)

1027
KELSEY, CALVIN.
Cabinetmaker.
Born c. 1833; w. 1850, Jefferson
Twp., Greene Co. Lived with
Stephen Lockwood, cabinetmaker.
(C)

1028
KENDALL, REUBEN.
Cabinetmaker.
W. 1849-, Rockville, Parke Co.
Died 1891. Started business in a
shop in a log building on a site
later used by the National Bank.
After his death the business was
carried on by his sons William
and Harry J. Kendall. (CH 48)
See also BONSAL, VINCENT P.

1029
KENNEDY, ELIJAH.
Cabinetmaker.
Born c. 1825, Kentucky; w. 1850,
Carroll Co. (C)

1030
KENNEDY, JAMES.
Chairmaker and painter.

W. 1820, Washington Co. Although James Kennedy was listed in the industrial census, the census taker remarked "None in operation, no sales." (MC)

1031
KENOWER, JOHN.
Cabinetmaker.
Born 1820; w. Huntington, Huntington Co., 1847-1863. Still living in 1914. In 1850 his shop employed three men who used water-powered machinery. Their annual product that year was valued at $1,500. (MC, CH 2)

1032
KENSICK, FRANKLIN G.
Chairmaker.
Born c. 1818, Pennsylvania; w. 1850, Adams Twp., Allen Co. (C)

1033
KENYON, WILOY.
Cabinetmaker.
Born c. 1821, Indiana; w. 1850, Union Twp., Montgomery Co. (C) See KENYON & ROSS.

1034
KENYON & ROSS.
Furniture makers and undertakers. Wiloy Kenyon and Thomas J. T. Ross; w. 1850, Union Twp., Montgomery Co. Three men worked in this shop which in 1850 produced furniture and coffins valued at $2,500. (C, MC)

1035
KEPNER, BARNETT. Painter.
Born c. 1829, Pennsylvania; w. 1850, New Albany, Floyd Co. Lived with John Shrader, cabinetmaker. (C) See also SANDERSON & SHRADER.

1036
KERR, JOHN. Cabinetmaker.
Born c. 1820, South Carolina; w. 1850, Jackson Twp., Fayette Co. In same household, Simon Kerr, cabinetmaker. (C)

1037
KERR, SIMON. Cabinetmaker.
Born c. 1832, Maryland; w. 1850, Jackson Twp., Fayette Co. Lived with John Kerr, cabinetmaker. (C)

1038
KERR, TAYLOR C.
Cabinetmaker.
Born c. 1827, Tennessee; w. 1850, Blue River Twp., Henry Co. (C)

1039
KERR & COMPANY.
Cabinet Shop.
W. 1850, Jackson Twp., Fayette Co. Three men worked in this shop; in 1850 they produced 75 bedsteads, 20 bureaus, 20 tables, and miscellaneous items. (MC)

1040
KERSON, WILLIAM.
Chairmaker.
Born c. 1823, Indiana; w. 1850, Lafayette, Tippecanoe Co. Lived with James Wallace, chairmaker, q.v. (C)

1041
KESSNER, JACOB. Chairmaker.
Born c. 1813, Tennessee; w. 1850, Rockport, Spencer Co. Three chairs made by him are known. (C)

1042
KEYES, JOHN F.
Chairmaker and painter.

W. 1827, Salem, Washington Co.
Adv. in *Annotator of News,
Politics and Literature,* 24 November 1827: "CHAIR FACTORY/
JOHN F. KEYES, Still continues to carry on the Chair Making Business in all its various branches, on South-Main Street in Salem, . . . He also does all kinds of *House & Sign Painting, &c. &c."*

1043
KIMBALL, CHARLES G.
Cabinetmaker.
> Born c. 1816, Indiana; w. 1850, Greencastle, Putnam Co. (C)

1044
KINCAID, JOHN. Cabinetmaker.
> Born c. 1826, Kentucky; w. 1850, Fugit Twp., Decatur Co. (C)

1045
KINNEY, JACOB B.
Bedstead maker.
> W. -1841-, Goshen, Elkhart Co. (CH 14)

1046
KIRK, EDWARD J.
Cabinetmaker.
> Born c. 1820, Pennsylvania; w. 1850, Portage Twp., Porter Co. (C)

1047
KIRK, THOMAS F.
Cabinetmaker.
> Born c. 1832, Pennsylvania; w. 1850, Shelbyville, Shelby Co. Lived with Joseph Cummins, cabinetmaker, q.v. (C)

1048
KIRKPATRICK, WILLIAM.
Chairmaker.
> Born c. 1789, South Carolina; w. 1850, Morristown, Shelby Co. (C)

1049
KITCHEN, ANDREW.
Chairmaker.
> Born c. 1817, Indiana; w. 1850, Rush Co. (C)

1050
KLIPSTA, GUSTAVUS.
> Born c. 1823, Germany; w. 1850, Cabinetmaker.
> Haw Creek Twp., Bartholomew Co. (C)

1051
KNECHE, DOMINIC.
Cabinetmaker.
> Born c. 1826, Switzerland; w. 1850, Wayne Twp., Allen Co. Lived with David Wurstein, cabinetmaker. (C)

1052
KNOTHE, TICTUS.
Cabinetmaker.
> Born c. 1818, Germany; w. 1850, Wayne Twp., Allen Co. (C)

1053
KNOX, GEORGE GILL.
Cabinetmaker.
> W. c. 1815-, Vevay, Switzerland Co. Had worked previously in Frankfort, Kentucky. Two-drawer square table and chest of drawers are extant. Knox also built houses, two of which were still standing in 1961 in Vevay, one a "two story frame of New Orleans French architecture. . ." (Julie LeClerc Knox, *Some Interesting Pioneer Homesteads In and*

Around Vevay, Indiana, 2d ed., 1948). Said to have been the first cabinetmaker to work in Vevay. (CH 16)

1054
KONTZ, GEORGE. Chairmaker.
Born c. 1818, Maryland; w. 1850, Jefferson, Clinton Co. (C)

1055
KOONTZ, BENJAMIN. Cabinetmaker.
Born c. 1810, Maryland; w. 1850, Peru, Miami Co. (C)

1056
KRANELE, FRANCIS. Cabinetmaker.
Born c. 1817, Germany; w. 1850, Evansville, Vanderburgh Co. (C)
See also KRANELE & GILLS.

1057
KRANELE (KRAENLE) & GILLS. Cabinetmakers.
Francis Kranele and——Gills; w. 1850, Evansville, Vanderburgh Co. Five men worked in this shop; in 1850 they produced cabinet furniture worth $2,000. The second member of the firm may have been Leonard Gills, recorded in 1850 census as carpenter, age 34, and born in Germany. (C, MC)

1058
KREIDER, HENRY. Cabinetmaker.
Born c. 1814, Pennsylvania; w. 1850, Clay Twp., Kosciusko Co. (C)

1059
KREPS, GOTLIEB. Cabinetmaker.

Born c. 1824, Germany; w. 1850, Bloomfield Twp., La Grange Co. (C)

1060
KRISHER, WILLIAM. Cabinetmaker.
Born c. 1832, Pennsylvania; w. 1850, Chester Twp., Wabash Co. Listed twice in census, once in household of John F. Smith, cabinetmaker, to whom he may have been an apprentice. (C)

1061
KRUSE, HENRY. Cabinetmaker.
Born c. 1817, Hesse, Germany; w. 1850, Madison, Jefferson Co. (C)

1062
KUHLMAN (COLEMAN), PETER. Cabinetmaker.
Born c. 1825, Germany; w. 1850, Evansville, Vanderburgh Co. Four men were employed in this shop; in 1850 they produced cabinet furniture worth $2,100. (C, MC)

1063
KUMES, HARRY. Cabinetmaker.
Born c. 1818; w. 1850, Lafayette, Tippecanoe Co. (C)

1064
KUNGLE, MICHAEL. Cabinetmaker.
Born c. 1815, Germany; w. 1850, Lawrenceburg, Dearborn Co. (C)

1065
KURTZ, JACOB. Cabinetmaker.
Born c. 1791, Kentucky; w. 1850, Floyd Twp., Putnam Co. (C)

1066
LACY, BENJAMIN.
Chairmaker.
> Born c. 1819, New York; w.
> 1850, Perrysville, Vermillion Co.
> In same household, McClary
> Harris, chairmaker. (C)

1067
LACY (?), RANDOLPH.
Cabinetmaker.
> Born c. 1818, Ohio; w. 1850,
> Anderson Twp., Madison Co.
> Four men worked in this shop
> using machinery powered by
> horse. Their product in 1850 was
> valued at $2,000. The other
> employees of the shop, who also
> lived in the Lacy(?) household,
> were Thomas Danahoo and
> Arsemus Collis, cabinetmakers,
> and Benjamin Clark, chairmaker.
> (C, MC)

1068
LACY, WILLIAM. Chairmaker.
> Born c. 1820, Indiana; w. 1850,
> Robinson Twp., Posey Co. (C)

1069
LAMAN (LAYMAN), JAMES S.
Chairmaker.
> Born c. 1812, Pennsylvania; w.
> 1850, Parke Co. Two men work-
> ing in this shop made chairs,
> settees, etc., worth $800 in 1850.
> The other worker was William
> Crawford, chairmaker. (C, MC)

1070
LAMB, ALBERSON.
Cabinetmaker.
> Born c. 1826, North Carolina; w.
> 1850, New Garden Twp., Wayne
> Co. Lived with Robert Curtis,
> cabinetmaker. (C)

1071
LAMB, BENJAMIN. Chairmaker.
> Born c. 1825, North Carolina; w.
> 1850, Dalton Twp., Wayne Co.
> (C)

1072
LAMB, NATHAN. Chairmaker.
> Born c. 1826, Indiana; w. 1850,
> Noble Twp., Wabash Co. (C)

1073
LAMBERT, HENRY.
Cabinetmaker.
> Born c. 1802, Pennsylvania; w.
> 1850, Columbus Twp., Bartholo-
> mew Co. (C)

1074
LAMBERT, JOSEPH.
Cabinetmaker.
> Born c. 1810, Indiana; 1842, ar-
> rived in Rockville, Parke Co.
> w. -1850-, Rockville. (C, CH 48)

1075
LAMON, WESTLEY.
Chairmaker.
> Born c. 1834, Indiana; w. 1850,
> Harrison Co. (C)

1076
LAMPERY, LEWIS.
Cabinetmaker.
> Born c. 1816, Germany; w. 1850,
> Lawrenceburg, Dearborn Co. (C)

1077
LANCASTER, JESSE.
Chairmaker.
> Born c. 1798, South Carolina; w.
> 1850, Green Twp., Howard Co.
> (C)

1078
LANDIS, SAMUEL.
Cabinetmaker.
    Born c. 1794, Pennsylvania; w.
    1850, Johnson Twp., Ripley Co.
    (C)

1079
LANDON, ROBERT.
Cabinetmaker.
    W. -1838-1846-, South Bend, St.
    Joseph Co. Associated with Ben-
    jamin F. Price 1838-40, q.v. Adv.
    South Bend Free Press, January
    1841: Landon shop on Washing-
    ton Street at the sign of the
    bedstead. Adv. in *St. Joseph Val-
    ley Register* December 1845:
    "Robert Landon's old stand . . .
    selling all kinds of cabinet work
    . . . sofas, tables, bedsteads," etc.
    Advertises cheapness of product;
    also makes coffins. Adv. in *St.
    Joseph Valley Register*, May-
    October 1846: associated with
    Alfred Wright, painter; they
    employ an experienced workman,
    Abraham Wilson. They make
    coffins and do painting on Michi-
    gan Street one door south of the
    Post Office.

1080
LANE, ——. Cabinetmaker.
    Born c. 1825, Ohio; w. 1850,
    Jeffersonville, Clark Co. Lived
    with William Guy, chairmaker.
    (C)

1081
LANE, ENOCH M. W.
Cabinetmaker.
    Born c. 1798, Ohio; w. 1850,
    Eugene Twp., Vermillion Co. (C)

1082
LANE, WILLIAM.
Cabinetmaker.
    Born c. 1825, Virginia; w. 1850,
    Clinton Twp., Elkhart Co. (C)

1082a
LARSH, T. J., & CO. Turners.
    W. 1835, Richmond, Wayne Co.
    Adv. in the *Palladium*, 4 April
    1835, that they would do "all
    manner of Turning" in "the best
    possible style, and on the shortest
    notice—Bed posts, Chair stuffs,
    Columns large or small, Waggon
    hubs, Table legs. . . ."

1083
LASSLEY, AARON.
Cabinetmaker.
    Born c. 1832, Indiana; w. 1850,
    New Garden Twp., Wayne Co.
    (C)

1084
LATHROP, EZRA R.
Cabinetmaker.
    Born c. 1831, Indiana; w. 1850,
    Greencastle, Putnam Co. Lived
    with Junia Lathrop, cabinetmaker.
    (C)

1085
LATHROP, JUNIA.
Cabinetmaker.
    Born c. 1793, New York; w.
    1850, Greencastle, Putnam Co. In
    same household, Ezra R. Lathrop,
    cabinetmaker. (C)

1086
LAWRENCE—*see* JAMISON &
LAWRENCE.

1086a
LAYMAN, JAMES T.—*see*
BLAIN, WILLIAM.

1087
LEACH, ELIAS. Cabinetmaker.
Born c. 1815, Kentucky; w. 1850, Pittsboro, Hendricks Co. In 1850 he produced furniture worth $500. (C, MC, CH 22)

1088
LEACHMAN, JAMES F. Chairmaker.
Born c. 1827, Ohio; w. 1850, Sugar Creek Twp., Hancock Co. Lived with William Leachman, chairmaker, q.v. (C)

1089
LEACHMAN, WILLIAM. Chairmaker.
Born c. 1827, Indiana; w. 1850, Hancock Co. James F. Leachman worked with him in his shop; their machinery was powered by horse. In 1850 they made 700 chairs worth $1,200. (C, MC)

1090
LEARNING, JEREMIAH. Cabinetmaker.
Born c. 1832, New York; w. 1850, Lauramie Twp. Tippecanoe Co. Lived with Nathaniel S. Barnes, cabinetmaker, q.v. (C)

1091
LEATHERMAN, JOHN. Cabinetmaker.
Born c. 1811, Ohio; w. 1850, Fountain Co. In 1850 he made 10 bureaus, 25 tables, 60 bedsteads, 10 stands, 15 coffins, and other articles. (C, MC)

1092
LEE, CHARLES M. Cabinetmaker.
Born c. 1831, Ohio; w. 1850, Madison, Jefferson Co. (C)

1093
LEE, GREENUP. Cabinetmaker.
Born c. 1816, Kentucky; w. 1850, Greencastle, Putnam Co. In same household, Augustine Elliott, cabinetmaker. (C)

1094
LEE, JAMES. Chairmaker.
Born c. 1820, Ohio; w. 1850, Vernon Twp., Jennings Co. (C)

1095
LEE, MITCHEL. Cabinetmaker.
Born c. 1798, Kentucky; w. 1850, Monroe Twp., Putnam Co. (C)

1096
LEE, RALPH. Chairmaker, cabinetmaker, and miller.
Born c. 1808, England; w. 1850, Jefferson Twp., Carroll Co. Three men were employed in this shop, using water power to make 493 chairs and 123 pieces of furniture valued at $1,000 in 1850. (C, MC)

1097
LEIGHTY, HENRY. Cabinetmaker.
W. 1850, Fountain Co. He worked alone, and in 1850 produced 8 bureaus, 30 tables, 60 bedsteads, 6 stands, 30 coffins, and other work. (MC)

1098
LENCE, JOHN. Cabinetmaker.
Born c. 1820, Indiana; w. 1850, Harrison Co. (C)

1099
LENTZ, JOHN. Cabinetmaker.
Born c. 1825, Pennsylvania; w. 1850, Harrison Co. (C)

1100
LEONARD, GEORGE W.
Chairmaker.
Born c. 1829, Ohio; w. 1850,
Portage Twp., St. Joseph Co. (C)

1101
LEPPER, HENRY. Cabinetmaker.
Born c. 1817, Germany; w. 1850,
Wayne Twp., Allen Co. Lived
with William Paul, chairmaker.
(C)

1102
LERING, ISAAC M.
Cabinetmaker.
Born c. 1805, Kentucky; w. 1850,
Liberty, Union Co. (C)

1103
LERY, ALFRED. Cabinetmaker.
Born c. 1810, Kentucky; w. 1850,
Jeffersonville, Clark Co. In same
household, John J. Lery, cabinet-
maker. (C)

1104
LERY, JOHN J. Cabinetmaker.
Born c. 1832, Ohio; w. 1850,
Jeffersonville, Clark Co. Lived
with Alfred Lery, cabinetmaker.
(C)

1105
LESSIG, CHRISTIAN.
Chairmaker and painter.
Born c. 1818, Pennsylvania; w.
1850, Noble Twp., Wabash Co.
(C)

1106
LETERS, ROBERT P.
Chairmaker.
Born c. 1821, Kentucky; w. 1850,
Morgantown, Morgan Co. (C)

1107
LEVING, LEWIS. Cabinetmaker.
Born c. 1827, North Carolina; w.
1850, Haw Creek Twp., Bartholomew Co. (C)

1108
LEWELLEN, DAVID.
Cabinetmaker.
Born c. 1817, Pennsylvania; w.
1850, Noblesville, Hamilton Co.
(C)

1109
LEWIS, DAVID. Cabinetmaker.
Born c. 1825, New York; w.
1850, Jefferson Twp., Miami Co.
(C)

1110
LEWIS, DAVID. Cabinetmaker.
Born c. 1804, Kentucky; w. 1850,
Newburgh, Warrick Co. (C)

1111
LEWIS, E. & J. Chair factory.
Ezekial and Joseph Lewis; w.
1850, Madison, Jefferson Co. Eight
men were employed in this shop;
their raw materials included "125
Stands Chair Stuff" and paint.
In 1850 they made 500 dozen
chairs valued at $5,000. (C, MC)

1112
LEWIS, EZEKIAL. Chairmaker.
Born c. 1814, Ohio; w. 1850,
Madison, Jefferson Co. (C) *See
also* LEWIS, E. & J.

1113
LEWIS, HALSEY. Chair factory.
W. 1830s, York Twp., Noble Co.
Used water power. Firm in busi-
ness for a few years; made crude
furniture. (CH 12)

1114
LEWIS, JOHN H. Cabinetmaker.
Born c. 1808, Pennsylvania; w.
1850, Rising Sun, Ohio Co. In
same household, Samuel Lewis,
painter. (C)

1115
LEWIS, JONAS C. Cabinetmaker.
Born c. 1814, Ohio; w. 1850,
Liberty Twp., Parke Co. (C)

1116
LEWIS, JOSEPH. Chairmaker.
Born c. 1810, Ohio; w. 1850,
Madison, Jefferson Co. (C) *See
also* LEWIS, E. & J.

1117
LEWIS, SAMUEL. Painter.
Born c. 1831, Indiana; w. 1850,
Rising Sun, Ohio Co. Lived with
John H. Lewis, cabinetmaker. **(C)**

1118
LEWIS, STEPHEN R.
Cabinetmaker and chairmaker.
Born c. 1812, New York; **w.**
1850, Haw Creek Twp., Barthol-
omew Co. (C)

1119
LIENTZ, ELHANAN.
Chairmaker.
Born c. 1826, Indiana; w. 1850,
Pleasant Twp., Switzerland Co.
(C)

1120
LIFE, JOHN S. Cabinetmaker.
Born c. 1828, Virginia; w. 1850,
Emmettsville, Randolph Co. (C)
See LIFE & GORDON.

1121
LIFE & GORDON. Cabinetmakers.
John S. Life and Silas Gordon;
w. 1850, Emmettsville, Randolph

Co. In 1850 they made 18 bureaus,
125 bedsteads, and "sundries,"
totaling $1,073 in value. (C, MC)

1122
LIGHTFOOT, JAMES.
Cabinetmaker.
W. 1820, Corydon, Harrison Co.
Adv. in *Indiana Gazette* 2 Novem-
ber 1820, for return of runaway
apprentice Lewis Shryoch.

1123
LIGON, JNO. B. Cabinetmaker.
Born c. 1823, Kentucky; w. 1850,
Rush Co. (C)

1124
LILINY, JOHN. Cabinetmaker.
Born c. 1800, Virginia; w. 1850,
Huntington Co. (C)

1125
LILPOP, CHRISTOPHER.
Cabinetmaker.
Born c. 1817, Germany; w. 1850,
Hall Twp., Dubois Co. (C)

1126
LINCH, JAMES. Cabinetmaker.
Born c. 1831, Ohio; w. 1850,
Noble Twp., Noble Co. (C)

1127
LINCH, SAMUEL. Chairmaker.
Born c. 1805, Virginia; w. 1850,
Union Twp., Parke Co. (C)

1128
LINCOLN, THOMAS.
Cabinetmaker.
In Indiana 1816-1830. Thomas
Lincoln, father of President Abraham Lincoln, made several pieces
of furniture still extant, including
a cherry hutch, cherry sugar chest,
cherry day bed, cherry desk and
bookcase, inlaid cherry chest of

drawers, and several corner cupboards. (Plates III and IV).
These are illustrated in articles by
R. Gerald McMurtry in *Antiques,*
LXXXV, No. 2 (February 1964),
pp. 206-208; LXXXVII, No. 3
(March 1965), p. 337, and in
Lincoln Lore (The Lincoln National Life Foundation, Fort
Wayne, Ind.), nos. 1476 (February 1961) and 1512 (February
1964). See also Louis A. Warren,
Lincoln's Youth in Indiana (Indianapolis: Indiana Historical Society, 1959), pp. 139-40.

1129
LINDLEY & LISTON.
Cabinetmakers.
 W. 1837, Paoli, Orange Co. (Adv.
 in *Torch-Light* 1 December 1837.)
 See William A. Liston, possibly
 same.

1130
LINDSEY, DANIEL T.
Cabinetmaker.
 Born 6 February 1815, Guilford
 Co., North Carolina; c. 1845
 moved to Delaware Co. Worked
 in North Carolina and Delaware
 Co. as cabinetmaker; later turned
 to carpentry, building, and farm-
 ing. Died 1899, Franklin Twp.,
 Grant Co. **(CH 45)**

1131
LINDSEY, FESTUS.
Cabinetmaker.
 Born c. 1831, Virginia; w. 1850,
 Bluffton, Wells Co. Lived with
 William McBride, cabinetmaker,
 q.v. (C)

1132
LINES, CHARLES. Cabinetmaker.
 Born c. 1816, Indiana; w. 1850,
 Rush Co. (C)

1133
LINES, JOHN. Chairmaker.
 Born c. 1820, Indiana; w. 1850,
 Stony Creek Twp., Henry Co.
 (C)

1134
LINK, LEWIS. Cabinetmaker.
 Born c. 1826, Germany; w. 1850,
 Logan Twp., Fountain Co. (C)

1134a
LINKS(?), JAMES—*see* SINKS
(or LINKS?), JAMES.

1135
LINLEY, HENRY. Cabinetmaker.
 Born c. 1825, North Carolina; w.
 1850, Greensboro Twp., Henry Co.
 (C)

1136
LINSEY, W. H. Cabinetmaker.
 Born c. 1824, Indiana; w. 1850,
 Gosport, Owen Co. (C)

1137
LINTNER, CHARLES.
Cabinetmaker.
 Born c. 1805, Germany; w. 1850,
 New Albany, Floyd Co. (C)

1138
LINTON, ALBERT. Chairmaker.
 Born c. 1807, Maryland; w. 1850,
 Orange Twp., Fayette Co. In
 same household, Thomas L.
 Linton, chairmaker. (C)

1139
LINTON, THOMAS L.
Chairmaker.
 Born c. 1834, Ohio; w. 1850,

Orange Twp., Fayette Co. Lived with Albert Linton, chairmaker. (C)

1140
LIPTON, PETER. Cabinetmaker.
Born c. 1822, Ohio; w. 1850, Sheffield Twp., Tippecanoe Co. (C)

1141
LIST, JOHN. Cabinetmaker.
Born c. 1814, Paris; w. 1850, Mt. Tabor, Monroe Co. (C)

1142
LIST, SILAS. Cabinetmaker.
Born c. 1811, Kentucky; w. 1850, Wayne Twp., Randolph Co. (C)

1143
LISTON, WILLIAM A. Cabinetmaker.
Born c. 1813, Delaware; w. 1850, Paoli, Orange Co. Had three apprentices (two of them, William Murphy and William Cloud); in 1850 they made 352 bureaus and cupboards, 105 tables and bedsteads. (C, MC) *See also* LINDLEY & LISTON.

1144
LITTLEFIELD, JOHN. Cabinetmaker.
Born c. 1814, Pennsylvania; w. 1850, Cotton Twp., Switzerland Co. His annual product was valued at $500 in 1850. (C, MC)

1145
LIVINGSTON, PETER F. Cabinetmaker.
Born c. 1818, Virginia; w. 1850, Clay Twp., Owen Co. (C)

1146
LOCKRIDGE, JAMES. Chairmaker.
Born c. 1812, Virginia; w. 1850, Danville, Hendricks Co. (C)

1147
LOCKWOOD, STEPHEN. Cabinetmaker.
Born c. 1809, New York; w. 1850, Jefferson Twp., Greene Co. In same household, Calvin Kelsey, cabinetmaker. (C)

1148
LONEY, RICHARD. Cabinetmaker.
Born c. 1820, Ohio; w. 1850, Warsaw, Kosciusko Co. Two men worked in this shop; in 1850 they made 76 bedsteads and bureaus as well as other furniture. (C, MC)

1149
LONG, GEORGE. Cabinetmaker.
W. -1839-, Lafayette, Tippecanoe Co. Adv. in *Indiana Eagle*, 2 January 1839 and later, that he had a shop on the south side of South Street between Ohio and Wabash.

1150
LONG, HAMILTON. Chairmaker.
Born c. 1831, Ohio; w. 1850, Rochester Twp., Fulton Co. (C)

1151
LONGE, JASPER—*see* WHEAT & LONGE.

1152
LOOMIS, EPHRAIM. Cabinetmaker.

Born c. 1813, New Jersey; w. 1850, Liberty Twp., Union Co. (C)

1153
LORING, CHARLES.
Cabinetmaker.
Born c. 1801, Kentucky; w. 1850, Portage Twp., St. Joseph Co. (C)

1154
LOVE, LABAN. Cabinetmaker.
Born c. 1828, North Carolina; w. 1850, Winchester, Randolph Co. (C)

1155
LOVELACE, WILLIAM.
Cabinetmaker.
W. 1841-, Franklin, Johnson Co. (CH 29)

1156
LOW, WILLIAM. Chairmaker.
W. 1850, Madison Co. Five men worked in this shop; their 1850 product was listed (probably incorrectly) as "30 Chairs $800." (MC)

1157
LOW & THAYER. Cabinetmakers.
———— Low & Alvin Thayer; W. 1850, Miami Co. Five men worked in this shop, using machinery powered by water. Their annual product was listed as "various" and worth $2,500. (MC) Thayer's partner may have been John Low, Peru, born c. 1804, Maryland, who is listed as a machinist in the 1850 census.

1158
LOZIER, ARPHAXID.
Cabinetmaker.

Born c. 1826, Ohio; w. 1850, Brown Twp., Hancock Co. (C)

1159
LUCUS, ANDREW I.
Cabinetmaker.
Born c. 1829, Ohio; w. 1850, Hagerstown, Wayne Co. Lived with Elijah Castator, cabinetmaker. (C)

1160
LUELLEN, ALPHEUS I.
Cabinetmaker.
Born c. 1825, Virginia; w. 1850, Liberty Twp., Delaware Co. (C)

1161
LUMN, ALFRED. Cabinetmaker.
Born c. 1830, Ohio; w. 1850, Bethel Twp., Posey Co. (C)

1162
LUMN, F. Cabinetmaker.
Born c. 1810, Virginia; w. 1850, Bethel Twp., Posey Co. (C)

1163
LUMN, HARRISON.
Cabinetmaker.
Born c. 1833, Pennsylvania; w. 1850, Bethel Twp., Posey Co. (C)

1164
LUSE, FLEMING T.
Cabinetmaker.
W. -1826-40, Indianapolis, Marion Co. Adv. in *Indianapolis Gazette* 11 April 1826: ". . . wishes to inform his friends and the public that he has again rebuilt his shop on the same lot on which his former shop stood that was burnt, and has commenced business a few

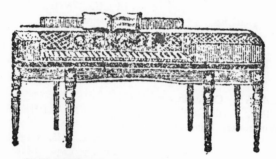

CABINET MAKING.

FLEMING T. LUSE

GRATEFUL for past favors, informs his friends and the public that he still continues to carry on the above-business at his old stand, a few feet south of Washington-street and one door east of M'Carty's Store, where the public can be accommodated with almost every kind of work in his line, of the best materials and executed in a workmanlike manner. Persons wishing any descriptions of furniture can be accomodated as low for CASH as at any other shop in town.

Indianapolis, Oct. 15, 1831.   451

Fig. 5.   From Indianapolis *Indiana Journal*

doors east of the Washington Hall tavern . . ."; adv. *Indiana Journal* 2 January 1830—"FLEMING T. LUSE, Still continues to carry on the [cabinet making] business at his old stand, a few feet South of Washington street and one door east of M'Carty's store, where the public can be accommodated with almost every kind of work in his line, of the best materials, and executed in a workmanlike manner. Persons wishing any description of furniture can be accommodated, and at a fair price. [Apprentice wanted]" A d v. *Indiana Journal* 29 October 1831, illustrating a piano. Adv. *ibid.* 16 October 1835, cabinet and plane making; F.T. Luse does cabinet work, S. Cook makes planes. Adv. *Indiana State Gazette* 3 November 1838. Succeeded by Tucker & Weaver in 1840, q.v.

1165
LYCAN, GEORGE.
Chairmaker.
> Born c. 1830, Illinois; w. 1850, Harrison Twp., Vigo Co. Lived with Lewis (Louis) Smith, chairmaker. (C)

1166
LYNASS, JOSEPH.
Cabinetmaker.
> Born c. 1792, England; w. 1850, Miller Twp., Dearborn Co. (C)

1167
LYONS, CHARLES T.
Cabinetmaker.
> Born c. 1826, New York; w. 1850, York Twp., Noble Co. (C)

1168
LYONS, J. A. Cabinetmaker.
> Born c. 1828, Indiana; w. 1850, Gosport, Owen Co. (C) *See* SCOTT & LYONS.

1169
LYSER, URIAH. Wood turner.
> Born c. 1809, Ohio; w. 1850, Pike Twp., Warren Co. (C)

1170
LYTLE, LEVI M. Cabinetmaker.
> Born c. 1815, Indiana; w. 1850, St. Omer, Decatur Co. In 1850 he produced $1,000 worth of cabinetware. (C, MC)

1171
McADAMS, JAMES.
Cabinetmaker.
> Born c. 1826, Kentucky; w. 1850, Jefferson Twp., Greene Co. (C)

1172
McBRIDE, JOHN. Cabinetmaker.
> W. 1850, Clay Twp., Owen Co. In 1850 he produced 12 bureaus, 6 cupboards, 25 bedsteads, 6 tables and "other work." (MC)

1173
McBRIDE, WILLIAM.
Cabinetmaker and undertaker.
> Born c. 1805, Pennsylvania; w. 1834-1841, Salem, Ohio; w. 1841-1871, Bluffton, Wells Co. Taught nephew Gabriel Schrock cabinetmaking and both came to Wells County together in 1841; Shrock was still living with him in 1850. Son William Warren McBride was associated with him and carried on the business in Bluffton. J. A. McBride & Son Funeral Directors, celebrated their 100th anniversary in 1940. Account books (microfilm) in library of Indiana Historical Society indicate William McBride made bureaus, stands, dining tables, desks, chairs, beds, including French bedsteads, chests, cupboards, safes, and cradles, in addition to the usual miscellany of household objects.

Woods listed include **walnut,** cherry, poplar, and sycamore. (C, CH 4)

1174
McCALLIE, CHRISTOPHER M.
Cabinetmaker.
Born c. 1830, South Carolina; w. 1850, Bloomington, Monroe Co. Lived with George W. Batterton, cabinetmaker. **(C)**

1175
McCALLY, JAMES.
Cabinetmaker.
Born c. 1801, Kentucky; w. 1850, Rush Co. In same household, William McCally, cabinetmaker. (C)

1176
McCALLY, WILLIAM.
Cabinetmaker.
Born c. 1825, Indiana; w. 1850, Rush Co. Lived with James Mc-Cally, cabinetmaker. (C)

1177
McCLAREN, HUGH.
Apprentice cabinetmaker.
Born c. 1831, Indiana; w. 1850, Corydon, Harrison Co. Apprenticed to John Peter. (C)

1178
McCLURE, A[NDREW].
Chairmaker.
W. 1834-1835, **Indianapolis,** Marion Co. Adv. in *Indiana D e m o c r a t* 4 May 1834: "INDIANAPOLIS C H A I R M A N U F A C T O R Y / A. McClure . . . has, and intends keeping constantly on hand a large and general assortment of *FANCY AND WIND-SOR CHAIRS, SETTEES, &C.*

of the latest patterns, which he warrants to be equal, in durability or elegance, to any manufactured in the Western or Eastern cities . . . [located two doors east of Bates' store on Washington Street]." Adv. in *Indiana Democrat* 2 January 1835: "Indianapolis Fancy and Windsor Chair Manufactory . . . also . . . a large and general assortment of CABINET FURNITURE. A. McCLURE & CO." Adv. *ibid.* 29 June 1835: "A. McCLURE & JAS. E. WHEAT dissolve the partnership which was called A. McClure & Co." Patrons asked to settle with A. McClure. *See* WHEAT, JAMES E.

1179
McCLURE, ANDREW.
Cabinetmaker.
Born c. 1810, Ohio; w. 1850-, Logansport, Cass Co. In 1850, three men worked in this shop; they produced 500 chairs, 48 tables, 24 bureaus, and 100 bedsteads. Andrew McClure was listed in the census as a cabinetmaker, therefore probably not the same as A. McClure, q.v. His manufactory was located on the corner of Oak and Duret streets in Logansport. (C, MC, CH 25)

1180
McCLURE, JAMES. Chairmaker.
Born in Pennsylvania; w. 1850, Benton Co. (C)

1181
McCOLLOUGH & WEIR.
Cabinetmakers.
W. 1824, Bloomington, Monroe Co. Adv. in *Indiana Gazette* 11 December 1 8 2 4 : "M'COL-

LOUGH AND WEIR RE-SPECTFULLY informs their friends and the public generally, that they carry on the CABINET Business in all its various branches, in the west end of a brick building on south main street in Bloomington, fronting the court house:—And as they are in possession of all the newest fashions, they flatter themselves that they will be able to give general satisfaction to all who may favor them with their custom."

1182
McCORMICK, JOHN.
Chairmaker.
> Born c. 1833, Ohio; w. 1850, Portland, Jay Co., Lived with William McCormick, chairmaker. (C)

1183
McCORMICK, RUFUS.
Chairmaker.
> Born c. 1828, Ohio; w. 1850, Portland, Jay Co. Lived with William McCormick, chairmaker. (C)

1184
McCORMICK, WILLIAM.
Chairmaker.
> Born c. 1801, Ohio; w. 1850, Portland, Jay Co. Three men worked in this shop using machinery powered by horse. In 1850 they made chairs and bedsteads valued at $800. The other two men were probably Rufus and John McCormick both of whom lived in the William McCormick household. (C, MC)

1185
McCOULLOUCK, JOHN.
Chairmaker and painter.
> W. 1820, Washington Co. His annual product was listed as "Windsor Chairs, Signs &c. Chairs two Dollars, Signs various prices." (MC)

1186
McCOULLOUGH, JEREMIAH.
Cabinetmaker.
> Born c. 1820, Pennsylvania; w. 1850, Vernon Twp., Washington Co. (C)

1187
McCRACKEN, WILLIAM.
Chairmaker and wheelmaker.
> W. 1850, Washington Twp., Knox Co. His tools included a turning lathe; his product was listed as "windsor Chairs & Wheels." The census taker remarked that he worked in a log shop. (MC)

1188
McCRANER, WILLIAM.
Cabinetmaker.
> Born c. 1819, Pennsylvania; w. 1850, Wayne Twp., Henry Co. (C)

1189
McCREARY, ALBERT.
Chairmaker.
> Born c. 1834, Ohio; w. 1850, Deer Creek Twp., Miami Co. Lived with Jno. McCreary, chairmaker. (C)

1190
McCREARY, JNO. Chairmaker.
> Born c. 1806, Virginia; w. 1850, Deer Creek Twp., Miami Co. In same household, Albert McCreary, chairmaker. (C)

1191
McCULLA, JAMES.
Cabinetmaker.
  Born c. 1785, Ireland; w. 1850,
  Boone Twp., Warrick Co. (C)

1192
McCULOUGH, WALTER R.
Chairmaker.
  Born c. 1820, Indiana; w. 1850,
  Madison Twp., Jefferson Co. (C)

1193
McDANIEL, WILLIAM.
Chairmaker.
  Born c. 1821, Ohio; w. 1850,
  Auburn, De Kalb Co. (C)

1194
McDOUGLE, LEVI. Chairmaker.
  Born c. 1798, Maryland; w. 1826,
  New Albany, Floyd Co.; w. 1838-
  1850, Corydon, Harrison Co. Adv.
  Indiana Recorder and Public Advertiser 6 January 1826: "WINDSOR CHAIR *MANUFACTORY*/LEVI M'DOUGLE respectfully informs the citizens of this place, and the public generally, that he has opened a shop on lower Market-street, at the house formerly occupied as a Wool Carding Establishment, where he will keep constantly on hand, a good assortment of Windsor Chairs. He flatters himself that his work will not be inferior to any made in Louisville; and respectfully solicits a share of the public patronage." Adv. repeated 23 Oct. 1826 for "Plain and Fancy Chairs." Adv. in Corydon, *The Investigator* 29 March 1838: "LEVI McDOUGLE commences CHAIR MAKING business again . . .

[will] have a good supply of WINDSOR CHAIRS on hand. . . ."

1195
McDOWELL, FRANCIS M.
Chairmaker.
  Born c. 1831, Indiana; w. 1850,
  New Castle, Henry Co. (C)

1196
McENTIRE, DANIEL.
Cabinetmaker.
  Born c. 1826, Ohio; w. 1850,
  Liberty Twp., Shelby Co. (C)

1197
McFARLANE, ARCHIBALD D.
Cabinetmaker.
  Born c. 1830, Pennsylvania; w.
  1850, Carroll Co. (C)

1198
McGAHA, JAMES. Cabinetmaker.
  W.-1829, Centerville, Wayne Co.
  Adv. in *Western Times* 5 September 1829: "J. M'GAHA RESPECTFULLY informs his old customers, and the public generally, that he has again commenced the CABINET MAKING Business, at the shop adjoining the Printing Office, in Centreville, where he will be ready and willing to accommodate those who may favor him with their custom, on the shortest notice and most reasonable terms. Produce of all kinds will be taken in payment for work. A quantity of cherry and poplar plank, and cherry scantling, suitable for cabinet work, is wanted immediately." Adv. 26 September 1829 for 2 or 3 journeymen.

1199
McGILL, JOHN. Cabinetmaker.
Born c. 1822, Pennsylvania; w.
1850, Washington Twp., Owen Co.
(C)

1200
McGINNEY, DANIEL.
Apprentice cabinetmaker.
Born c. 1834, Indiana; w. 1850,
Bainbridge Twp., Dubois Co. Apprenticed to Henry W. Barker.
(C)

1201
McGINNIS, FRANKLIN.
Chairmaker.
W. 1835, Brookville, Franklin Co.
Adv. in *Indiana American* 25
December 1835, "C H A I R
MANUFACTORY/T H E Subscriber respectfully informs the
citizens of Franklin county, that
he continues the business of
CHAIR MAKING in the town
of Brookville . . . [makes common or fancy chairs]. . . . His
shop is immediately north of R. &
S. Tyner's Store. Call and see."

1202
McGUFFEY, SOLOMON.
Chairmaker.
Born c. 1824, Kentucky; w. 1850,
Huff Twp., Spencer Co. (C)

1203
McKAY, ROBERT.
Cabinetmaker.
Born c. 1809, Scotland; w. 1850,
Jackson Twp., Putnam Co. (C)

1204
McKEE, JOHN. Chairmaker.
Born c. 1795, Pennsylvania; w.
1850, Manchester Twp., Dearborn
Co. (C)

1205
McKEE, PETER. Cabinetmaker.
Born c. 1800, Ohio; w. 1850,
Washington Twp., Benton Co.
(C)

1206
McKEE, WILLIAM A.
Cabinetmaker.
Born c. 1828, Indiana; w. 1850,
Madison Twp., Putnam Co. (C)

1207
McKELVY, J. P. Cabinetmaker.
Born c. 1814, Pennsylvania; w.
1850, Waltz Twp., Wabash Co.
(C)

1208
McKEY, JOSHUA. Chairmaker.
Born c. 1830, Ohio; w. 1850,
Marion, Grant Co. (C)

1209
McKINNEY, GUINN.
Cabinetmaker.
Born c. 1831; w. 1850, Haw Creek
Twp., Bartholomew Co. (C)

1210
McKINNY, WILLIAM.
Cabinetmaker.
Born c. 1810, Ohio; w. 1850,
Fugit Twp., Decatur Co. (C)

1211
McKINNY, WILLIAM.
Cabinetmaker.
Born c. 1827, Indiana; w. 1850,
Greensburg, Decatur Co. (C)

1212
McLAIN, GEORGE. Cabinetmaker.
Born c. 1800, Tennessee; w. 1850,
Jackson Twp., Fountain Co. In
same household, John McLain,
cabinetmaker. (C)

1213
McLAIN, JOHN. Cabinetmaker.
Born c. 1832, Indiana; w. 1850,
Jackson Twp., Fountain Co. Lived
with George McLain, cabinet-
maker. (C)

1214
McLAUGHLIN, DANIEL.
Cabinetmaker.
Born c. 1822, Pennsylvania; w.
1850, Bloomfield Twp., La Grange
Co. (C)

1215
McMICHAEL, JNO.
Cabinetmaker.
Born c. 1804, North Carolina; w.
1850, Rush Co. (C)

1216
McMILLEN, WILLIAM.
Cabinetmaker.
Born 1793, Virginia; to Fayette
Co., Kentucky, by 1817; w. 1817-
1841, Charlestown, Clark Co. (CH
33)

1217
McNOBB, DAVID.
Cabinetmaker.
Born c. 1815, Kentucky; w. 1850,
Indianapolis, Marion Co. (C)

1218
McNOWN, HUGH. Cabinetmaker.
Born c. 1818, Ireland; w. 1850,
Lagro Twp., Wabash Co. (C)

1219
McPHEETERS, HUGH.
Cabinetmaker.
W. 1820, Washington Co. Two
men and one boy worked in this
shop. In 1820 they produced goods
priced as follows: "Clock cases
$30; Side boards $60 to $250;

Sacraterys [sic] from 30 to
$65; Desks from 25 to $30 & all
other in proportion." They remarked, "Dull Sales." (MC)

1220
McQUINN, SAMUEL S.
Cabinetmaker.
Born c. 1818, Kentucky; w. 1850,
Carter Twp., Spencer Co. (C)

1221
McTEER, ROBERT.
Cabinetmaker.
Born c. 1828, Tennessee; w. 1850,
Tippecanoe Twp., Carroll Co. In
same household, Nicholas Van
Pelt, cabinetmaker. (C)

1222
MACK, ——. Cabinetmaker.
W. 1825, Crawfordsville, Mont-
gomery Co. (CH 3)

1223
MACY, TRISTRAM.
Cabinetmaker.
Born c. 1803, North Carolina; w.
1850, Posey Twp., Rush Co. (C)

1224
MAGEE, MARTIN. Cabinetmaker.
Born c. 1829, Indiana; w. 1850,
Greenville Twp., Floyd Co. (C)

1225
MAGEE, WILLIAM.
Cabinetmaker.
Born c. 1825, Indiana; w. 1850,
Greenville Twp., Floyd Co. (C)

1226
MAHAN, ANDREW.
Cabinetmaker.
Born c. 1790, Pennsylvania; w.
1850, Owen Twp., Jackson Co.
(C)

1227

MAHONEY, THOMAS.
Cabinetmaker.
  Born 29 August 1821, Washington Co., Tennessee; 1831, moved
  to Rush County, Indiana. Apprenticed in New Salem to
  William Miller, cabinetmaker. In
  1841 or 1842 moved to Huntington Co.; 1843-1855, w. Mount
  Etna; 1855, moved out of the
  town; still living 1887. The 1850
  census records two men employed
  in his shop, making stands and
  tables. (C, MC, CH 28)

1228

MAINS, JOEL S. Chairmaker.
  Born c. 1819, Ohio; w. 1850,
  Huntington Co. (C)

1229

MALLERY, HENRY C.
Cabinetmaker.
  Born c. 1832, Indiana; w. 1850,
  Noblesville Twp., Hamilton Co.
  (C)

1230

MALLERY, JOSIAH M.
Cabinetmaker.
  Born c. 1806, New York; w.
  1850, Noblesville, Hamilton Co.
  In 1850 he made 12 bureaus and
  100 bedsteads. (C, MC)

1231

MALONE, JOHN. Cabinetmaker.
  Born c. 1825, Ohio; w. 1850,
  New Albany, Floyd Co. (C)

1232

MANDERBAUGH, WILLIAM.
Chairmaker.
  Born c. 1800; w. 1850, Jefferson-
  ville, Clark Co. (C)

1233

MANLY, WILLIAM T. S.
Cabinetmaker.
  Born 10 April 1813, near Pooles-
  ville, Maryland; moved to
  Virginia; to Springfield, Ohio;
  to Richmond, Indiana, and
  Indianapolis. October 1837, settled
  in Logansport, Cass Co. W. 1837-
  1850-, Logansport. In 1838, with
  Israel Neal ran a furniture and
  undertaking establishment. Adv.
  in *Logansport Telegraph* in 1840:
  "FURNITURE WARE-ROOM
  . . . established a CABINET SHOP
  . . . CABINET FURNITURE
  . . . he has also attached to his
  Shop a Power Lathe, on which he
  will do all kinds Turning in best of
  style . . . ." "During the year
  1841, William T.S. Manly operated a furniture factory on Third
  Street, south of North. He also
  made coffins and later moved his
  shop to the corner of Sixth and
  Broadway."
  In 1850 three men were working
  in his shop (the other two were
  John Christman and James De-
  Wolf); that year they produced
  100 tables, 40 bureaus, 100 bedsteads, and other work. A later
  partner was Leopold Smith, when
  the firm was known as W.T.S.
  Manly & Co. They erected large
  factory buildings north of the Eel
  River on the canal in Logansport.
  Manly died in November 1879,
  and Smith continued the business.
  (C, CH 25, MC)

1234

MANN, P. A.
Cabinetmaker and chairmaker.

FURNITURE
WARE-ROOM.
—.ooo—

THE subscriber would respectfully in- form the citizens of Logansport and its vicinity that he has established a CABINET SHOP, on Bridge street, between Market and Broadway, where he will keep constantly on hand an assortment of CABINET FURNITURE which he will war- rant to be equal with any made in the west.

All old work repaired and varnished or painted at the shortest notice—he has also attached to his Shop a Power Lathe, on which he will do all kinds Turning in best of style. Most kinds of Country produce will be taken in exchange for Furniture or Turning·   W. T. S. MANLY.

Logansport, Aug. 29, 1840   18ly

Fig. 6.   From *Logansport Telegraph*

Born c. 1821, Massachusetts; w. 1850, Rochester, Fulton Co. Two men worked in this shop; in 1850 they produced 50 bedsteads, 50 sets of chairs, 25 bureaus, and 25 tables. (C, MC)

1235
MANTZ (MONTZ), JACK.
Chairmaker.

Born c. 1824, Pennsylvania; w. 1850, New Albany, Floyd Co. Lived with George W. Porter, cabinetmaker.   (C)   *See also* PORTER & MANTZ (MONTZ)

1236
MAPES, WILLIAM H.
Chairmaker.

Born c. 1815; w. -1838-1850-, Rising Sun, Ohio Co. Adv. in *Rising Sun Journal* in the fall of 1838: that he continued to manu- facture "Family Chairs in all their variety; Windsor do; Com- mon do; Fancy, Windsor and common Settees; Fancy, Windsor and common Rocking Chairs; Cradle Settees and Sociables in all their varieties of style and sizes. Fancy and Windsor Sewing Chairs. do do Writing Chairs and

RISING SUN
CHAIR MANUFACTORY.

WILLIAM H. MAPES, being thankful for past favors, would hereby inform his customers and the public generally, that he continues to carry on the business of Chair manufacturing in all of its various branches, at his old stand, on the West side of Main street, between Front and Market streets, where he keeps on hand and manufactures to order the following articles:

Family Chairs in all their variety.
Windsor   do
Common   do
Fancy, Windsor, and common Settees.
Fancy, Windsor, and common Rocking Chairs.
Cradle Settees and Sociables in all their varieties of style and sizes.
Fancy and Windsor Sewing Chairs.
     do   do   : Writing Chairs,
and every article in the line of chair making.

He assures all who may patronize him that he uses none but the best kind of stock in all his manufacture, and as he employs none but the first class of workmen; he is willing that his work may be adjudged by competent judges, and if not found equal to any in the market, he asks not for continuance of patronage.

All orders from town or country thankfully received, and promptly attended to.

He hopes that by past experience and by a close attention to business, to receive a liberal share of patronage, and no trouble or expense shall be spared on his part to give satisfaction, or at least to do justice to all that may favor him with a call.

He continues to repair old work as usual.
The above articles may be obtained on accommodating terms.

Rising Sun, Sept. 29, 1838.—3-tf.

Fig. 7. From *Rising Sun Journal*

every article in the line of chair making." Adv. in Wilmington *Dearborn County Register* 27 March 1841: "CHAIR FACTORY . . . FANCY AND WINDSOR Chairs, also Settees, Sociables, Boston and fancy Rocking Chairs, Sewing Chairs with drawers, children's chairs of all descriptions, also, Cane and Rush bottom Chairs, split bottom Chairs . . . ." In 1845 he had a shop on the west side of Main Street near the river in Rising Sun. (C, CH 26)

1237
MAPES & ARMSTRONG.
Chair factory.
William H. Mapes and ——— Armstrong; w. after 1833, Rising Sun, Ohio Co. (CH 26)

1238
MARBLE, JONATHON.
Cabinetmaker.
Born c. 1812, Pennsylvania; w. 1850, Rising Sun, Ohio Co. (C) *See* HOOLE & MARBLE.

1239
MARINE, JAMES. Cabinetmaker.
Born c. 1827, North Carolina; w. 1850, Mooresville, Morgan Co. (C)

1240
MARION, FREDERICK.
Cabinetmaker.
Born c. 1820, France; w. 1850, Addison Twp., Shelby Co. (C)

1241
MARK, HUGH S. Chairmaker.
Born c. 1815, Virginia; w. 1850, Greencastle, Putnam Co. (C)

1242
MARKER, CURTIS. Chairmaker.
Born c. 1805, Delaware; w. 1850, Belleville, Hendricks Co. In 1850 he made $500 worth of chairs. (C, MC)

1243
MARKLE (MARKEL),
NATHAN. Cabinetmaker.
Born c. 1819, Pennsylvania; w. 1850, Concord Twp., Elkhart Co. In same household, Edward Broombaugh and John James, cabinetmakers. (C, CH 14)

1244
MARR, JOHN. Cabinetmaker.
Born c. 1810, Ireland; w. 1850, Shawnee Twp., Fountain Co. Robert H. Thompson worked with him; in 1850 they produced 30 bureaus, 50 tables, 60 bedsteads, 20 stands, 15 coffins, and other work. (C, MC)

1245
MARSH, JOHN. Cabinetmaker.
Born c. 1835, Connecticut; w. 1850, Madison, Jefferson Co. (C)

1246
MARTEL, DAVID L. (or T.).
Cabinetmaker.
Born c. 1819, Ohio; w. 1850, Mount Vernon, Posey Co. (C)

1247
MARTIN, EDMUND.
Cabinetmaker.
Born c. 1822, Kentucky; w. 1850, Wild Cat Twp., Tipton Co. (C)

1248
MARTIN, ELISHA.
Cabinetmaker.
  Born c. 1818, Indiana; w. 1850,
  Martinsburg, Washington Co. (C)

1249
MARTIN, JOSEPH.
Cabinetmaker.
  Born c. 1815, Kentucky; w. 1850,
  Franklin Twp., Johnson Co. (C)

1250
MARTIN, R. Chairmaker.
  W. 1850, Indianapolis, Marion Co.
  Three men worked in this shop,
  using machinery powered by
  steam. In 1850 they produced
  2,500 chairs worth $2,175. (MC)

1251
MARTIN, ROBERT.
Cabinetmaker.
  Born c. 1822; w. 1850, Lafayette,
  Tippecanoe Co. (C)

1252
MARTIN, WILLIAM.
Cabinetmaker.
  Born c. 1822, Ohio; w. 1850,
  Parke Co. (C)

1253
MARTINDALE, JAMES.
Chairmaker.
  Born c. 1829, Ohio; w. 1850,
  Deer Creek Twp., Miami Co. (C)

1254
MASON, JAMES E.
Cabinetmaker.
  W. 1850, Portage Twp., St.
  Joseph Co. Two men worked in
  this shop; in 1850 they made
  cabinet ware valued at $1,200.
  (MC) *See also* MASON, JOHN
  E., possibly same.

1255
MASON, JOHN E. Cabinetmaker.
  Born c. 1813, New York; w. 1850,
  Portage Twp., St. Joseph Co. In
  same household, C. G. Ferdinand
  Fogel, cabinetmaker. (C) *See
  also* MASON, JAMES E., pos-
  sibly same.

1256
MASON, THOMAS.
Cabinetmaker.
  Born c. 1812, New York; w. 1850-
  1860-, Wayne Twp., and/or
  Boston Twp., Wayne Co. Two
  men worked in this shop; in 1850
  they produced 100 coffins and
  other articles totaling in value
  $1,000. Adv. in the Richmond
  Jeffersonian 28 October 1852:
  "Thomas Mason, U N D E R -
  TAKER, AND MANUFAC-
  TURER OF FURNITURE,
  . . . has removed his shop to
  the South-West corner of Main
  and Front streets, . . . where he
  manufactures Cabinet-Ware of
  every variety . . . . He is also
  manufacturing a superior article
  of Patent Screw Bedsteads."
    In the 1860 industrial census he
  listed his raw materials as walnut,
  poplar, cherry, mahogany, glue,
  and varnish, from which he made
  "cabinet furniture asst'd" worth
  $8,000. (C, MC)

1257
MASTERS, WILLIAM.
Cabinetmaker.
  Born c. 1820, Pennsylvania; w.
  1850, Fairfield Twp., Franklin Co.
  (C)

1258
MATTHEW—*see* PECK &
MATTHEW.

1258a
MATTHEWS, W., &
I. L. JOHNSTON. Chairmakers.
W. 1834, Richmond, Wayne Co.
Adv. in the *Palladium,* 4 October
1834, that they "have established
themselves in this place, in the
chairmaking business, on Pearl
street . . . where they intend
to manufacture and keep constantly on hand a large and
splendid assortment of fancy and
winsor chairs, settees, sociables,
&c. . . ." *See also* MATTHEWS,
WILLIAM.

1258b
MATTHEWS, WILLIAM.
Chairmaker and cabinetmaker.
W. 1835, Richmond, Wayne Co.
Adv. in the *Palladium,* 7 March
1835, that he had in his shop two
doors east of Burk's Hotel chairs
bureaus, tables, and bedsteads of
different prices and qualities. *See
also* MATTHEWS, W., & I. L.
JOHNSTON;   MATTHEWS,
WILLIAM & JONATHAN.

1259
MATTHEWS, WILLIAM &
JONATHAN. Cabinetmakers.
W. after 1825, Washington Twp.,
Wayne Co. (CH 34)

1260
MATTOX, JAMES. Cabinetmaker.
Born c. 1829, Ohio; w. 1850,
Liberty, Union Co. (C)

1261
MAY, GEORGE W. Cabinetmaker.
Born c. 1809, Virginia; w. 1850,
Washington Twp., Owen Co. (C)

1262
MAYES, JAMES F. Cabinetmaker.
Born c. 1829, Tennessee; w. 1850,
Bloomington, Monroe Co. (C)

1263
MEAD, WILLIAM CHANCY.
Cabinetmaker.
Born c. 1827, New York; w.
1850, Pleasant Twp., Switzerland
Co. (C)

1264
MEEK, JACOB A. Cabinetmaker.
Born c. 1813, Kentucky; w. 1850,
Greencastle, Putnam Co. (C)

1265
MEEKER, D. L. Cabinetmaker.
Born c. 1811, New Jersey; w.
1850, Fayette Co. Two men
worked in this shop; in 1850 they
made 30 tables, 30 bedsteads, 10
bureaus, 6 bookcases, and other
articles. (C, MC)

1266
MEEKS, I.—*see* MEEKS, R. & I.

1267
MEEKS, ISAAC—*see* MEEKS,
ROBERT.

1268
MEEKS, JOSEPH. Cabinetmaker.
W. -1810-1818, New York, N. Y.;
1818, moved to Brookville, Frank-
lin Co.; adv. in *Brookville En-
quirer and Indiana Telegraph* 5
February 1819: "JOSEPH
MEEKS CABINET-MAKER,
Late from the City of N. York,
where he has conducted a small

business for the last eight years, takes this method of informing the inhabitants of Brookville, and the vicinity that he intends following the above Business at this place. He has brought with him a quantity of *Superior Mahogany,* which he will manufacture in the newest fashion and workman like manner; likewise other woods natural to the growth of this country. His residence is at the House of Mrs. Cooper, in the rear of Mr. Ray's tavern. N.B. An Apprentice wanted immediately." In 1821 he married Miss Lucinda Adair of Brookville, his second wife.

Adv. in *Indiana American* 1 August 1834, "Joseph Meeks, Cabinet Maker. R E S P E C T - FULLY informs his friends and the public in general, that he still continues to carry on the above business in all its various branches at his old stand where he has resided for the last fifteen years. He warrants his work to be of the best materials, and workmanship, and has now on hand two Mahogany Sideboards, — ALSO — BUREAUS, DINING TABLES, TEA TABLES, Stands, and Bedsteads of various descriptions, which he will dispose of in exchange for Cash, or country produce, likewise, Lumber of all kinds will be received."

Joseph Meeks undoubtedly was related to Joseph Meeks (1771-1868), a prominent furniture maker of New York City (*see Antiques,* LXXXV, No. 4 [April 1964], pp. 414-20; and XC, No. 1 [July 1966], pp. 69-73). The Indiana Joseph Meeks died December 3, 1843, and is buried at Brookville (Franklin County Cemetery Inscriptions, compiled by Mrs. Roscoe C. O'Byrne).

In the library of the Indiana Historical Society is the scrapbook of Martha S. Goodwin (microfilm), which contains the scrapbook of Phoebe Ann Meeks, daughter of Joseph Meeks. This illustrates the house which Joseph Meeks built on North Main Street in Brookville. A local history of 1915 stated, "There are many pieces of his handiwork to be seen in the homes of Brookville people today," and called him a "cabinetmaker and wood-working genius." (C, CH 43) *See above,* pp. 12-13.

1269
MEEKS, R. & I. Cabinetmakers. Robert and Isaac Meeks; w. 1844-1890, Muncie, Delaware Co. Business founded in 1844; said to have had nine or ten workmen, natives of West Virginia. They made "parlor, drawing-room, bed-room and library sets." Another source states they made all types of furniture "from the old-fashioned bedpost down to latest improved spring-bottom, and from the old-fashioned rocking chair, with its great high back, down to the modern, convenient, upholstered rocker, from the old-fashioned Dutch bureau down to the modern fancy dressing case." The 1850 census reported two men employed in this shop; they produced that year cabinet ware worth $1,200. In 1871 the firm name was

changed to R. & I. Meeks & Co. The factory burned in 1890 and was never rebuilt. (CH 1, 36, 37, C) *See also* MEEKS, ROBERT.

1270
MEEKS, ROBERT. Cabinetmaker. Born 8 July 1822, West Virginia; 1839, moved from West Virginia; w. 1844-1871-, Muncie, Delaware Co. Joined business begun by James Hodge; was an apprentice to firm of Nottingham & Swain to learn the trade of cabinet-making. Later was a partner of Job Swain (less than one year); then bought out Nottingham. In 1848 the firm was called Nottingham & Meeks, according to one source. However, the firm became known as R. & I. Meeks at some point, and by 1871 was known as R. & I. Meeks & Co. It is not known whether these Meekses were related to Joseph Meeks and the famous New York City family of cabinetmakers. (CH 1, 36, 37, 41) *See also* MEEKS, R. & I.

1271
MEEKS, THEODORE. Cabinetmaker. Born c. 1822, Indiana; w. 1850, Brookville, Franklin Co. Son of Joseph Meeks, cabinetmaker, q.v. Died 1854. In 1850, two men worked in this shop and made furniture valued at $800. (C, MC, *Antiques*, XCVIII, No. 1 [July 1970], pp. 122, 127)

1272
MEEKS, WILLIAM. Cabinetmaker. W. late 1840s -1850-, Cass Co.

Two men worked in this shop in 1850; their annual product was valued at $1,200. (MC, CH 25)

1273
MELDRUM, HENRY. Cabinetmaker. Born c. 1829, Pennsylvania; w. 1850, Harrison Twp., Fayette Co. In same household, William Calloway, cabinetmaker. (C)

1274
MELEA (MEALY), WILLIAM A. Chair factory. Born 1813, Pennsylvania; w. 1850, Madison, Jefferson Co. Three men worked in this shop; their raw materials included "53 Stands Chair Stuff, paints." In 1850 they made 364 dozen chairs valued at $2,548. (C, MC)

1275
MENEAR (or MINEAR), CHARLES. Cabinetmaker. Born c. 1826, Indiana; w. 1850, Pike Twp., Warren Co. (C)

1276
MENTZA, CONRAD. Cabinetmaker. Born c. 1821, Germany; w. 1850, Wayne Twp., Allen Co. (C)

1277
MEREDITH, JAMES. Cabinetmaker. Born c. 1832, Kentucky; w. 1850, Connersville, Fayette Co. (C)

1278
MERICK, MELAKIAH. Cabinetmaker. Born c. 1799, Virginia; w. 1850, Petersburg, Pike Co. (C)

1279
MERRIMAN, WILLIAM.
Cabinetmaker.
> Born c. 1801, Connecticut; w.
> 1850, Harrison Twp., Vigo
> County. (C)

1280
MESSACK, MICHAEL.
Cabinetmaker.
> Born c. 1829, Indiana; w. 1850,
> Paoli, Orange Co. (C)

1281
MICHAEL, EDWARD.
Cabinetmaker.
> Born c. 1819, Indiana; w. 1850,
> Clay Twp., Decatur Co. (C)

1282
MICHAEL, GEORGE W.
Chairmaker.
> **Born c. 1823**, Kentucky; w. 1850,
> Franklin Twp., Montgomery **Co.**
> (C)

1283
MICHAELS (MICHALS),
WILLIAM. Cabinetmaker.
> Born 2 February 1809, North
> Carolina; **w.** -1850-, Rockville,
> Parke Co.; died 1892. His shop
> was on Ohio Street in Rockville;
> he is said to have made excellent
> furniture. Later he set up his
> business in Piattsville (8 miles
> southeast of Rockville), where
> his sons John and Benjamin
> worked with him. (MC, CH 48)

1284
MICHELTREE, GEORGE W.
Cabinetmaker.
> Born c. 1822, Kentucky; w. 1850,
> Scott Twp., Montgomery Co. (C)

1285
MILAM, WALKER A.
Apprentice cabinetmaker.
> W. 1828, Carlisle, Sullivan Co.
> Apprenticed to Benson Riggs, Sr.,
> who advertised Milam as a run-
> away apprentice in the Vincennes
> *Western Sun and General Ad-*
> *vertiser* on 6 September 1828.

1286
MILLER, ALEXANDER.
Cabinetmaker.
> Born c. 1829, Pennsylvania; w.
> 1850, Portage Twp., St. Joseph
> Co. Lived with Henry Miller,
> cabinetmaker, q.v. (C)

1287
MILLER, AUGUSTUS.
Chairmaker.
> Born c. 1811, Ohio; w. 1850,
> Union Twp., Union Co. (C)

1288
MILLER, DANIEL. Cabinetmaker.
> Born c. 1812, Pennsylvania; w.
> 1850, Huntington Co. (C)

1289
MILLER, DANIEL. Cabinetmaker.
> Born c. 1826, Germany; w. 1850,
> Indianapolis, Marion Co. (C)

1290
MILLER, DAVID. Cabinetmaker.
> Born c. 1827, France; w. 1850,
> Indianapolis, Marion Co. (C)

1291
MILLER, ELI. Cabinetmaker.
> Born c. 1801, Virginia; w. 1850,
> Harrison Co. (C)

1292
MILLER, GEORGE. Chairmaker.
> Born c. 1814, Indiana; w. 1850,
> Madison, Jefferson Co. (C)

1293

MILLER, HENRY. Cabinetmaker. Born c. 1810, Germany; w. 1850, Haw Creek Twp., Bartholomew Co. (C)

1294

MILLER, HENRY. Cabinetmaker. Born c. 1811, Kentucky; w. 1850, Paoli, Orange Co. In same household, Ebenezer Doane, cabinetmaker. Miller and 2 apprentices made 100 bedsteads, 25 bureaus, 40 tables, and 20 cupboards in 1850. (C, MC)

1295

MILLER, HENRY. Cabinetmaker. Born c. 1806, Pennsylvania; w. 1837-1850, South Bend, St. Joseph Co. Adv. *South Bend Free Press,* April 1837 through June 1838: had a shop two doors north of the courthouse on Main Street. Finished work offered included tables, bedsteads, bureaus, secretaries, and sideboards. Cabinet timber taken in exchange for furniture. Adv. *St. Joseph Valley Register,* December 1846: operates a "cabinet ware-room"; wishes to inform old friends he is still in business. ". . . latest patterns and models of furniture used in the Eastern Cities . . . music stools, ottomans of Black Walnut & Maple, sofas with spring seats, sideboards . . . piano cases dressed over and polished anew; coffins made to order; black walnut, cherry, maple, poplar & pine plank & scantling will be taken in exchange. . . ."

In 1850 three men worked in this shop and made cabinet ware

valued at $2,000. One of these men was Alexander Miller, cabinetmaker, who lived in the Henry Miller household. (C, MC)

1296

MILLER, HIRAM. Cabinetmaker. Born c. 1827, Pennsylvania; w. 1850, Springfield Twp., La Porte Co. (C)

1297

MILLER, ISRAEL. Chairmaker. Born c. 1816, Pennsylvania; w. 1850, German Twp., Bartholomew Co. (C)

1298

MILLER, J. LEWIS. Cabinetmaker. Born c. 1824, Ohio; w. 1850, Middletown, Henry Co. (C)

1299

MILLER, JAMES. Cabinetmaker. Born c. 1769, Pennsylvania; w. 1850, Fugit Twp., Decatur Co. (C)

1300

MILLER, JOHN. Cabinetmaker. Born c. 1818, Pennsylvania; w. 1850, Wayne Twp., Allen Co. Twelve men worked in his shop, using horse-powered machinery. Their raw materials included "veneering." In 1850 they made furniture worth $8,000. (C, MC)

1301

MILLER, JOHN. Chairmaker. Born c. 1804, Pennsylvania; w. 1850, Harrison Co. (C)

1302

MILLER, JOHN. Cabinetmaker. Born c. 1824, Virginia; w. 1850,

Jefferson Twp., Miami Co. Lived with Hen Olinger, cabinetmaker. (C)

1303
MILLER, JOHN. Cabinetmaker.
Born c. 1821, Kentucky; w. 1850, Russell Twp., Putnam Co. (C)

1304
MILLER, JOHN W. Cabinetmaker.
Born c. 1810, Kentucky; w. 1850, Shawswick Twp., Lawrence Co. (C)

1305
MILLER, JONATHAN.
Chairmaker.
Born c. 1819, Kentucky; w. 1850, Harrison Co. (C)

1306
MILLER, LEWIS. Cabinetmaker.
Born c. 1812, Pennsylvania; w. 1850, Whitewater Twp., Franklin Co. (C)

1307
MILLER, MICHAEL. Chairmaker.
Born c. 1828, Germany; w. 1850, Mishawaka, St. Joseph Co. Lived with A. M. Wing, cabinetmaker. (C)

1308
MILLER, OLIVER. Cabinetmaker.
Born c. 1826, Massachusetts; w. 1850, Mill Grove Twp., Steuben Co. (C)

1309
MILLER, PETER. Cabinetmaker.
Born c. 1830, Germany; w. 1850, Harrison Twp., Vigo Co. (C)

1310
MILLER, SAMUEL.
Chairmaker and wheelmaker.
W. 1820, Palmyra Twp., Knox Co. He worked alone to produce chairs and spinning wheels; he commented on the census return that the demand and sales were dull. (MC)

1311
MILLER, WILLIAM.
Cabinetmaker.
Born c. 1818, Virginia; w. 1850, Winchester, Randolph Co. (C)

1312
MILLER, WILLIAM R.
Cabinetmaker.
Born c. 1808, Kentucky; w. 1850, Rush Co. (C)

1313
MILLIKEN, SAMUEL.
Cabinetmaker.
Born c. 1805, Pennsylvania; w. 1850, Jefferson Twp., Wells Co. (C)

1314
MILLS, EPHRAIM. Cabinetmaker.
Born c. 1800, Kentucky; w. 1850, Jennings Twp., Fayette Co. (C)

1315
MILLS, JACOB C. Cabinetmaker.
Born c. 1817, Ohio; w. 1850, Harrison Twp., Miami Co. (C)

1316
MILLS, THOMAS. Cabinetmaker.
Born c. 1822, Ohio; w. 1850, Adams Twp., Hamilton Co. (C)

1317
MILTON, ARTHUR.
Cabinetmaker.
Born c. 1825, Ireland; w. 1850, Bloomfield Twp., La Grange Co. (C)

1318
MINER, JAMES. Cabinetmaker.
Born c. 1830, Indiana; w. 1850,
Hamilton Twp., Sullivan Co. (C)

1319
MINICK, JAMES P.
Cabinetmaker.
Born c. 1815, Virginia; w. 1850,
Jennings Twp., Owen Co. (C)

1320
MINTER, WILLIAM. Chairmaker.
Born c. 1828, Indiana; w. 1850,
Harrison Co. (C)

1321
MITCHEL, THOMAS.
Cabinetmaker.
Born c. 1800, Tennessee; w. 1850,
Harrison Twp., Morgan Co. (C)

1322
MITCHELL, ANDREW T.
Cabinetmaker.
Born c. 1801, New York; w.
1850, Olive Twp., Elkhart Co.
(C)

1323
MITCHELL, JOSEPH A.
Chairmaker.
Born c. 1813, Kentucky; w.
1850, Posey Twp., Franklin Co.
(C)

1324
MODDRELL, JAMES A.
Cabinetmaker.
Born c. 1824, Kentucky; w. 1850,
also MOODRELL, J. A., possibly
Montgomery Twp., Owen Co. See
same man, listed in Wayne Twp.;
double listing may indicate journeyman cabinetmaker. (C)

1325
MOLEAR, CHARLES.
Cabinetmaker.
Born c. 1827, Ohio; w. 1850,
Jackson Twp., Clinton Co. (C)

1326
MOLNING, ERNEST.
Cabinetmaker.
Born c. 1833, Germany; w. 1850,
Lawrenceburg, Dearborn Co.
Lived with Lewis Schrater, cabi-
netmaker. (C)

1327
MONMAN, JESSE. Cabinetmaker.
Born c. 1821, Indiana; w. 1850,
Columbus, Bartholomew Co. (C)

1328
MONROE, DUNCAN.
Cabinetmaker.
Born c. 1806, Scotland; w. 1850,
Michigan City, La Porte Co. (C)

1329
MONROE, WILLIAM.
Chairmaker.
Born c. 1820, Kentucky; w. 1850,
Madison, Jefferson Co. (C)

1330
MONTGOMERY, SAMUEL.
Cabinetmaker.
Born c. 1818, Pennsylvania; w.
1850, Covington, Fountain Co.
(C)

1331
MONTGOMERY, WILLIAM.
Chairmaker.
Born c. 1796, Kentucky; w. 1850,
Perry Twp., Martin Co. (C)

1332
MOODRELL, J. A. Cabinetmaker.
Born c. 1825; w. 1850, Wayne
Twp., Owen Co. (C) See also

James A. Moddrell, possibly same man, listed in Montgomery Twp.; double listing may indicate journeyman cabinetmaker.

1333
MOORE, ALLEN. Cabinetmaker.
Born c. 1813, Kentucky; w. 1850, Columbia Twp., Martin Co. (C)

1334
MOORE, CHARLES W.
Cabinetmaker.
Born c. 1824, Ohio; w. 1850, Lagro Twp., Wabash Co. (C)

1335
MOORE, DANIEL.
Chairmaker and painter.
W. 1814, Vincennes, Knox Co. Adv. in *Western Sun and General Advertiser* 2 July 1814, "Daniel Moore /Chair Maker & Painter Has commenced business in the corner house below C. Graeter's Inn, where all orders in his line shall be particularly & expeditiously attended to—he flatters himself from his experience, and attention to business to be able to give general satisfaction." Adv. *ibid.,* 26 November 1814,"WANTED, a smart active lad between the age of 14 & 16, as an apprentice to the *Chair Making & Painting Business*—one of good morals and steady habits, will receive advantageous terms by a speedy application to *D. Moore."*

1336
MOORE, DAVID. Chairmaker.
W. 1814, Vincennes, Knox Co. Adv. in *Western Sun,* October 1814, for apprentice to chairmaking business (as mentioned in *Fine Furniture in Indiana* [Indi-anapolis: Public Service Company, n.d.]). *See* MOORE, DANIEL, possibly same.

1337
MOORE, JAMES. Cabinetmaker.
Born c. 1823, Indiana; w. 1850, Jonesboro, Grant Co. (C)

1338
MOORE, JAMES H. Chairmaker.
Born c. 1829, Kentucky; w. 1850, Greencastle, Putnam Co. Lived with Samuel M. Moore, chairmaker. (C)

1339
MOORE, JAMES M. Chairmaker.
Born c. 1835, Kentucky; w. 1850, Greencastle, Putnam Co. Lived with Samuel M. Moore, chairmaker. (C)

1340
MOORE, JOHN. Cabinetmaker.
W. 1820, Vincennes, Knox Co. Four men worked in this shop; their product was listed as "Cabinett ware, houses &c." (MC)

1341
MOORE, SAMUEL. Chairmaker.
Born c. 1797, Pennsylvania; w. 1850, Fugit Twp., Decatur Co. Edward Wallace, chairmaker, worked with him; their raw materials included timber and paint. In 1850 they made 500 chairs which sold for $1 each. (C, MC)

1342
MOORE, SAMUEL M.
Chairmaker.
Born c. 1785, Pennsylvania; w. 1850, Greencastle, Putnam Co. In

same household, c h a i r m a k e r s
James M. Moore and James H.
Moore. (C)

1343

MOORE, WILLIAM.
Cabinetmaker.
   Born c. 1828, Ohio; w. 1850,
   Perry Twp., Noble Co. (C)

1344

MOORMAN, ERNST.
Cabinetmaker.
   Born c. 1823, Germany; w. 1850,
   Lawrenceburg, Dearborn Co. (C)

1345

MORELAND, WILLIAM.
Chairmaker.
   Born c. 1812, Pennsylvania; w.
   1850, Niles Twp., Delaware Co.
   (C)

1346

MORGAN, ABEL. Chairmaker.
   Born c. 1822, Massachusetts; w.
   1850,   Addison Twp., Shelby Co.
   (C)

1347

MORGAN, ARTHUR B.
Cabinetmaker.
   Born c. 1811, Ohio; w. 1850,
   Nineveh Twp., Johnson Co. (C)

1348

MORGAN, CALVIN.
Cabinetmaker.
   Born c. 1822, Tennessee; w. 1850,
   Indianapolis, Marion Co. (C)

1349

MORGAN, NATHAN.
Cabinetmaker.
   Born 9 October 1792, Blackwood,
   N. J.; apprenticed to Nehemiah
   Fowler of Haddonfield, N. J.;
   he moved in 1823 to Richmond,

Wayne Co., where he operated a
cabinetmaking and undertaking
shop until 1850. (C, CH 34)

1350

MORISON, CHARLES.
Cabinetmaker.
   Born c. 1822, Ohio; w. 1850,
   Jennings Twp., Crawford Co.
   Two men worked in this shop;
   their product in 1850 was valued
   at $1,500. (C, MC)

1351

MORLEY, ALBERT.
Cabinetmaker.
   Born c. 1833, New York; w.
   1850, Richland Twp., Steuben Co.
   Lived with James Everhart,
   cabinetmaker. (C)

1352

MORRIS, E. C. Cabinetmaker.
   Born c. 1826, Pennsylvania; w.
   1850, Deerfield, Randolph Co. In
   same household, R. M. Morris,
   cabinetmaker.   (C) *See also*
   MORRIS, E. C. & T. M.

1353

MORRIS, E. C. & T. M.
Cabinetmakers.
   W. 1850, Deerfield, Randolph Co.
   Three men worked in this shop;
   in 1850 they made 30 tables, 60
   bedsteads, 5 bureaus, and cupboards valued at $164. (MC)

1354

MORRIS, JAMES. Cabinetmaker.
   Born c. 1830, Indiana; w. 1850,
   Shelbyville, Shelby Co. Lived with
   George Carruthers, cabinetmaker,
   q.v. (C)

1355
MORRIS, N. L. (or P.).
Cabinetmaker.
> Born c. 1800, Virginia; w. 1850, Mount Auburn, Shelby Co. (C)

1356
MORRIS, OWEN. Cabinetmaker.
> Born c. 1812, Pennsylvania; w. 1841-1850, Centerville, Wayne Co. Adv. in *Wayne County Record*, 1 December 1841. In same household, Allen Tollbott and Henry Clay Noble, cabinetmakers. (C, CH 46)

1357
MORRIS, R. M. Cabinetmaker.
> Born c. 1832, Pennsylvania; w. 1850, Deerfield, Randolph Co. Lived with E. C. Morris, cabinetmaker. (C)

1358
MORRIS, THOMAS M.
Cabinetmaker.
> Born c. 1828, Pennsylvania; w. 1850, Deerfield, Randolph Co. (C)
> *See also* MORRIS, E. C. & T. M.

1359
MORRISON, A. R.
Cabinetmaker and chairmaker.
> W. 1850, Fayette Co. In 1850 he made 30 bedsteads, 20 tables, 5 bureaus, chairs valued at $300, and other articles worth $190. (MC)

1360
MORRISON, GEORGE C.
Chairmaker.
> Born c. 1830, Virginia; w. 1850, Shelbyville. Lived with John Morrison, chairmaker and turner. (C)

1361
MORRISON, JOHN.
Chairmaker and turner.
> Born c. 1794 or 1800, Pennsylvania; w. 1850, Shelbyville. In same household, George C. Morrison, chairmaker. In 1850 they made chairs valued at $1,500. (C, MC)

1362
MORROW, B. B. Cabinetmaker.
> Born c. 1804, Kentucky; w. 1850, Rush Co. (C)

1363
MORROW, WILLIAM.
Chairmaker.
> Born c. 1812, Kentucky; w. 1850, Madison, Jefferson Co. (C)

1364
MORSE, ALLEN. Cabinetmaker.
> Born c. 1827, New York; w. 1850, Mill Grove Twp., Steuben Co. In same household, Allen Sheldon, cabinetmaker. (C)

1364a
MORTON, JOSEPH.
Chairmaker and turner.
> W. 1844, near Centerville, Wayne Co. Adv. in *Wayne County Record*, 3 July 1844: "Chair making and Turning. The subscriber respectfully informs the public that he has commenced the manufacture of COMMON SPLIT BOTTOMED CHAIRS at the Saw Mill of Mr. T. G. Noble, three quarters of a mile West of Centerville . . . . He will also have in readiness, in a few days, a TURNING LATHE . . . ."

1365
MOSS, JOHN. Cabinetmaker.
Born c. 1819, North Carolina; w.
1850, Monroe Twp., Howard Co.
(C)

1366
MOSS, MARTIN. Cabinetmaker.
Born c. 1826, North Carolina; w.
1850, Monroe Twp., Howard Co.
(C)

1367
MOUNCE, SMITH. Cabinetmaker.
W. 1820, Lawrence Co. His products were priced as follows:
desks $40; bureaus $18; tables
$8; cupboards, $20. (MC)

1368
MOUNT, WILLIAM.
Cabinetmaker.
Born c. 1832, Indiana; w. 1850,
Washington Twp., Washington
Co. Lived with Benjamin Jones,
cabinetmaker, q.v. (C)

1369
MOWREY, EMUEL I.
Cabinetmaker.
Born c. 1828, Ohio; w. 1850,
Chester Twp., Wabash Co. (C)

1370
MOZELY, JEROME.
Cabinetmaker.
Born c. 1833, New York; w.
1850, Lauramie Twp., Tippecanoe
Co. Lived with Nathaniel S.
Barnes, cabinetmaker, q.v. (C)

1371
MRANDLE (?), STEPHEN.
Cabinetmaker.
Born c. 1832, Indiana; w. 1850,
Richland Twp., Miami Co. (C)

1372
MUHLER, CHARLES M.
Cabinetmaker.
Born c. 1810, Germany; w. 1850,
Wayne Twp., Allen Co. (C) *See
also* MUHLER & GRAFFE.

1373
MUHLER & GRAFFE.
Cabinetmakers.
Charles M. Muhler and Frederick
Graffe; w. 1850, Wayne Twp.,
Allen Co. Two men worked in
this shop; mahogany was listed
as one of their raw materials.
In 1850 they produced cabinet
work worth $2,000. (C, MC)

1374
MULFORD, H. J. Cabinetmaker.
Born c. 1808, Ohio; w. -1839-
1850, Lafayette, Tippecanoe Co.
Adv. in *Indiana Eagle* 2 January
1839 and in *The Lafayette Free
Press* 27 October 1840: "H.J.
MULFORD respectfully informs
the citizens of Lafayette and
vicinity, that he still continues to
carry on the *CABINET MAK-
ING* [business] in the stand on
the south side of Main street
. . . . He keeps constantly on
hand a good s u p p l y o f
*B U R E A U S, T A B L E S,
STANDS* and *BEDSTEADS,*
and is prepared to manufacture to
order, all kinds of Furniture needed in this country . . . . he is
provided with a Hearse and will
attend at all times to the business
of an Undertaker."
    In 1850 his shop employed five
men, one of whom was William
Mulford. That year their product
was valued at $3,500. (C, MC)

1375
MULFORD, WILLIAM.
Cabinetmaker.
> Born c. 1830, Ohio; w. 1850,
> Lafayette, Tippecanoe Co. Lived
> with H. J. Mulford, cabinet-
> maker, q.v. (C)

1376
MULL, DANIEL H.
Cabinetmaker.
> Born c. 1821, Indiana; w. 1850,
> Eel Twp., Cass Co. (C)

1377
MULL, JAMES. Chairmaker.
> Born c. 1820, Ohio; w. 1850,
> Madison, Jefferson Co. (C)

1378
MULL, JOHN A. Cabinetmaker.
> Born c. 1820, Indiana; w. 1850,
> Washington Twp., Owen Co. (C)

1379
MULLIKIN, JAMES G.
Cabinetmaker.
> Born c. 1823, Kentucky; w. 1850,
> Danville, Hendricks Co. (C)

1380
MUNROE, HENRY.
Cabinetmaker.
> Born c. 1810, Scotland; w. 1850,
> Michigan City, La Porte Co.
> Three men worked in this shop;
> in 1850 they produced 20 tables,
> 12 bureaus, 30 bedsteads, 70 cof-
> fins, and other articles. (C, MC)

1381
MUNSON, LUIS. Chairmaker.
> Born c. 1795, New York; w.
> 1850, Jefferson Twp., Switzerland
> Co. (C)

1382
MURDOCK, JOSEPH.
Cabinetmaker.
> Born c. 1794, Virginia; w. 1850,
> Jefferson Twp., Switzerland Co.
> (C)

1383
MURDOCK, WILLIAM.
Upholsterer.
> Born c. 1820, Ohio; w. 1850,
> Wayne Twp., Tippecanoe Co. (C)

1384
MURPHY, JOHN D.
Cabinetmaker.
> Born c. 1814, Virginia; w. 1850,
> Delaware Twp., Delaware Co.
> (C)

1385
MURPHY, THOMAS.
Cabinetmaker.
> Born c. 1810, Kentucky; w. 1850,
> Monroe Twp., Morgan Co. (C)

1386
MURPHY, THOMAS.
Cabinetmaker.
> Born c. 1815, Kentucky; w. 1850,
> Ray Twp., Morgan Co. (C)

1387
MURPHY, WILLIAM.
Apprentice cabinetmaker.
> Born c. 1833, Indiana; w. 1850,
> Paoli, Orange Co. Apprenticed to
> William A. Liston, cabinetmaker,
> q.v. (C)

1388
MURY, MICHEL. Chairmaker.
> Born c. 1825, Ohio; w. 1850,
> Jackson Twp., Elkhart Co. (C)

1389
MYERS, CHRISTIAN.
Cabinetmaker.
Born c. 1812, Germany; w. 1850, Marion Twp., Allen Co. (C)

1390
MYERS, GEORGE.
Apprentice cabinetmaker.
Born c. 1832, Germany; w. 1850, Muncie, Delaware Co. Apprenticed to Isaac Gramly. (C)

1391
MYERS, GEORGE C.
Chairmaker.
Born c. 1808, Pennsylvania; w. 1850, York Twp., Noble Co. In same household, John Myers, chairmaker. (C)

1392
MYERS, JOHN. Chairmaker.
Born c. 1835, Ohio; w. 1850, York Twp., Noble Co. Lived with George C. Myers, chairmaker. (C)

1393
MYERS, UMPHRA.
Cabinetmaker.
Born c. 1822, Pennsylvania; w. 1850, Lawrenceburg, Dearborn Co. (C)

1394
NAPP, AUGUST. Cabinetmaker.
Born c. 1800, Germany; w. 1850, Washington Twp., Noble Co. (C)

1395
NARDIN, FREDERICK P.
Cabinetmaker.
Born c. 1804, France; w. 1850, New Albany, Floyd Co. (C)

1396
NEAL, ISRAEL. Chairmaker.
Born c. 1811, Ohio; w. -1838-1850, Logansport, Cass Co. In 1838 he was working with William T. S. Manly, q.v., who ran a furniture and undertaking business. In 1840 he was a partner in the firm of Aldrich, Neal & Co., q.v.; in 1850 the firm was known as Neal & Burch, a cabinet- and chairmaking business, q.v. (C, MC, CH 25)

1397
NEAL & BURCH.
Cabinetmakers and chairmakers.
Israel Neal and Bernard Z. Burch; w. 1850, Logansport, Cass Co. These two men were the sole workers in their shop which in 1850 produced 100 tables, 30 bureaus, 50 dozen chairs, and 100 pairs of [i.e., 50] bedsteads. (C, MC) See also ALDRICH, NEAL & CO.

1398
NEET, JOSEPH. Cabinetmaker.
Born c. 1822, Kentucky; w. 1850, Jackson Twp., Parke Co. (C)

1399
NEIHARD, JOHN. Cabinetmaker.
Born c. 1830, Ohio; w. 1850, Ross Twp., Clinton Co. Lived with Moses Neihard, cabinetmaker. (C)

1400
NEIHARD, MOSES.
Cabinetmaker.
Born c. 1807, Pennsylvania; w. 1850, Ross Twp., Clinton Co. In same household, John Neihard, cabinetmaker. (C)

1401
NEUCOMB, JOHN T.
Cabinetmaker.
> Born c. 1823, District of Columbia; w. 1850, Indianapolis, Marion Co. (C)

1402
NEW, HECKMAN.
Cabinetmaker.
> W. 1850, Union Twp., Jennings Co. He worked alone, and in 1850 produced "160 Bureaus, Tables &c," worth $1,000. (MC)

1403
NEWBANKS, GEORGE H.
Cabinetmaker.
> Born c. 1826, Ohio; w. 1850, Corydon, Harrison Co. (C)

1404
NEWBANKS, JONATHAN.
Cabinetmaker.
> Born c. 1800, Virginia; w. 1850, Harrison Co. (C)

1405
NEWBY, THOMAS.
Cabinetmaker.
> Born c. 1831, Indiana; w. 1850, Washington Twp., Washington Co. Lived with Benjamin Jones, cabinetmaker, q.v. (C)

1406
NEWELL, HUGH.
Chairmaker and wheelmaker.
> Born c. 1802, New Jersey; w. 1850, Union Twp., Montgomery Co. He worked alone and in 1850 made wheels and chairs worth $1,000. (C, MC)

1407
NEWHOUSE, B. W. Chairmaker.
> Born c. 1816, Tennessee; w. 1850, Columbia Twp., Fayette Co. (C)

1408
NEWKIRK, BENJAMIN.
Cabinetmaker.
> Born c. 1812, Indiana; w. 1850, Flinn Twp., Lawrence Co. In same household, Benjamin Newkirk, Jr., cabinetmaker. (C)

1409
NEWKIRK, BENJAMIN, JR.
Cabinetmaker.
> Born c. 1829, Indiana; w. 1850, Flinn Twp., Lawrence Co. Lived with Benjamin Newkirk, Sr., cabinetmaker. (C)

1410
NEWLAND, JAMES.
Cabinetmaker.
> Born 29 December 1782, Pennsylvania; 1794, moved to Lexington, Ky., where learned trade; w. 1820, Jennings Twp., Fayette Co. Died January 1849. In 1820 his products were priced as follows: "Desks $30; Bureaus from $16 to $50; Cupboards $20; Dining Tables $10; Breakfast Tables $6; Candle Stands $3; Clock Cases $25; Coffins raised lid $10; flat lids Dto $5." (CH 1, MC)

1411
NICHOLAS (or NICHALAS), H. C. Cabinetmaker.
> Born c. 1830, Indiana; w. 1850, Rush Co. In same household, Jno. Hufford, chairmaker. (C)

1412
NICHOLS, ANDREW.
Cabinetmaker.

Born c. 1814, Pennsylvania; w. 1850, Tippecanoe Twp., Kosciusko Co. In the same household, Isaac Jarrard and Eli Bathel, cabinetmakers. (C)

1413
NICHOLSON, HENRY.
Cabinetmaker.
Born c. 1822, Ohio; w. 1850, Union Twp., Montgomery Co. (C)

1414
NICHOLSON, JOHN.
Windsor chairmaker.
Born 1825, Jefferson Co.; w. 1845-, Columbus, Bartholomew Co. Later became a painter of signs and portraits. (Wilbur D. Peat, *Pioneer Painters of Indiana* [Art Association of Indianapolis, 1954]).

1415
NIHART, PHILIP.
Chair Manufactory.
Born c. 1816, Ohio; w. 1850, Boone Twp., Porter Co. (C)

1416
NIXON, JOSHUA. Cabinetmaker.
Born c. 1815, Ohio; w. 1850, Vermillion Twp., Vermillion Co. He worked alone and in 1850 made furniture worth $800. (C, MC)

1417
NOBLE, GEORGE R.
Chairmaker.
Born c. 1803, Pennsylvania; w. 1850, Van Buren Twp., Grant Co. (C)

1418
NOBLE, HENRY A.
Cabinetmaker.
Born c. 1831, Indiana; w. 1850, Center Twp., Wayne Co. (C)

1419
NOBLE, HENRY CLAY.
Cabinetmaker and undertaker.
Born c. 1832, Indiana; w. -1850-, Centerville, Wayne Co.; died 1907, Indianapolis. In 1850 he lived with Owen Morris, cabinetmaker. (C, unidentified newspaper obituary)

1420
NORRIS, JOHN. Cabinetmaker.
Born c. 1810, Pennsylvania; w. 1850, Harrison Co. (C)

1421
NORRIS, OLIVER P.
Cabinetmaker.
Born c. 1826, Ohio; w. 1850, Center Twp., Howard Co. (C)

1422
NORRIS, WESTLEY.
Cabinetmaker.
Born c. 1823, Ohio; w. 1850, Center Twp., Howard Co. (C)

1423
NORTON, THOMAS.
Cabinetmaker.
Born c. 1818, Pennsylvania; w. 1850, Monroe Twp., Morgan Co. (C)

1424
NOTEMAN, W. W.
Cabinetmaker.
Born c. 1820, Ohio; w. 1850, Noble Twp., Noble Co. (C)

1425
NOTTINGHAM, J. W.
Cabinetmaker.
   Born c. 1819, Ohio; w. 1850,
   Lagro Twp., Wabash Co. (C)

1426
NOTTINGHAM, JAMES.
Cabinetmaker.
   Born 1811, Pennsylvania; 1817,
   moved near Muncie, Delaware
   Co., where he learned his trade.
   Died 1885. (C, CH 36) *See also*
   NOTTINGHAM & MEEKS and
   NOTTINGHAM & SWAIN.

1427
NOTTINGHAM & MEEKS.
Cabinetmakers.
   James Nottingham and Robert
   Meeks; w. 1848, Muncie, Dela-
   ware Co. (CH 36) *See also*
   MEEKS, ROBERT, for evolu-
   tion of firm.

1428
NOTTINGHAM & SWAIN.
Cabinetmakers.
   James Nottingham and Job
   Swain; w. prior to 1850, Muncie,
   Delaware Co. *See also* MEEKS,
   ROBERT, for evolution of firm.

1429
NUNEMACHER, ALFRED.
Cabinetmaker.
   Born c. 1831, Pennsylvania; w.
   1850, New Albany, Floyd Co. (C)

1430
NUNNALLY, LEVI B.
Cabinetmaker.
   Born c. 1814, North Carolina; w.
   1850, Shawswick Twp., Lawrence
   Co. In same household, Jno. M.
   Anderson, cabinetmaker. (C)

1431
NUTMIRE, CHRISTIAN.
Cabinetmaker.
   Born c. 1833, Germany; w. 1850,
   Indianapolis, Marion Co. (C)

1432
OAKLEY, JAMES. Cabinetmaker.
   Born c. 1816, North Carolina; w.
   1850, Chester Twp., Wabash Co.
   (C)

1433
OATS, MICHAEL. Cabinetmaker.
   Born c. 1817, Ohio; w. 1850,
   Warren, Huntington Co. Working
   with him in his shop were Samuel
   G. Fleming and Henry Ream. In
   1850 they made bedsteads, stands,
   and tables worth $550. (C, MC)

1434
OBERHOUSEN, NICHOLAS.
Cabinetmaker.
   Born c. 1830, Germany; w. 1850,
   Rockport, Spencer Co. Lived with
   Daniel Willmot, cabinetmaker, q.v.
   (C)

1435
OGDEN, ISAAC C.
Chairmaker.
   Born c. 1821, Ohio; w. 1850,
   Rush Co. Two men worked in
   this shop; in 1850 they made
   "Chairs &c" valued at $600. (C,
   MC)

1436
O'HARROW, WILLIAM.
Cabinetmaker.
   Born c. 1821, Alabama; w. 1850,
   Clear Creek Twp., Monroe Co.
   He worked alone, making all
   kinds of furniture; his 1850 prod-
   uct was valued at $500. (C, MC)

1437
OKEL, JOEL. Cabinetmaker.
Born c. 1809, Pennsylvania; w.
1850, Dudley Twp., Henry Co.
(C)

1438
OLDS, JOSHUA A.
Millwright and cabinetmaker.
B. Salem, Mass.; w. before 1848,
Vigo Co.; died 1848, Montezuma,
Parke Co. Said to have made the
first chairs seen in the Vigo
County area. (CH 9)

1439
OLERICK, FREDERICK.
Cabinetmaker.
Born c. 1827, Pennsylvania; w.
1850, Lafayette, Tippecanoe Co.
(C)

1440
OLINGER, DANIEL.
Cabinetmaker.
Born c. 1805, Virginia; w. 1850,
Harrison Co. (C)

1441
OLINGER, HEN. Cabinetmaker.
Born c. 1819, Maryland; w. 1850,
Jefferson Twp., Miami Co. In
same household, John Miller,
cabinetmaker. (C)

1442
OLIPHANT, JOSEPH.
Chairmaker.
Born c. 1834, Ohio; w. 1850, Eel
Twp., Cass Co. Lived with Nuttar
Oliphant, chairmaker, q.v. (C)

1443
OLIPHANT, NUTTAR.
Chairmaker.
Born c. 1807, Delaware; w. 1850,
Eel Twp., Cass Co. In 1850 he

produced 120 sets of chairs worth
$600. In the same household,
Joseph Oliphant, chairmaker. (C,
MC)

1444
OLLEMAN, EZRA. Cabinetmaker.
Born c. 1829, Kentucky; w. 1850,
Mooresville, Morgan Co. (C)

1445
ONEAL, WILLIAM.
Cabinetmaker.
Born c. 1817, Pennsylvania; w.
1850, Pipe Creek Twp., Madison
Co. (C)

1446
OPP, REUBEN. Cabinetmaker.
Born c. 1823, Pennsylvania; w.
1850, Pittsburg, Carroll Co. Two
men worked in this shop; in 1850
they produced cabinet furniture
worth $1,800. (C, MC)

1447
ORAFF, GATLIF. Cabinetmaker.
Born c. 1823, Germany; w. 1850,
Wayne Twp., Allen Co. (C)

1448
OSBORN, ALFRED.
Turner and cabinetmaker.
Born c. 1827, Ohio; w. 1850, La
Porte, La Porte Co. (C)

1449
OSBORN, ISAAC. Cabinetmaker.
Born c. 1801, North Carolina; w.
1850, Plainfield, Hendricks Co.
(C)

1450
OSBORN, JOSIAH. Cabinetmaker.
W. 1825-, Perry Twp., Wayne
Co. (CH 34)

1451
OSBORN, LEMUEL.
Cabinetmaker.
Born c. 1816, Tennessee; w. 1850, Chili, Miami Co. (C, CH 30)

1452
OSBORNE, JOHN H.
Cabinetmaker.
Born c. 1821, Tennessee; w. 1850, Haddon Twp., Sullivan Co. (C)

1453
OSGOOD, MELANCTON.
Cabinetmaker.
Born c. 1824, New York; w. 1850, Henry Twp., Fulton Co. (C)

1454
OSGOOD & DENNETT. Sash and blind factory; furniture makers.
W. 1839, Lafayette, Tippecanoe Co. Adv. in *Indiana Eagle* 8 May 1839: "LAFAYETTE SASH & BLIND MANUFACTORY . . . They will, also, attend to all orders for joinering, carpentering, turning, sawing, &c., and intend keeping constantly on hand Sashes, Bedsteads, Split Bottom Chairs, &c. . . ."

1455
OSMAN, IRA. Chairmaker.
Born c. 1824, New York; w. 1850, Sand Creek Twp., Bartholomew Co. (C)

1456
OSMAN, JAMES. Chairmaker.
Born c. 1795, Pennsylvania; w. 1850, Sand Creek Twp., Bartholomew Co. (C)

1457
OTT, JOHN. Cabinetmaker.
Born c. 1824, Bavaria, Germany; 1850, established furniture business in Indianapolis, Marion Co. He was succeeded in business by his son Lewis W. Ott, who died in 1885; in 1885 the firm was known as the L.W. Ott Manufacturing Company. By 1890 the firm had moved to Chicago, Illinois, where it was known as the Ott Lounge Company, operated by Ott & Schoen. They manufactured there "single and bed lounges and Ott's Patent Sofa Bed." While the firm was located in Indianapolis, it produced some finely carved elaborate furniture. John Ott's original drawing books reveal designs of furniture made by him, probably in the 1880s. The Ott chair illustrated in Plates XIV and XV could have been made around 1850. (TH 18, C)

1458
OTTER, THOMAS.
Chairmaker.
Born c. 1819, New York; w. 1850, Harrison Twp., Fayette Co. (C)

1459
OVERMAN, THOMAS.
Cabinetmaker.
Born c. 1807, North Carolina; w. 1850, Sand Creek Twp., Bartholomew Co. (C)

1460
OWENS, THOMAS.
Cabinetmaker.
Born c. 1810, Kentucky; w. 1850, Brown Twp., Montgomery Co. (C)

1461
PAGE, CHARLES. Cabinetmaker.
Born c. 1829, Pennsylvania; w.
1850, La Porte, La Porte Co.
Lived with Willard N. Ball,
cabinetmaker. (C)

1462
PAGE, GEORGE. Cabinetmaker.
Born c. 1834, Ohio; w. 1850,
Vernon Twp., Jennings Co. Lived
with William Page, cabinetmaker.
(C)

1463
PAGE, WILLIAM. Cabinetmaker.
Born c. 1802, Pennsylvania; w.
1850, Vernon Twp., Jennings Co.
In same household, George Page,
cabinetmaker. (C)

1464
PALMER, ALEN. Cabinetmaker.
Born c. 1814, South Carolina; w.
1850, Petersburg, Pike Co. (C)

1465
PALMER, JOHN. Cabinetmaker.
Born c. 1812, South Carolina; w.
1850, Petersburg, Pike Co. (C)

1466
PALMER, P. Chairmaker.
W. 1837, Brookville, Franklin
Co. Adv. in *Indiana American*
20 October 1837, "P. PALMER
/CHAIR MAKING . . .
[common and fancy chairs, also
house and sign painting; shop
located] directly opposite the
Franklin Hotel."

1466a
PALMITER—*see* SMITH &
PALMITER

1467
PANKEY, JOHN B.
Cabinetmaker.
Born c. 1797, Virginia; w. 1850,
Union Twp., Fulton Co. (C)

1468
PARAMORE, THOMAS.
Chairmaker.
Born c. 1784, Pennsylvania; w.
1850, Salt Creek Twp., Decatur
Co. (C)

1469
PARINE, J. N. Cabinetmaker.
Born c. 1815, New York; w.
1850, New Albany, Floyd Co. (C)

1470
PARISH, JOHN W.
Cabinetmaker.
Born c. 1825, Kentucky; w. 1850,
Franklin Twp., Johnson Co. (C)

1471
PARKER, JACOB. Chairmaker.
Born c. 1817, Kentucky; w. 1850,
Jackson Twp., Wells Co. (C)

1472
PARKER, JOHN. Cabinetmaker.
Born c. 1830, Ohio; w. 1850,
Lagro Twp., Wabash Co. (C)

1473
PARKER, WILLIAM H.
Cabinetmaker.
Born c. 1828, Ohio; w. 1850,
North Bend Twp., Starke Co.
(C)

1474
PARKS, GEORGE. Chairmaker.
Born c. 1824, Indiana; w. 1850,
Carroll Co. (C)

1475
PARKS, JOHN. Chairmaker.
Born c. 1822, Ohio; w. 1850,
Carroll Co. (C)

1476
PARMALEE, ROBERT.
Piano-forte factory.
W. 1844, Indianapolis, Marion Co.
Adv. in *Semi-Weekly State
Journal* 23 February 1844.

1477
PARRISH, RICHARD.
Cabinetmaker.
Born c. 1833, Kentucky; w. 1850,
Franklin Twp., Johnson Co. (C)
See also PARRISH (PARISH)
& COBB.

1478
PARRISH (PARISH) & COBB.
Cabinetmakers.
Richard Parrish and Joseph Cobb;
w. 1850, Franklin Twp., Johnson
Co. Three men worked in this
shop; in 1850 they produced furni-
ture worth $1,200. (C, MC)

1479
PASKER (or PARKER?), H.
Cabinetmaker.
Born c. 1825, Indiana; w. 1850,
Lafayette, Tippecanoe Co. (C)

1480
PATRICK, DAVID. Cabinetmaker.
Born c. 1807, Pennsylvania; w.
1850, Eel Twp., Cass Co. Two
men worked in this shop; in 1850
they made furniture valued at
$1,200. (C, MC)

1481
PATRIDGE, RICHARD.
Upholsterer.
Born c. 1806, Virginia; w. 1850,
Evansville, Vanderburgh Co. (C)

1482
PATTERSON, JAS. R.
Cabinetmaker.
Born c. 1821, North Carolina; w.
1850, Parke Co. (C)

1483
PATTERSON, ULM.
Cabinetmaker.
Born c. 1809, Germany; w. 1850,
Laurel Twp., Franklin Co. (C)

1484
PAUL, HENRY. Cabinetmaker.
Born in Germany; 1847, arrived
in Fort Wayne, Allen Co.; died
1882. (TH 21)

1485
PAUL, JOHN. Chairmaker.
Born c. 1823, New York; w.
1850, Wayne Twp., Allen Co.
Lived with William Paul, chair-
maker. (C) *See also* PAUL,
W. & J.

1486
PAUL, W. & J. Chairmakers and
cabinetmakers.
William Paul and John Paul; w.
1850, Wayne Twp., Allen Co.
Eight men worked in this shop
using horse-powered machinery;
in 1850 their product was listed
as "Chairs and Cabinet Work
worth $3,500." (C, MC)

1487
PAUL, WILLIAM. Chairmaker.
Born c. 1795, Scotland; w. 1850,
Wayne Twp., Allen Co. In same

household, John Paul, Henry Lepper, and George Deffler. (C) *See also* PAUL, W. & J.

1488
PAUL, WILLIAM. Cabinetmaker.
Born c. 1812, England; w. 1850, Vernon Twp., Washington Co. (C)

1489
PAXSON, HESTON.
Cabinetmaker.
Born c. 1821, Ohio; w. 1850, Penn Twp., Jay Co. (C) *See* PAXSON (PAXON) & BEEDY.

1490
PAXSON, JESSE. Cabinetmaker.
Born c. 1811, Pennsylvania; w. 1850, Penn Twp., Jay Co. (C) *See* PAXSON (PAXON) & BEEDY.

1491
PAXSON (PAXON) & BEEDY.
Cabinetmakers.
W. 1850, Jay Co. Three men worked in this shop, using horse-powered machinery. In 1850 they produced cabinet ware worth $1,500. (MC)

1492
PAYNE, M. R. Cabinetmaker.
W. 1838, Indianapolis, Marion Co. Adv. in *Indiana State Gazette*, 3 November 1838.

1493
PAYNE, THOMAS F.
Cabinetmaker.
Born c. 1827, Virginia; w. 1850, Noble Twp., Wabash Co. (C)

1494
PEACELY (or PEUCELY),
HENRY W. Chairmaker.
Born c. 1829, Indiana; w. 1850, Jeffersonville, Clark Co. (C)

1495
PEACOCK, SAMUEL.
Chairmaker.
Born c. 1815, New Jersey; w. 1850, West River Twp., Randolph Co. (C)

1496
PEAK, JOSEPH. Cabinetmaker.
Born c. 1821, Indiana; w. 1850, Monroe Twp., Howard Co. Two men worked in his shop; in 1850 they made furniture valued at $575. (C, MC)

1497
PEARSON, WILLIAM.
Cabinetmaker.
Born c. 1808, Kentucky; w. 1850, Salem, Washington Co. (C)

1498
PEASE, HENRY C. Chairmaker.
Born c. 1810, Massachusetts; w. 1850, La Porte, La Porte Co. (C)

1499
PEASE, JACOB W. Cabinetmaker.
Born c. 1827, New Jersey; w. 1850, Noble Twp., Wabash Co. (C)

1500
PECK, ——. Cabinetmaker.
W. 1825, Washington Twp., Wayne Co. Recorded as the first cabinetmaker in that area. (CH 34)

1501
PECK, DANIEL. Cabinetmaker.
Born c. 1820, Kentucky; w. 1850,
Shelby Twp., Jefferson Co. (C)

1502
PECK, JOHN W. Cabinetmaker.
Born c. 1825, Indiana; w. 1850 for
Elisha L. Cunningham, Putnam-
ville, Putnam Co. (C)

1503
PECK & MATTHEW.
Cabinetmakers.
W. 1829-, Dublin, Wayne Co.
This was the first cabinetmaking
firm in Dublin. They were
succeeded by Eli Pittman and
Thomas Allen in 1832, although
it is not clear whether Pittman
took over the same business or
started independently. (CH 34)

1504
PEDIGO, JOHN D. Cabinetmaker.
Born c. 1819, Kentucky; w. 1850,
Perry Twp., Lawrence Co. (C)

1505
PEELMAN, JOSEPH.
Cabinetmaker.
W. 1833, Vevay, Switzerland Co.
(CH 16)

1506
PEGG, AMOS. Chairmaker.
Born c. 1818, Ohio; w. 1850,
Harrison Twp., Kosciusko Co.
(C)

1507
PELKEY, LEWIS. Cabinetmaker.
Born c. 1816, Indiana; w. 1850,
Wayne Twp., Allen Co. Two men
worked in this shop; their raw
materials included "veneering." In
1850 they produced cabinet work

worth $1,800. In same household,
Peter Rolle, cabinetmaker. (C,
MC)

1508
PENCH, CHRISTIAN.
Cabinetmaker.
Born c. 1813, Pennsylvania; w.
1850, Sheffield Twp., Tippecanoe
Co. (C)

1509
PENNINGTON, DENNIS.
Farmer, schoolteacher, politician,
and cabinetmaker.
Born 19 May 1776, Virginia;
1797, moved to Kentucky; 1804
moved to Corydon, Harrison Co.;
died 2 September 1854. Contractor
for old courthouse at Corydon
which became the first state
capitol and where a cherry desk
and a "Jackson press" made by
him are located. (Indiana Biog-
raphy [bound newspaper clippings
in Indiana State Library], IV,
222-23, 316-18.) See Plate X.

1510
PENNINGTON, JOEL.
Cabinetmaker.
Born c. 1834, Ohio; w. 1850,
Westport, Decatur Co. Lived with
Joshua Pennington, cabinetmaker.
(C)

1511
PENNINGTON, JOHN.
Cabinetmaker.
Born c. 1828, Ohio; w. 1850,
Westport, Decatur Co. Lived with
Joshua Pennington, cabinetmaker.
(C)

1512
PENNINGTON, JOSHUA.
Cabinetmaker.

Born c. 1804, Pennsylvania; w. 1850, Westport, Decatur Co. In same household, cabinetmakers John and Joel Pennington. (C)

1513
PENNINGTON, LORENZO. Chairmaker.
Born c. 1827, Ohio; w. 1850, Westport, Decatur Co. (C)

1514
PENNY, RICHARD H.
Bedstead manufacturer.
W. 1850, Harrison Twp., Dearborn Co. Eight men worked in this shop, using water-powered machinery to produce 3,000 bedsteads in 1850. (MC)

1515
PEREMAN (PEARMAN), JOHN. Cabinetmaker.
Born c. 1816, Kentucky; w. 1850, Helt Twp., Vermillion Co. He worked alone and in 1850 made "Bedsteads &c." worth $600. (C, MC)

1516
PERKINGS, HORACE S.
Cabinetmaker.
Born c. 1811, New York; w. 1850, Angola, Steuben Co. (C)

1517
PERRY, JOHN. Cabinetmaker.
Born c. 1821, Ohio; w. 1850, Madison, Jefferson Co. (C)

1518
PERRY, RICHARD.
Cabinetmaker.
Born c. 1802, South Carolina; w. 1850, Cambridge City, Wayne Co. (C)

1519
PERRY, T. W. Cabinetmaker.
Born c. 1818, Ohio; w. 1850, Lawrence Twp., Marion Co. (C)

1520
PETER, JOHN [J. D.?].
Cabinetmaker.
Born c. 1814, Indiana; w. 1850, Corydon, Harrison Co. In the same household, his apprentice Hugh McClaren. (C) Probably the J. D. Peter who worked with John Rice, q.v.

1521
PETERMAN, HENRY.
Chairmaker.
Born c. 1831, Germany; w. 1850, Lawrenceburg, Dearborn Co. Lived with Cyrus Armstrong, q.v. (C)

1522
PETERMAN, WM. H.
Cabinetmaker.
Born c. 1815, Virginia; w. 1850, Brown Twp., Montgomery Co. (C)

1523
PEUCELY, HENRY, see PEACELY (PEUCELY), HENRY.

1524
PEUGH, ISAIAH, see PUGH (PEUGH), ISAIAH.

1525
PHILIPS (PHILLIPS), ABRAM (ABRAHAM). Cabinetmaker.
Born c. 1812, Pennsylvania; 1836, moved to Macomb, Illinois; 1838, moved to Richmond, Wayne Co. W. 1838-1852-, Richmond. Had shop on South Pearl Street and later on the west side of

Main Street near Marion. Adv. in *Jeffersonian* 21 September 1839 and 11 January 1840: "CABINET WARE-ROOM./ The subscriber respectfully informs the public, that he continues the CABINET MAKING BUSINESS, at his old stand on Pearl Street, near the Market house, where all articles in the way of FURNITURE, can be had on as good terms, as they can be any where, this side of the Alleghany Mountains. His work is executed in the most substantial and fashionable style . . . . A. Philips." By 1852 he was advertising his cabinetmaking business on Main Street where he emphasized his patent screw bedsteads and ready-made coffins (*ibid.*, 28 October 1852).

1526
PHILIPS, JOHN. Chairmaker.
  Born c. 1779, Virginia; w. 1850, Adams Twp., Decatur Co. (C)

1527
PHILLIPS, M. H. Cabinetmaker.
  Born c. 1817, Alabama; w. 1850, Perry Twp., Lawrence Co. Lived with William C. Pipher, cabinetmaker. (C)

1528
PIATT—*see* RIDEOUT (RIDOUT) & PIATT.

1529
PIATT, JOSIAH. Cabinetmaker.
  Born c. 1828, Pennsylvania; w. 1850, La Porte, La Porte Co. (C)

1530
PIATT, WILLIAM.
Cabinetmaker.
  Born c. 1823, Pennsylvania; w. 1850, La Porte, La Porte Co. (C)

1531
PICKERING, JORDAN.
Cabinetmaker.
  Born c. 1821, Ohio; w. 1850, Harrison Twp., Henry Co. (C)

1532
PIKE, JESSE.
Cabinetmaker and undertaker.
  Born 1810 (C) or 1807 (CH), North Carolina; moved to Salem, Indiana; 1825, moved to Milton, Indiana; 1832, arrived Dublin, Wayne Co. W. 1832- 1884-, Dublin. Began working as a journeyman for Thomas Allen; then went into business alone. In his household in 1850 was David Taylor, cabinetmaker. Mr. Pike was still in business in 1884. (C, CH 34)

1533
PIKE, WILSON. Cabinetmaker.
  Born c. 1819, North Carolina; w. 1850, Dublin, Wayne Co. (C)

1534
PILES, WILLIAM. Cabinetmaker.
  Born c. 1782, Virginia; w. 1850, Shelby Twp., Ripley Co. (C)

1535
PIPHER (PIPER), WILLIAM C.
Cabinetmaker.
  Born c. 1814, Pennsylvania; w. 1850, Perry Twp., Lawrence Co. In same household, M. H. Phillips, cabinetmaker. The product of this shop in 1850 was listed as "Furniture & Coffins $2,000." (C, MC)

1536
PITTMAN, ELI. Cabinetmaker.
  W. 1832-, Dublin, Wayne Co.
  Succeeded Peck & Matthew, q.v.
  (CH 34)

1537
PITTMAN, JAMES P.
Cabinetmaker.
  Born c. 1800, Virginia; w. 1850,
  New Albany, Floyd Co. (C)

1538
PLANT, LEWIS. Chairmaker.
  Born c. 1831, North Carolina (?);
  w. 1850, Vernon Twp., Jennings
  Co. (C)

1539
PLUMMER, WILLIAM.
Cabinetmaker.
  Born c. 1828, Ohio; w. 1850,
  Connersville, Fayette Co. (C)

1540
POLK—see BUTLER & POLK
(POLKE).

1541
POLK, GEORGE W.
Cabinetmaker.
  Born c. 1817, Kentucky; w. 1850,
  Princeton, Gibson Co. In 1850
  his shop produced 25 bureaus, 40
  cupboards, 75 tables, 100 bedsteads, and other articles totaling
  in value $2,450. (C, MC)

1542
POLK, JAMES W. Chairmaker.
  Born c. 1824, North Carolina;
  w. 1850, Lewisville, Henry Co.
  (C) See BUTLER & POLK
  (POLKE).

1543
POLK, JOHN. Cabinetmaker.
  Born c. 1810, North Carolina; w.
  1850, Greensboro Twp., Henry Co.
  In 1850 he made 75 bureaus and
  tables valued at $1,200. (C, MC)

1544
POLSLEY, ROBERT W.
Carpenter and cabinetmaker.
  Born 1824, probably in Virginia;
  grew up in Henry Co., and
  learned trades of carpenter and
  cabinetmaker. W. c. 1826-, Jefferson Twp., Grant Co. Died 1862.
  (CH 45)

1545
POLTZ, CONRAD, see POTTS
(POLTZ), CONRAD.

1546
POMROY, LUCIUS F.
Chairmaker.
  Born c. 1808, New York; w.
  1850, Greensboro Twp., Henry Co.
  (C)

1547
PORTER, GEORGE W.
Cabinetmaker.
  Born c. 1824, Ohio; w. 1850,
  New Albany, Floyd Co. In same
  household: Philip Sudlow, painter;
  Jack Mantz, Joseph Tanner, and
  George Bratten, chairmakers; and
  Barny Christy, cabinetmaker. (C)
  See PORTER & MANTZ
  (MONTZ).

1548
PORTER & MANTZ (MONTZ).
Cabinetmakers and chairmakers.
  George W. Porter and Jack
  Mantz; w. 1850, New Albany,
  Floyd Co. Eight men worked in
  this establishment; their raw

materials included cherry, poplar, and walnut. In 1850 they made 100 bedsteads, 24 bureaus, 60 dozen chairs, and 144 tables. The men living in the Porter household were undoubtedly employees of this firm. (C, MC)

1549
POSEY, THOMAS. Cabinet shop. Born Virginia 1792, son of Thomas Posey, g o v e r n o r o f Indiana Territory; operated cabinet shop in Corydon, Harrison Co. date unknown; died 1863 in Henderson, Ky. (Information from Frederick P. Griffin, Corydon.)

1550
POSTON, AARON F. Cabinetmaker.
Born in Rush Co.; c. 1845, moved to Wabash Co. and began work as cabinetmaker. Later operated a dry goods business in La Fontaine. Died 1859, age 29. (CH 45)

1551
POTERE(?), W. Cabinetmaker.
Born c. 1830; w. 1850, Gosport, Owen Co. (C)

1552
POTTS (POLTZ), CONRAD. Cabinetmaker.
Born c. 1810, Germany; w. 1850, Wayne Twp., Allen Co. (C)

1553
POTTS, JOHN. Cabinetmaker.
Born c. 1831, Ohio; w. 1850, Clear Spring Twp., La Grange Co. (C)

1554
POWEL, CHARLES. Cabinetmaker.
Born c. 1831; w. 1850, Blue River Twp., Johnson Co. (C)

1555
POWEL, JOSEL F. Cabinetmaker.
Born c. 1820, Virginia; w. 1850, Marion, Grant Co. (C)

1556
POWERS, CYRUS. Cabinetmaker.
Born c. 1828, New York; w. 1850, Wayne Twp., Allen Co. (C)

1557
PRALLY, EARNEST. Cabinetmaker.
Born c. 1834, Germany; w. 1850, New Albany, Floyd Co. Lived with John Brindley, cabinetmaker. (C)

1558
PRICE, BENJAMIN F. Cabinetmaker.
Born 1807, Pennsylvania; w. Uniontown, Pa., until 1834; w. 1834-1884, South Bend, St. Joseph Co. In 1838 he adv. in *South Bend Free Press* that he was associated with a Mr. Inman and Robert Landon, q.v. Shop was located on Michigan Street opposite L. M. Taylor's trading post. They produced "side boards & sofas, center, loo, card, pier, dining & breakfast tables, secretaries & book cases, pillar & claw work stands, fancy, French & high post bedsteads, corner & square cupboards, wardrobes, etc." Adv. *ibid.* 1 January 1841, that his partnership with Landon was dis-

solved and he would continue at the old stand of Price & Landon. Adv. *St. Joseph Valley Register*, July 1846, that he had moved his shop to two doors north of Gilmore's store; offered coffins and services of a hearse. In 1850 two men were working in his shop; they produced cabinet ware valued at $1,500. Charles W. Price, cabinetmaker, was listed at the same address. (C, MC) See Plate V.

1559
PRICE, CHARLES W.
Cabinetmaker.
Born c. 1834, Pennsylvania; w. 1850, Portage Twp., St. Joseph Co. Lived with Benjamin F. Price, cabinetmaker, q.v. (C)

1560
PROTSMAN, LAWRENCE.
Cabinetmaker.
Born c. 1815, Kentucky; w. 1850, Troy Twp., Perry Co. (C)

1561
PUCKET, DAVID.
Furniture manufacturer.
W. c. 1838-, La Grange or Noble County. ". . . about 1838 David Pucket began manufacturing furniture . . . continued quite extensively several years." (CH 12)

1562
PUGH, DAVID D.
Cabinetmaker.
Born c. 1798, Virginia; w. 1850, Huntington Co. (C)

1563
PUGH (PEUGH), ISAIAH.
Cabinetmaker.
Born c. 1818, Kentucky; w. 1850,

Monroe Twp., Washington Co. He worked alone, using horse-powered machinery; in 1850 he produced furniture valued at $1,222. (C, MC)

1564
PULLIAM, ZACHARIAH.
Cabinetmaker.
Born c. 1796, Indiana; w. 1850, Knox Co. Two men worked in this shop; in 1850 they made 30 bedsteads, 10 bureaus, 150 tables, 15 coffins, and "sundrys." (C, MC)

1565
PUMPHREY, OLIVER.
Cabinetmaker.
Born c. 1829, Indiana; w. 1850, Milton, Wayne Co. (C)

1566
QUIER, WILLIAM. Cabinetmaker.
Born c. 1825, Pennsylvania; w. 1850, Marshall Co. (C)

1567
RADER, JEFFERSON.
Apprentice cabinetmaker.
Born c. 1830, Virginia; w. 1850, New Castle, Henry Co. Apprenticed to Adam Beam, cabinetmaker. (C)

1568
RAGAN, MICHAEL.
Cabinetmaker.
Born c. 1819, Ireland; w. 1850, Lagro Twp., Wabash Co. (C)

1569
RAHE, HENRY. Cabinetmaker.
Born c. 1822, Germany; w. 1850, Wayne Twp., Allen Co. (C)

1570
RALSTON, JAMES H.
Cabinetmaker.
  Born c. 1810, Kentucky; w. 1850,
  Center Twp., Howard Co. (C)

1571
RAMMAS, HERMAN.
Cabinetmaker.
  Born c. 1808, Germany; w. 1850,
  Vanderburgh Co. (C)

1572
RAMSEY (RAMSAY), JOHN F.
Cabinetmaker.
  Born 2 December, 1809, Lebanon,
  Ohio; apprenticed to Charles Leh-
  man of Cincinnati; worked in
  Louisville, New Orleans, and St.
  Louis, and near Madison and in
  Paris, Indiana. Came to Indianapolis in 1833. Adv. in *Indiana
  Democrat* 23 November 1833:
  "N E W ESTABLISHMENT/
  J. F. RAMSEY & CO./CABI-
  NET MAKERS . . . Having
  made arrangements to keep on
  hand a large supply of the best
  materials, and from the experience
  of one of the firm, in several of
  the best establishments in the
  west, they feel confident that the
  public will not be disappointed in
  giving them their custom. . ."
  Also wanted two or three journeymen; in 1834 needed an apprentice. Same advertisement carried
  in 1834 for J. F. Ramsey alone.
  In 1850 his shop employed three
  men and made 175 pairs of bedsteads, 100 tables, and other
  articles. He retired from the furniture business in 1870. (C, MC,
  TH 49) *See also* RAMSEY &
  GREER.

1573
RAMSEY & GREER.
Cabinetmakers.
  J. F. Ramsey and James Greer;
  w. 1838, Indianapolis, Marion Co.
  Adv. in *Indiana State Gazette* 3
  November 1838, that they operated
  a cabinet wareroom and also made
  coffins.

1574
RANAM, E. M. Cabinetmaker.
  W. 1850, Madison Co. Two men
  employed in this shop which pro-
  duced "Furniture worth $1,000."
  (MC)

1575
RANEY, JOHN M. Cabinetmaker.
  Born c. 1828, Indiana; w. 1850,
  Indianapolis, Marion Co. (C)

1576
RANKIN, DAVID. Cabinetmaker.
  Born c. 1809, Pennsylvania; w.
  1850, Harrison Twp., Vigo Co.
  Two men worked in this shop;
  in 1850 they made 50 bedsteads,
  25 tables, and 25 bureaus and
  stands. (C, MC)

1577
RANKIN, WILLIAM.
Cabinetmaker.
  W. 1841, Terre Haute, Vigo Co.
  Adv. in *Wabash Express*, 28
  December 1841, illustrating a
  sofa: "C A B I N E T W A R E-
  HOUSE/WILLIAM RANKIN
  has established a Cabinet Ware-
  House in Terre Haute, and is
  now prepared to execute any and
  all orders in his line at the short-
  est notice, and on accommodating
  terms. Those who may want
  Cabinet Furniture, of any descrip-

tion, from plain to fine, may always calculate on having it executed in a workmanlike manner, and at prices which will not be considered extravagant. His Room is on National Road Street, one door east above the Linton Bldg. All description of READY MADE FURNITURE kept on hand."

1578
RANNELS, GEORGE. Cabinetmaker.
Born c. 1826, Kentucky; w. 1850, New Albany, Floyd Co. (C)

1579
RASLER, GEORGE. Chairmaker.
Born c. 1809, Pennsylvania; w. 1850, Richland Twp., De Kalb Co. (C)

1580
RAVENSCROFF, JOHN. Cabinetmaker.
Born c. 1827, England; w. 1850, Eel River Twp., Greene Co. Lived with William Ravenscroff, cabinetmaker, q.v. (C)

1581
RAVENSCROFF, STEPHEN. Cabinetmaker.
Born c. 1830, England; w. 1850, Eel River Twp., Greene Co. Lived with William Ravenscroff, cabinetmaker, q.v. (C)

1582
RAVENSCROFF, WILLIAM. Cabinetmaker.
Born c. 1824, England; w. 1850, Eel River Twp., Greene Co. Four men worked in his shop (two of them were Stephen and John Ravenscroff); their raw materials

included mahogany; in 1850 they made cabinet ware valued at $1,500. (C, MC)

1583
RAY, SAMUEL. Chairmaker.
Born c. 1831, Indiana; w. 1850, Montgomery Twp., Jennings Co. Lived with Oskar A. Read, chairmaker. (C)

1584
RAYNES, JNO. Cabinetmaker.
Born c. 1801, Maine; w. 1850, Rush Co. (C)

1585
READ, OSKAR A. Chairmaker.
Born c. 1827, Kentucky; w. 1850, Montgomery Twp., Jennings Co. In same household, Samuel Ray, chairmaker. (C)

1586
READER, NICHOLAS. Chairmaker.
Born c. 1797, Virginia; w. 1850, Green Twp., Jay Co. (C)

1587
REAM, HENRY. Cabinetmaker.
Born c. 1817, Ohio; w. 1850, Warren, Huntington Co. Lived with Michael Oats, cabinetmaker. (C)

1588
REARE, CHRISTIAN. Cabinetmaker.
Born c. 1822, Germany; w. 1850, Harrison Twp., Vigo Co. (C)

1589
REATFORD, JACOB. Cabinetmaker.
Born c. 1826, Ohio; w. 1850, Turkey Creek Twp., Kosciusko Co. (C)

1590
RECTOR, W. H. Cabinetmaker.
W. 1836, Goshen, Elkhart Co.
Adv. in *South Bend Free Press*
October 1836, for journeyman;
adv. was placed by William
Hemphill.

1591
REDD, DANIEL. Cabinetmaker.
Born c. 1808, Pennsylvania; w.
-1839-1850-, Logansport, Cass Co.
"Daniel Redd ran a cabinet and
furniture factory in the 'Old Sem-
inary,' northeast corner of
Fourth & Market in 1839 and in
that year moved his shop to the
northeast corner of Sixth &
Broadway. . . ." In 1850 four
men were employed in his shop,
using machinery powered by hand
and horse; they made 40 bureaus,
150 tables, 150 pairs of bedsteads,
and 120 sets of chairs. (MC, CH
25)

1592
REDFORD, LEWIS.
Cabinetmaker.
W. 1830, Terre Haute, Vigo Co.
Adv. in *Western Register and
Terre-Haute Advertiser*, 31 July
1830 (illustrating sideboard):
"LEWIS REDFORD respect-
fully informs the public that he
carries on the CABINET MAK-
ING, one door north of his residence, in this village, where all
orders in his line will be thankfully received and promptly attended to . . . ."

1593
REDNER, NOAH. Chairmaker.
Born c. 1802, Virginia; w. 1850,
Bloomington Twp., Monroe Co.
(C)

1594
REED, ANDREW—*see* JONES,
JAMES.

1595
REED, ANDREW W.
Cabinetmaker.
W. 1824-, Indianapolis, Marion
Co. Adv. in *Indianapolis Gazette*,
8 June 1824, that he "Has commenced [business] . . . one
door north of Wilkins and
Yandes' Tan-Yard, where those
wishing furniture can be accommodated at the most reduced prices."
He would take cherry, poplar, and
scantling in payment "but for
ready *cash* his work will be sold
lower than any heretofore disposed
of in Indianapolis."

1596
REED, JOHN. Cabinetmaker.
Born c. 1824, Ohio; w. 1850,
Decatur, Adams Co. (C)

1597
REEL, HENRY. Cabinetmaker.
Born c. 1803, Virginia; w. 1850,
Washington Twp., Putnam Co.
(C)

1598
REEL, ZACHARIAH.
Cabinetmaker.
Born c. 1816, Ohio; w. 1850,
White Co. (C)

1599
REEVE, ALEXANDER.
Cabinetmaker.
  Born c. 1822, Kentucky; w. 1850,
  Brownsburg, Hendricks Co. (C)

1600
REEVE, POWELL. Chairmaker.
  Born c. 1818, Kentucky; w. 1850,
  Warren Twp., Warren Co. (C)

1601
REEVES, ASA. Cabinetmaker.
  Born c. 1827, Ohio; w. 1850, Jackson Twp., Hancock Co. (C)

1602
REINECKER, SAMUEL.
Cabinetmaker.
  Born c. 1814, Pennsylvania; w.
  1850, Perrysville, Vermillion Co.
  (C)

1603
REUEHART, A. Cabinetmaker.
  Born c. 1834, Germany; w. 1850,
  Indianapolis, Marion Co. (C)

1604
REYNOLDS, AUSTIN.
Chairmaker.
  Born c. 1826, Ohio; w. 1850,
  Vienna Twp., Scott Co. (C)

1605
REYNOLDS, JOHN B.
Cabinetmaker.
  Born c. 1813, Pennsylvania; w.
  1850, Columbus, Bartholomew Co.
  Two men worked in shop; in
  1850 they made 100 bedsteads and
  other furniture, totaling $1,200 in
  value. (C, MC)

1606
REYNOLDS, LORENZO D.
Chairmaker.
  Born c. 1825, Ohio; w. 1850,
  Vienna Twp., Scott Co. (C)

1607
REYNOLDS, LORENZO D.
Chairmaker.
  Born c. 1802, Indiana; w. 1850,
  Vienna Twp., Scott Co. (C)

1607a
REYNOLDS, WILLIAM L.
Cabinetmaker.
  W. 1820, Centerville, Wayne Co.
  (CH 53)

1608
RHEIN (RHINE), DAN.
Cabinetmaker.
  W. -1839-1850-, Lafayette, Tippecanoe Co. Adv. in *Indiana Eagle*
  2 January 1839, that he had a
  shop on the south side of Main
  Street between the public square
  and Wabash Street; adv. in
  Family Museum 2 March 1844.
  In 1850 seven men were working
  in his shop using machinery
  powered by horse; that year they
  made 1,000 bedsteads in addition
  to miscellaneous items valued at
  $2,000. (MC) *See also* BULLOCK, WILLIAM.

1609
RHODER, GEORGE.
Cabinetmaker.
  Born c. 1828, France; w. 1850,
  Indianapolis, Marion Co. (C)

1610
RHODES, EZEKIEL.
Cabinetmaker.
  Born c. 1811, Virginia; w. 1850,
  Liberty Twp., Wabash Co. (C)

1611
RHODES, JACOB. Cabinetmaker.
Born c. 1830, Indiana; w. 1850,
New Albany, Floyd Co. Lived
with John Shrader, cabinetmaker.
(C) *See also* SANDERSON &
SHRADER.

1612
RHODES, JACOB. Cabinetmaker.
Born c. 1831, Indiana; w. 1850,
Harrison Co. (C)

1613
RHODES, JAMES K.
Cabinetmaker.
Born c. 1813, Virginia; w. 1850,
Orange Twp., Fayette Co. (C)

1614
RICE, HENRY. Cabinetmaker.
Born 1762, Pennsylvania; w. 1823-
1834-, Corydon, Harrison Co. Adv.
in *Indiana Gazette* 22 January
1823: "NOTICE/THE under-
signed will give the highest market
price for country sugar, in exchange for cabinet furniture./
HENRY RICE Senr." Adv. *ibid.*,
26 May 1834: Sheriff's sale,
Harrison district court, s u i t
against Henry Rice. To be sold:
"Eight Beds and bedding, and
bedsteds, two pair of and irons,
nine chairs, one large Kettle, two
tables, all the cupboard furniture
in two cupboards, consisting of
plates, tea-cups and saucers,
knives and forks, —one teaboard,
three dutch-ovens, one waffle iron,
three buckets, and all the other
kitchen furniture in said Rices
kitchen, —three saws and all
other Cabinet tools in said Rices
shop, about two hundred feet of
Cherry plank, two fire shovels,

and two pair of tongs, one grind
stone; . . ." His son John also
made furniture in Corydon.

1615
RICE, JOHN.
Cabinetmaker and chairmaker.
Born c. 1805, Pennsylvania; w.
1836-1838-, Corydon, Harrison Co.
Son of Henry Rice, cabinetmaker,
q.v. Adv. in *Investigator* 14 January 1837: "ABSCONDED on the
25th of December, 1836, an in-
dented apprentice to the Cabinet
making business, by the name of
John Floyd." John Rice offered
ten mills reward. Adv. *ibid.*, 6 May
1837: "THE subscribers would
respectfully inform the public that
they have on hand a large supply
of Furniture of almost every description, and of the best quality
and workmanship, which they will
dispose of on the most reasonable
terms. Orders for any work in
their line will be thankfully received and promptly attended to
. . . JOHN RICE./J. D.
PETER." This advertisement
illustrated a four-drawer bureau.
Adv. *ibid.*, 20 May 1837, for turning. Adv. *ibid.*, 10 May 1838:
"RICE & PETER . . . CABINET
BUSINESS. . . ." Adv. *ibid.*, 7
June 1838: "CHAIR MAKING.
The Subscriber has commenced
the above business in the town of
Corydon, at his old stand, where
he intends to keep constantly on
hand a variety of WINDSOR,
ROCKING and S E W I N G
CHAIRS, SETTEES, &C., . . .
JOHN RICE." From these ad-
vertisements, one surmises that

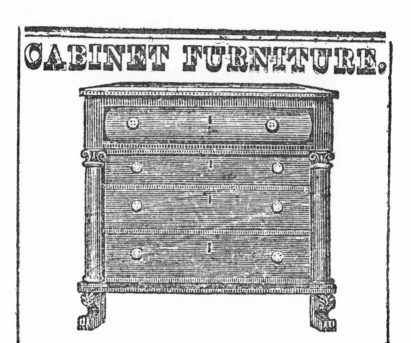

CABINET FURNITURE.

THE subscribers would respectfully inform the public that they have on hand a large supply of Furniture of almost every description, and of the best quality and workmanship, which they will dispose of on the most reasonable terms. Orders for any work in their line will be thankfully received and promptly attended to. They solicit the patronage of a generous public.

JOHN RICE,
J. D. PETER.

Corydon, May 6, 1837.—29-

Fig. 8. From *The Investigator* (Corydon)

John Rice was the turner and chairmaker of the Rice & Peter firm, Peter doing the cabinetwork.

1616
RICE & PETER—*see* RICE, JOHN.

1617
RICHARDS, JOHN.
Cabinetmaker.
    Born c. 1813, Pennsylvania; w. 1850, Hamilton Twp., Sullivan Co. (C)

1618
RICHARDSON, WILLIAM H.
Cabinetmaker.
    Born c. 1830, Ohio; w. 1850, Emmettsville, Randolph Co. (C)

1619
RICHEY, BARNEY.
Cabinetmaker.
    Born c. 1796, Kentucky; w. 1850, Cass Twp., Greene Co. (C)

1620
RICKETTS—*see* BELMONT & RICKETTS.

1621
RIDEOUT, SAMUEL.
Cabinetmaker.
    Born c. 1813, New Hampshire; w. 1850, La Porte, La Porte Co. (C)

1622
RIDEOUT (RIDOUT) & PIATT.
Cabinetmakers.
    Samuel Rideout (Ridout) and —— Piatt; w. 1850, La Porte, La Porte Co. Four men worked in this shop using machinery powered by hand and by steam power. In 1850 they made furniture worth $1,000. (MC)

1623
RIDER, DANIEL. Cabinetmaker.
    Born c. 1815, Pennsylvania; w. 1850, Lawrenceburg, Dearborn Co. (C)

1624
RIDGEWAY, DAVID.
    A child's chair and a footstool made by David Ridgeway in Indiana before 1850 are in the possession of a descendant.

1625
RIES, MARTIN. Cabinetmaker.
    Born c. 1810, Germany; w. 1850, Evansville, Vanderburgh Co. (C)

1626
RIGGS, BENSON [Sr.].
Cabinetmaker.
    Born c. 1800, Virginia; w. -1828-1850-, Haddon Twp., Sullivan Co. Five men worked in his shop; among them in 1850 were Daniel Davidson and Thomas K. Henderson, who lived in his household, and probably Benson Riggs, Jr. In 1850 they made "Miscellaneous" worth $1,500. (C, MC) *See also* MILAM, WALKER A., whom Riggs advertised as a runaway apprentice in September 1828.

1627
RIGGS, BENSON [Jr.].
Cabinetmaker.
    Born c. 1827, Indiana; w. 1850, Haddon Twp., Sullivan Co. Probably worked for Benson Riggs [Sr.], q.v. (C)

1628
RIGGS, GREENBERRY.
Cabinetmaker.
    Born c. 1805, Virginia; w. 1850, Turman Twp., Sullivan Co. (C)

1629
RIGHT, THOMAS I. (or J.).
Cabinetmaker.
Born c. 1829, Ohio; w. 1850, Pleasant View, Shelby Co. (C)

1630
RILEY, ZACHARIAH.
Cabinetmaker.
Born c. 1828, Kentucky; w. 1850, Clinton Twp., Decatur Co. (C)

1631
RINEER (RYNIER), AAREN.
Cabinetmaker.
Born c. 1806, New Jersey; w. 1850, Metamora, Franklin Co. Three men were employed in his shop; in 1850 they produced furniture worth $1,000. (C, MC)

1632
RIPLEY, MONOT. Cabinetmaker.
Born c. 1795, Massachusetts; w. 1850, Pipe Creek Twp., Madison Co. (C)

1633
RITCHER, LEWIS. Cabinetmaker.
Born c. 1812, Ohio; w. 1850, German Twp., Vanderburgh Co. (C)

1634
RITER, LEVI. Cabinetmaker.
Born c. 1821, Pennsylvania; w. 1850, Noble Twp., Wabash Co. (C)

1635
RITTER, ARTHUR C.
Cabinetmaker.
Born c. 1810, Pennsylvania; w. 1850, Noble Twp., Noble Co. (C)

1636
RITZ, CLEMENTS.
Cabinetmaker.
Born c. 1833, Germany; w. 1850, Vanderburgh Co. (C)

1637
RIZELY, JOSHUA S.
Cabinetmaker.
Born c. 1817, New Jersey; w. 1850, Washington Twp., Brown Co. (C)

1638
ROBERTS, GEORGE.
Chairmaker.
Born c. 1809, Indiana; w. 1850, Harrison Twp., Vigo Co. (C)

1639
ROBERTS, JAMES.
Cabinetmaker.
Born c. 1813, Pennsylvania; w. 1850, Lafayette, Tippecanoe Co. Four men worked in his shop, one of them, John Winship, lived in his household. In 1850 they produced 200 bedsteads, 25 bureaus, "Miscellaneous & Tables &c." (C, MC)

1640
ROBERTS, JOHN M.
Cabinetmaker.
Born c. 1818, Kentucky; w. 1850, Monroe Twp., Morgan Co. (C)

1641
ROBERTS, LARKEN F.
Cabinetmaker.
Born c. 1810, Kentucky; w. 1850, Plainfield, Hendricks Co. (C)

1642
ROBERTS, ROBERT R.
Chairmaker.
Came to Indiana in 1819; w. in

Bishop (near Paoli), Orange Co. Six chairs known, one illustrated in *Indianapolis Star* 2 November 1941.

1643
ROBERTS, WILLIAM H.
Apprentice cabinetmaker.
> Born c. 1833, Indiana; w. 1850, Center Twp., Hancock Co. Apprenticed to Prestley Guymon, cabinetmaker. (C)

1644
ROBERTSON, DANIEL.
Chairmaker.
> Born c. 1820, Indiana; w. 1850, Boone Co. (C)

1645
ROBERTSON, MILTON.
Cabinetmaker.
> Born c. 1829, Indiana; w. 1850, Lexington, Scott Co. Lived with Alfred Amick, cabinetmaker, q.v. (C)

1646
ROBERTSON, THOMAS.
Cabinetmaker.
> Born c. 1825, Ohio; w. 1850, Redding Twp., Jackson Co. (C)

1647
ROBINSON, GEORGE.
Cabinetmaker.
> Born c. 1804, New Jersey; w. 1850, Sugar Creek Twp., Hancock Co. In same household, Nathan Snodgrass, cabinetmaker. (C)

1648
ROBINSON, HORACE.
Cabinetmaker.
> Born c. 1815, Connecticut; w. 1850, Jackson Twp., Washington Co. (C)

1649
ROBINSON, P. F. Cabinetmaker.
> Born c. 1819, Pennsylvania; w. 1850, Adams Co. In 1850 his product was worth $600. (C, MC)

1650
ROBINSON, WILLIAM.
Cabinetmaker.
> Born c. 1823, Scotland; w. 1850, Union Twp., Montgomery Co. (C) *See also* WHITE & ROBINSON.

1651
ROCKY, DAVID. Cabinetmaker.
> Born c. 1821, Pennsylvania; w. 1850, Noble Twp., Noble Co. (C)

1652
RODARMEL, OSCAR F.
Cabinetmaker.
> Born c. 1833, Indiana; w. 1850, Washington Twp., Daviess Co. Lived with Samuel A. Rodarmel, cabinetmaker, q.v. (C)

1653
RODARMEL, SAMUEL A.
Cabinetmaker.
> Born c. 1810, Indiana; w. 1850, Washington Twp., Daviess Co. His raw materials included mahogany. In 1850 his shop made 125 bedsteads, 115 coffins, 30 bureaus, 15 cupboards and presses, 75 breakfast tables, and 40 dining tables. Working with him were Oscar F. Rodarmel, Daniel Vliet, and John Hymon. (C, MC)

1654
RODE, LODWICK. Cabinetmaker.
> Born c. 1820, Germany; w. 1850, Vanderburgh Co. (C)

1655
RODERFER, SAMUEL.
Cabinetmaker.
Born in Virginia; w. Woodstock,
Va., as carpenter and cabinet-
maker. April 1839, arrived
Rochester, Fulton Co.; worked
for Jacob Kitt. Still living in 1887
in Lebanon, Indiana. (CH 23)

1656
ROGERS, ISAAC. Cabinetmaker.
Born c. 1810, Tennessee; w. 1850,
Mount Auburn, Shelby Co. (C)

1657
ROLL, JACOB. Chairmaker.
Born c. 1800, Ohio; w. 1850,
Logan Twp., Dearborn Co. In
same household, Jacob J. Roll and
William J. M. Roll, chairmakers.
(C)

1658
ROLL, JACOB J. Chairmaker.
Born c. 1832, Ohio; w. 1850,
Logan Twp., Dearborn Co. Lived
with Jacob Roll, chairmaker. (C)

1659
ROLL, WILLIAM J. M.
Chairmaker.
Born c. 1828, Ohio; w. 1850,
Logan Twp., Dearborn Co. Lived
with Jacob Roll, chairmaker. (C)

1660
ROLLE, PETER. Cabinetmaker.
Born c. 1831, Germany; w. 1850,
Wayne Twp., Allen Co. Lived
with Lewis Pelkey, cabinetmaker,
q.v. (C)

1661
ROMNY, JOHN P. Cabinetmaker.
Born c. 1824, Germany; w. 1850,
York Twp., Noble Co. (C)

1662
ROOKER, SAMUEL S.
Painter and Chairmaker.
Born near Knoxville, Tenn., c.
1800; came to Indianapolis, Marion Co., 1821. Worked as sign and
house painter. Adv. in *Indiana
Democrat* 17 July 1835: "FANCY
CANE, FLAG AND WINDSOR
CHAIR MANUFACTORY.
SAMUEL S. ROOKER RE-
SPECTFULLY informs the public that he has removed his Ware
Room and Manufactory two doors
west of the Democrat printing
office, in Griffith's Row, where
he will be happy to accommodate
his old customers and all others
with FANCY AND WINDSOR
CHAIRS, SETTEES, &C. He
will also execute sign and ornamental painting as usual. His
prices will be moderate, and he
will spare no pains to render
general satisfaction to his
customers. Having just received a
supply of materials from the city
of New York, he will be able to
execute fancy work in a style
superior to any before offered in
this place. The public are invited
to give him a call." (Wilbur D.
Peat, *Pioneer Painters of Indiana*
[Art Association of Indianapolis,
1954], TH 17)

1663
ROOP, JEREMIAH.
Cabinetmaker.
Born c. 1822, Pennsylvania; w.
1850, Wayne Twp., Tippecanoe
Co. He worked alone, and in
1850 he produced cabinet ware
worth $1,050. (C, MC)

1664
RORETY, SAMUEL S.
Cabinetmaker.
Born c. 1805, Kentucky; w. 1850,
Morristown, Shelby Co. (C)

1665
ROSE, ENOS. Cabinetmaker.
Born c. 1825, Indiana; w. 1850,
Rochester Twp., Fulton Co. (C)

1666
ROSE, WILLIAM G.
Cabinetmaker.
Born c. 1807, Kentucky; w. 1850,
Robb Twp., Posey Co. (C)

1667
ROSEMAN, JOSEPH.
Chairmaker.
Born c. 1793, New Jersey; w.
1819-1820-, Vincennes, Knox Co.
Adv. in *Indiana Centinel* 11
December 1819 through 1 January
1820: "J. ROSEMAN, *WIND-
SOR and FANCY Chair
MAKER, Three doors below Mr.
Beamon's Hotel,* WILL give
ONE DOLLAR per bushel, for
any quantity of *Clean Flax Seed.*"
Adv. in *Western Sun & General
Advertiser* 29 July 1820: "RE-
MOVAL/J. ROSEMAN, *Wind-
sor and Fancy Chair Maker,* Has
removed to the corner of Vigo-
street, opposite Doctor M'Na-
mee's. . . ."

1668
ROSEMAN, THOMAS.
Cabinetmaker.
W. 1820, Vincennes, Knox Co.
Two men worked in this shop
and made sideboards and bedside
tables. The census taker noted
"Demand and Sale Bad." (MC)

1669
ROSS, ISAAC. Cabinetmaker.
Born c. 1790, Kentucky; w. 1850,
Liberty Twp., Crawford Co. (C)

1670
ROSS, JOHN F. Cabinetmaker.
Born c. 1829, Kentucky; w. 1850,
Marion Twp., Shelby Co. (C)

1671
ROSS, THOMAS J. T.
Cabinetmaker.
Born c. 1811, New York; w. 1850,
Union Twp., Montgomery Co.
(C) *See also* KENYON &
ROSS.

1672
ROTERAS, PHILIP.
Cabinetmaker.
Born c. 1809, Germany; w. 1850,
Harrison Twp., Vigo Co. (C)

1673
ROUDEBUSH, DAVID.
Cabinetmaker.
Born c. 1815, Ohio; w. 1850,
Leesburg, Kosciusko Co. (C)

1674
ROWE, EDWARD. Cabinetmaker.
Born c. 1835, Ohio; w. 1850,
Wayne Twp., Allen Co. Lived
with Charles Fink, cabinetmaker,
q.v. (C)

1675
ROWEN, ABRAHAM.
Cabinetmaker.
Born c. 1829, Indiana; w. 1850,
Ripley Twp., Rush Co. Lived
with David Coble, cabinetmaker.
(C)

1676
ROWLEY, SAMUEL. Chairmaker.
Born c. 1821, Connecticut; w.
1850, Deer Creek Twp., Perry
Co. (C)

1677
RUCH, CHARLES. Cabinetmaker.
Born c. 1809, Pennsylvania; w.
1850, Whitley Co. (C)

1678
RUFER, SAMUEL. Cabinetmaker.
Born c. 1825, Pennsylvania; w.
1850, Whitley Co. In same house-
hold, Tilghman I. Siling and
Milton Siling, cabinetmakers.
(C)

1679
RUGG, ROBERT. Cabinetmaker.
Born c. 1800, Pennsylvania; w.
1850, New Castle Twp., Fulton
Co. (C)

1680
RUTH, ADAM. Cabinetmaker.
Born c. 1825, Germany; w. 1850,
Shawswick Twp., Lawrence Co.
Lived with Henry Cline, cabinet-
maker. (C)

1681
RUTLIDGE, GEORGE.
Cabinetmaker.
Born c. 1823, Virginia; w. 1850,
Franklin Twp., Montgomery Co.
(C)

1682
RYNIER, AAREN, see RINEER
(RYNIER), AAREN.

1683
RYOR, JAMES. Chairmaker.
Born c. 1824, Ohio; w. 1850,
Liberty, Union Co. (C)

1684
SAID, JOSEPH. Chairmaker.
W. 1850, Madison Co. He worked
alone and in 1850 made 75 sets
of chairs worth $600. (MC)

1685
SANDERS, MATHEW.
Cabinetmaker.
Born c. 1800, North Carolina; w.
1850, Greensboro Twp., Henry Co.
In same household, Milton Bald-
win, cabinetmaker. (C)

1686
SANDERSON, WILLIAM L.
Cabinetmaker.
Born c. 1812, Pennsylvania; w.
1850, New Albany, Floyd Co. (C)
See S A N D E R S O N &
SHRADER

1687
SANDERSON & SHRADER.
Cabinetmakers.
William L. Sanderson, John
Shrader, and Jacob Rhodes, cabi-
netmakers; Barnett Kepner,
painter; w. 1850, New Albany,
Floyd Co. Total of eight em-
ployees; their raw materials in-
cluded cherry, poplar, and walnut.
In 1850 they made 100 bedsteads,
25 bureaus, and 75 tables. (C,
MC)

1688
SAP, HENRY. Cabinetmaker.
Born c. 1810, Germany; w. 1850,
Vanderburgh Co. (C)

1689
SAPP, ARNOLD.
Cabinetmaker.
W. 1837 to sometime before 1845,
La Porte Co. (CH 13)

1690
SCHAFTER, HENRY.
Cabinetmaker.
> Born c. 1828, Switzerland; w.
> 1850, Harrison Twp., Wells Co.
> Lived with David Bovine, cabinet-
> maker. (C)

1691
SCHAFTER, PAUL I.
Cabinetmaker.
> Born c. 1832, Germany; w. 1850,
> Harrison Twp., Wells Co. Lived
> with David Bovine, cabinetmaker.
> (C)

1692
SCHMALHOUS, FREDERICK.
Cabinetmaker.
> Born c. 1808, Germany; w. 1850,
> Wayne Twp., Allen Co. (C)

1693
SCHNEIDERHAM, VINZENZ.
Cabinetmaker.
> Born c. 1829, Germany; w. 1850,
> New Albany, Floyd Co. (C)

1694
SCHNUDDLE, JOHN.
Cabinetmaker.
> Born c. 1810, Germany; w. 1850,
> Vincennes, Knox Co. (C)

1695
SCHOOLEY, ELIAS.
Cabinetmaker.
> Born c. 1805, New Jersey; w.
> 1850, Manchester Twp., Dearborn
> Co. (C)

1696
SCHRATER, LEWIS.
Cabinetmaker.
> Born c. 1806, Germany; w. 1850,

Lawrenceburg, Dearborn Co. In
same household, Ernest Molning,
cabinetmaker. (C)

1697
SCHRIDER, THOMAS.
Cabinetmaker.
> W. 1850, Springfield Twp., Frank-
> lin Co. The number of employees
> listed was one and a half; in
> 1850 this shop produced 75
> bureaus "&c.," worth $545. (MC)

1698
SCOTT, ——. Cabinetmaker.
> W. 1825, Crawfordsville, Mont-
> gomery Co. (CH 3)

1699
SCOTT, DAVID. Cabinetmaker.
> Born c. 1824, Indiana; w. 1850,
> New Albany, Floyd Co. (C)

1700
SCOTT, S. J. Cabinetmaker.
> Born c. 1826, Indiana; w. 1850,
> Gosport, Owen Co. (C) *See also*
> SCOTT & LYONS.

1701
SCOTT, SAMUEL. Cabinetmaker.
> Born c. 1831, Indiana; w. 1850,
> Rising Sun, Ohio Co. Lived with
> John Whitlock. (C)

1702
SCOTT, SAMUEL F. (or T.).
Chairmaker.
> Born c. 1815, Tennessee; w. 1850,
> Mount Vernon, Posey Co. (C)

1703
SCOTT, SILVESTER.
Cabinetmaker.
> Born c. 1823, Crawford Co.; w.
> 1850, Ohio Twp., Crawford Co.
> (C)

1704
SCOTT, WILLIAM.
Cabinetmaker.
> Born c. 1804, Kentucky; w. 1850, Jennings Twp., Crawford Co. Three men worked in this shop; in 1850 they made 468 pieces of furniture valued at $2,808. (C, MC)

1705
SCOTT & LYONS. Cabinetmakers and brick makers.
> S. J. Scott and J. A. Lyons; w. 1850, Gosport, Owen Co. In 1850 they made furniture worth $1,800. (C, MC)

1706
SCRIVENER, EDWARD.
Cabinetmaker.
> Born c. 1812, Virginia; w. 1850, Whitley Co. (C)

1707
SCUDDER, CALEB.
Cabinetmaker.
> 1821, arrived in Indianapolis, Marion Co., from New Jersey via Dayton, Ohio. Adv. in *Indianapolis Gazette* 5 April 1823, that he was operating a cabinetmaking shop, concluding "The subscriber will receive for cabinet work good merchantable cherry, walnut, and poplar plank. . . . Cabinet work will be exchanged for a good work horse." Adv. in *Indiana Journal*, 18 December 1827: "WANTED 25000 feet of Cherry and Poplar Lumber, For which Cabinet Furniture will be exchanged at a fair price. . . ." Mr. Scudder was the third mayor of Indianapolis. His shop was on West Washington Street opposite the State House. The first trade sign in Indianapolis is said to have been that of "Kalop Skodder, Kabbinet Maker," painted by Samuel S. Rooker, q.v. In 1833 Scudder bought an interest in a drug store with William Hannaman; in 1831 he advertised that he was making wheat fans.
> Furniture known: arrow slatback chair (illustrated in *Indianapolis Star* 8 August 1943); bookcase on stand, made of cherry with crotch mahogany veneer (illustrated *ibid.* 21 February 1943); lyre-end table (illustrated *ibid.* 10 November 1940); mention of a tall rocking chair and washstand (*ibid.*); rocking chair (illustrated *ibid.* 7 January 1940), (AGI, TH 17)

1708
SCUDDER, CALEB R. Cabinetmaker, undertaker, and printer.
> Born 11 April 1828, Lafayette, Tippecanoe Co. Took over cabinetmaking establishment of his father Mathias S. Scudder before 1850. In 1850 two men were working in this shop; their annual product was valued at $1,200. (Undated obituary transcript, Tippecanoe Co. Hist. Assoc., C, MC)

1709
SCUDDER, MATHIAS S.
Cabinetmaker.
> W. -1826-1850-, Lafayette, Tippecanoe Co. Adv. in *Indiana Eagle* 16 October 1839: "MATHIAS SCUDDER, Cabinet Maker, opposite the Globe Hotel, corner of Main and Mississippi streets." (CH 8a, 15, MC)

1710
SELEC, JACOB. Cabinetmaker.
　Born c. 1786, Prussia; w. 1850,
　Madison, Jefferson Co. (C)

1711
SELF, PHILLIP. Cabinetmaker.
　Born c. 1816, Kentucky; w. 1850,
　Southeast Twp., Orange Co. (C)

1712
SELLERS, JOHN A.
Cabinetmaker.
　Born c. 1799, Virginia; w. 1850,
　Huntington Co. (C)

1713
SENECA, SYRUS. Chairmaker.
　Born c. 1828, Ohio; w. 1850,
　Adams Twp., Parke Co. (C)

1714
SENECHEUH, DANIEL.
Chairmaker.
　Born c. 1796, Pennsylvania; w.
　1850, Adams Twp., Parke Co. (C)

1715
SETTLE, WILLIAM H.
Chair painter.
　Born c. 1833, Indiana; w. 1850,
　Madison, Jefferson Co. (C)

1716
SHAFFER, JOSEPH.
Cabinetmaker.
　Born c. 1833, Ohio; w. 1850,
　Union Twp., Montgomery Co.
　Average number of employees in
　this shop was one and a half;
　their equipment included "1 lathe"
　and their machinery was powered
　by horse. In 1850 the product of
　this shop was valued at $1,000.
　(C, MC)

1717
SHANEFELT, SOLOMON.
Cabinetmaker.
　Born c. 1826, Ohio; w. 1850,
　possibly as journeyman, Moores-
　ville and Monroe Twp., Morgan
　Co. (C)

1718
SHAW, JOHN N. (?)
Chairmaker.
　Born c. 1821, Ohio; w. 1850,
　Lafayette Twp., Madison Co. (C)

1718a
SHEARMAN, G. S.—see TEAS,
GIBSON.

1719
SHELDON, ALLEN.
Cabinetmaker.
　Born c. 1830, New York; w.
　1850, Mill Grove Twp., Steuben
　Co. Lived with Allen Morse,
　cabinetmaker. (C)

1720
SHELDON, WILLIAM.
Wheelmaker and chairmaker.
　W. 1850, Steuben Co. Four men
　worked in this shop; their prod-
　uct in 1850 was worth $3,000.
　(MC)

1721
SHELLER, DAVID H.
Cabinetmaker.
　Born c. 1821, Ohio; w. 1850,
　Delaware Twp., Delaware Co.
　(C)

1722
SHELLERS, JOHN R.
Chairmaker.
　Born c. 1829, Indiana; w. 1850,
　New Albany, Floyd Co. (C)

1723
SHELTON, SYLVESTER R., &
DAVID BRANSON.
Cabinetmakers.
> W. -1842-, Hartford City, Blackford Co. Shelton born Virginia 1819; to Rush Co., 1827; Blackford Co., 1842. These men built houses, made coffins and furniture. An 1842 business listing records them as carpenters and joiners. (CH 5)

1724
SHERER, FREDERICK.
Cabinetmaker.
> Born c. 1818, Germany; w. 1850, Wayne Twp., Allen Co. (C)

1725
SHERER, JACOB. Cabinetmaker.
> Born c. 1820, Germany; w. 1850, Vanderburgh Co. (C)

1726
SHERIDAN, WILLIAM.
Cabinetmaker.
> Born c. 1812, Ohio; came to La Porte, La Porte Co., 1833; opened cabinet shop in Lakeport (now Hudson) in 1837; w. 1850, Hudson Twp., La Porte Co. Died 1873. In 1850 two men were working in this shop using machinery powered by horse; their raw materials included paints. That year they made 12 bureaus, 25 tables, 50 bedsteads, 8 coffins, 350 chairs, and other articles. (C, CH 13, MC)

1727
SHERLOCK, JOHN.
Cabinetmaker.
> Born c. 1815, Ohio; w. 1850, Union Twp., De Kalb Co. (C)

1728
SHERMAN, HENRY.
Apprentice chairmaker.
> Born c. 1832, New York; w. 1850, Mishawaka, St. Joseph Co. Apprenticed to Albert Cap, chairmaker. (C)

1729
SHERN, JOHN. Cabinetmaker.
> Born c. 1820; w. 1850, Lafayette, Tippecanoe Co. (C)

1730
SHERN, JOSEPH. Cabinetmaker.
> Born c. 1824, Indiana; w. 1850, Lafayette, Tippecanoe Co. Five men worked in this shop; in 1850 they made 250 bedsteads, 25 bureaus, 200 tables, and other miscellaneous items. (C, MC)

1731
SHERRIN, JOHN. Cabinetmaker.
> Born c. 1826; w. 1850, Logan Twp., Fountain Co. (C)

1732
SHEUMIRE, HENRY.
Cabinetmaker.
> Born c. 1815, Germany; w. 1850, Lawrenceburg, Dearborn Co. (C)

1733
SHIDLER, ABRAM.
Cabinetmaker.
> Born c. 1826, Ohio; w. 1850, Wayne Twp., Wayne Co. (C)

1734
SHIDLER, FRANKLIN.
Cabinetmaker.
> Born c. 1827, Ohio; w. 1850, Liberty, Union Co. (C)

1735
SHIELDS, ABIJAH.
Cabinetmaker.

W. 1820, Jennings Twp., Fayette Co. He worked alone; his raw materials included walnut and cherry. He listed the prices of his products as follows: desks $25; bureaus $16; cupboards $14; clock cases $18; tables $7; bedsteads $3; wheat fans $25; wool carding machines $400. (MC)

1736
SHINGLE, JOSHUA.
Cabinetmaker.
Born c. 1815, Indiana; w. 1850, Anderson Twp., Madison Co. (C)

1737
SHIRELY, LEWIS H.
Cabinetmaker.
Born c. 1827, Pennsylvania; w. 1850, Columbus, Bartholomew Co. (C)

1738
SHIRLE, ADAM. Cabinetmaker.
Born c. 1815, Germany; w. 1850, Vanderburgh Co. (C)

1739
SHIRLEY, JOHN. Cabinetmaker.
W. 1820, Columbia Twp., Fayette Co. He listed the prices of his products as follows: desks $25; bureaus $15; cupboards $15; bedsteads $3; dining tables $10; breakfast tables $6; large coffins $6. (MC)

1740
SHOOK, ALLEN W.
Cabinetmaker.
Born c. 1830, Indiana; w. 1850, New Albany, Floyd Co. Lived with C. A. Dorsey, cabinetmaker. (C)

1741
SHOUP, CONRAD. Cabinetmaker.
Born c. 1819, Germany; w. 1850, Lawrenceburg, Dearborn Co. (C)

1742
SHOW, SAMUEL. Cabinetmaker.
Born c. 1773, Pennsylvania; w. 1850, Perry Twp., Tippecanoe Co. (C)

1743
SHOWER, DAVID. Cabinetmaker.
Born c. 1821, Pennsylvania; w. 1850, Pleasant Mills, Adams Co. (C)

1744
SHRADER, JOHN. Cabinetmaker.
Born c. 1821, Germany; w. 1850, New Albany, Floyd Co. In same household: Jacob Rhodes, cabinetmaker; Barnett Kepner, painter. (C) See also SANDERSON & SHRADER.

1745
SHROCK, GABRIEL.
Cabinetmaker.
Born 18 November 1831, Somerset Co., Pennsylvania; w. after 1841-1850-, Bluffton, Wells Co. He learned cabinetmaking from his uncle, William McBride, with whom he was living in 1850. He worked as a journeyman until establishing his own business in 1856. After 1873 he turned to carpentry, and in 1881 moved to a farm. He was still living in 1887. (C, CH 4)

1746
SHROYER, JOHN.
Painter and chairmaker.
Born c. 1806, Pennsylvania; w.

1850, New Castle, Henry Co. In same household, painters John Hoover and David Thomas. (C)

1747
SHRYOCH, LEWIS.
Apprentice cabinetmaker.
  W. 1820, Corydon, Harrison Co. Was apprenticed to James Lightfoot, q.v. (C)

1748
SILING, MILTON. Cabinetmaker.
  Born c. 1829, Ohio; w. 1850, Whitley Co. Lived with Samuel Rufer, cabinetmaker. (C)

1749
SILING, TILGHMAN I.
Cabinetmaker.
  Born c. 1826, Maryland; w. 1850, Whitley Co. Lived with Samuel Rufer, cabinetmaker. (C)

1750
SIMANS, FRANCIS.
Cabinetmaker.
  Born c. 1830, Ohio; w. 1850, Deerfield, Randolph Co. Lived with Francis M. Avery, cabinetmaker. (C)

1751
SIN (?), JESSE. Cabinetmaker.
  Born c. 1830, Indiana; w. 1850, Marion Twp., Jasper Co. (C)

1752
SINKS (or LINKS?), JAMES.
Cabinetmaker.
  Born c. 1822, Ohio; w. 1850, Pike Twp., Warren Co. (C)

1753
SIPE, ABRAHAM. Cabinetmaker.
  Born c. 1824, Pennsylvania; w. 1850, Huntsville, Randolph Co. (C)

1754
SISSON, JOHN. Cabinetmaker.
  Born c. 1814, Ohio; w. 1850, Marion Twp., Jennings Co. (C)

1755
SITZ, JACOB. Cabinetmaker.
  Born c. 1823, Germany; w. 1850, Harrison Twp., Vigo Co. (C)

1756
SKINNER, C. C. Chairmaker.
  Born c. 1802, New Jersey; w. 1850, Peru, Miami Co (C)

1757
SLOAN, JOHN. Cabinetmaker.
  Arrived 1836, Indianapolis, Marion Co.; w. 1836-1850-, Indianapolis. He made the first sofa manufactured in Indianapolis in 1837. This sofa was still in existence in 1876 when it was said "There is material enough in it to make three of the ordinary sofas of the present day." He was probably the Sloan of the firm of Espy & Sloan, q.v. (CH 39) *See also* STONE, JOHN, and SLOAN & INGERSOLL, possibly the same.

1758
SLOAN, MILTON. Cabinetmaker.
  Born c. 1806, Kentucky; w. 1850, Jackson Twp., Decatur Co. (C)

1759
SLOAN & INGERSOLL. Furniture and chair factory.

W. 1850-, Indianapolis, Marion Co. Perhaps John Sloan and Henry Ingersoll, q.v. (TH 17)

1760
SMART, ANDREW.
Cabinetmaker.
> Born c. 1797, New York; w. 1850, Wayne Twp., Henry Co. (C)

1761
SMILEY, JONATHAN.
Chairmaker.
> W. 1837, Vincennes, Knox Co. Adv. in *The Western Sun & General Advertiser* 14 October 1837: "Remova1/The sub-scriber would respectfully inform the citizens of this place, and the public in general, that he has re-moved his/Chair Shop/to the building formerly occupied by John Ewing, Esq. where he is prepared to furnish and will keep constantly on hand, or make to order, Windsor Chairs and Settees in the greatest variety of patterns and colors, on the shortest notice, and in the very best style of workmanship. *Rocking Chairs* of all sizes and patterns made to order. Old Chairs repaired and painted. JONATHAN SMILEY."

1762
SMITH, A. K. Cabinetmaker.
> Born c. 1817, Ohio; w. 1850, Rush Co. (C) *See* SMITH, A. K. & T. I.

1763
SMITH, A. K. & T. I.
Cabinetmakers.
> A. K. Smith and Thomas I. Smith; w. 1850, Rush Co. In 1850 these two men produced furniture worth $900. (C, MC)

1763a
SMITH, AARON. Chairmaker.
> W. 1840, Richmond, Wayne Co. Adv. in the *Palladium,* 11 April 1840: ". . . he is prepared to manufacture CHAIRS, SET-TEES, &c. &c., on liberal terms. . . ."

1764
SMITH, ADDISON.
Cabinetmaker.
> Born c. 1827, Indiana; w. 1850, Van Buren Twp., Monroe Co. (C)

1765
SMITH, CHARLES.
Cabinetmaker.
> Born in Indiana; w. 1850, Clay Twp., Dearborn Co. (C)

1766
SMITH, CHARLES.
Cabinetmaker.
> Born c. 1822, Germany; w. 1850, Indianapolis, Marion Co. (C)

1767
SMITH, CHARLES.
Cabinetmaker.
> Born c. 1828, Indiana; w. 1850, Evansville, Vanderburgh Co. Lived with Thomas Smith, cabinetmaker and turner, q.v. (C)

1768
SMITH, CHRISTOPHER H.
Piano maker.
> Born c. 1809, Germany; w. 1850, New Albany, Floyd Co. (C)

1769
SMITH, ELIJAH. Cabinetmaker.
  Born c. 1825, New York; w.
  1850, Bluffton, Wells Co. (C)

1770
SMITH, ERATUS.
Cabinetmaker.
  W. 1825, Richmond, Wayne Co.
  Adv. in *Public Leger* 15 January 1825: "Great Bargains!
  MUST and will be sold by
  ERATUS SMITH, C a b i n e t-
  maker, at his old stand, one door
  north of the Market house, an
  extensive assortment of MA-
  HOGANY & PLAIN FURNI-
  TURE, made in a superior man-
  ner, and of the best seasoned
  materials, among which, are
  Secretaries, columned and plain,
  Bureaus, Clock Cases, High Post,
  French, Fancy and Plain Bed-
  steads, Tables, Stands, &c. . . .
  [offers to take in payment]
  Cherry and Poplar Plank and
  Scantling . . . [has commenced
  making] WOOL CARDING
  MACHINES . . . CLOCKS
  cleaned and repaired, and for sale
  as usual. . . ."

1771
SMITH, GEORGE. Cabinetmaker.
  Born c. 1819, Ohio; w. 1850,
  Aboit Twp., Allen Co. (C)

1772
SMITH, GEORGE M.
Cabinetmaker.
  W. 1820, Brownsville, Union Co.
  In the industrial census Mr. Smith
  listed the prices of his wares as
  follows: "Bureaus $14; Cup-
  boards $14; Desks $23; Candle
  stands & Cradles $3; Breakfast

Tables $5; Dining Tables $8;
Clock Cases $20; Coffins from
Six to Ten Dollars; Side boards
$80; Bedsteads from $2.50 to Ten
Dollars." He remarked "Establishment has been and now is new
and in good order, and the demand
for Articles good and Sales Toler-
able Dull because money is
scarce."

1773
SMITH, GEORGE M., SR.
Cabinetmaker.
  Born c. 1798, South Carolina; w.
  1850, New Albany, Floyd Co. In
  same household, George M. Smith,
  Jr., cabinetmaker. (C)

1774
SMITH, GEORGE M., JR.
Cabinetmaker.
  Born c. 1825, New York; w. 1850,
  New Albany, Floyd Co. Lived
  with George M. Smith, Sr., cabi-
  netmaker. (C)

1775
SMITH, GUILFORD.
Cabinetmaker.
  Born c. 1831; w. 1850, Lafayette,
  Tippecanoe Co. (C)

1776
SMITH, HENRY. Cabinetmaker.
  W. 1839, Brookville, Franklin Co.
  Adv. in *Indiana American* 26 July
  1839, "MAHOGANY FURNI-
  TURE: *No. 1, New Building
  north east of public square,* Henry
  Smith, . . . intends to keep con-
  stantly for sale, all descriptions
  of CABINET FURNITURE,
  such as *Side Boards, Plain and
  Fancy Bureaus, Breakfast, Dining
  Side and Pier Tables;* Fancy,

Common *and French Bedsteads*;
Stands and sofas. . . . Any of
the above articles will be made to
order at the shortest notice. A
good supply on hand." Also adv.
that he wished to purchase cabinet
lumber, including cherry.

1777
SMITH, JACOB. Cabinetmaker.
    Born c. 1785, Pennsylvania; w.
    1850, Logan Twp., Fountain Co.
    (C)

1778
SMITH, JAMES. Chairmaker.
    Born c. 1801, Kentucky; w. 1850,
    Greencastle, Putnam Co. (C)

1779
SMITH, JAMES. Chairmaker.
    Born c. 1804, Pennsylvania; w.
    1850, Hagerstown, Wayne Co.
    (C)

1780
SMITH, JOHN. Cabinetmaker.
    W. 1822, Brookville, Franklin Co.
    Adv. in *Brookville Enquirer*, 24
    September 1822: "Two Journey-
    men To the Cabinet business may
    find employment by applying im-
    mediately to the subscriber in
    Brookville. JOHN SMITH."

1781
SMITH, JOHN. Cabinetmaker.
    Born c. 1818, Germany; w. 1850,
    Montgomery Twp., Gibson Co.
    (C)

1782
SMITH, JOHN. Cabinetmaker.
    Born c. 1790, Pennsylvania; w.
    1850, Wayne Twp., Randolph Co.
    (C)

1783
SMITH, JOHN F. Cabinetmaker.
    Born c. 1826, Ohio; w. 1850,
    Chester Twp., Wabash Co. In
    same household, William Krisher
    and David M. Story, cabinet-
    makers. (C)

1784
SMITH, JOSEPH. Cabinetmaker.
    Born c. 1825, Pennsylvania; w.
    1850, New Albany, Floyd Co. (C)

1785
SMITH, LEWIS (LOUIS).
Chairmaker.
    Born c. 1826, Ohio; w. 1850,
    Harrison Twp., Vigo Co. In the
    same household was George
    Lycan, chairmaker. These two
    men operated a shop whose raw
    materials included "8 Stands
    Timber" and paint. In 1850 they
    made 800 chairs valued at $900.
    (C, MC)

1786
SMITH, MOSES. Cabinetmaker.
    W. 1850, Greenville Twp., Floyd
    Co. Two men worked in this
    shop; in 1850 they made furniture
    worth $1,000. (MC)

1787
SMITH, REUBEN. Cabinetmaker.
    Born c. 1804, Kentucky; w. 1850,
    Greenville Twp., Floyd Co. (C)

1788
SMITH, RICHARD.
Cabinetmaker.
    Born c. 1813, Ohio; w. 1839-1850-,
    Lafayette, Tippecanoe Co. In
    January 1839 he was a member of
    the firm of Smith & Heatly, q.v.
    Later that year he was listed alone

at the same address: Ohio between Ferry and North streets. (C)

1789
SMITH, ROBERT. Cabinetmaker. Born c. 1829, Indiana; w. 1850, Pleasant Twp., Johnson Co. (C)

1790
SMITH, S. J. Chairmaker.
W. 1839-1840, Lafayette, Tippecanoe Co. Adv. in *Lafayette Free Press* 30 September 1840 and in the *Indiana Eagle* 2 January 1839 that he carried on a Windsor chair making and painting business. For a brief period in early 1840 he advertised with a partner as Smith & Kelley. His shop was on Mississippi between North and Brown streets in Lafayette.

1791
SMITH, STEPHEN. Chairmaker.
Born c. 1810; w. 1850, Lafayette, Tippecanoe Co. (C)

1792
SMITH, T. I.—*see* SMITH, THOMAS I.

1793
SMITH, THOMAS.
Cabinetmaker and turner.
Born c. 1785, England; w. 1837-50, Evansville, Vanderburgh Co. In 1837 he was said to be operating a "large cabinet making establishment." In 1850 Charles Smith, cabinetmaker, lived in his household. John Ingle, Jr., learned the cabinetmaking trade from Thomas Smith. (C, TH 19)

1794
SMITH, THOMAS I.
Cabinetmaker.
Born c. 1819, Ohio; w. 1850, Rush County. (C) *See also* SMITH, A. K. & T. I.

1795
SMITH, WASHINGTON.
Chairmaker.
Born c. 1828, Ohio; w. 1850, Franklin Twp., Montgomery Co. (C)

1796
SMITH, WESTLEY.
Cabinetmaker.
Born c. 1815, New Jersey; w. 1850, Salem, Washington Co. Working with him were William Jones and William Emery, cabinetmakers. In 1850 these three men made furniture worth $2,000. (C, MC)

1797
SMITH, WILLIAM.
Cabinetmaker.
Born c. 1827, Georgia; w. 1850, Brown Twp., Hancock Co. His apprentice Robert Haney lived in the same household. (C)

1798
SMITH, ZEBULON C.
Cabinetmaker.
Born c. 1807, Kentucky; w. 1850, Orleans Twp., Orange Co. (C)

1799
SMITH & HEATLY.
Cabinetmakers.
Richard Smith and —— Heatly; w. 1839, Lafayette, Tippecanoe Co. Adv. in *Indiana Eagle* 2 January 1839. Later in the year Richard

Smith was listed alone at the same address: Ohio between Ferry and North streets.

1800
SMITH & KELLEY. Windsor chairmakers and painters.

S. J. Smith and —— Kelley; w. 1840, Lafayette, Tippecanoe Co. Smith, q.v., listed alone in 1839 and later in 1840. Smith & Kelley had their shop on Mississippi between North and Brown streets in Lafayette (*Indiana Eagle,* January 1840).

1800a
SMITH & PALMITER.
Cabinetmakers.

W. 1822-, Richmond, Wayne Co. Adv. in *Weekly Intelligencer* 2 February 1822: "Smith & Palmiter, CABINET-MAKERS, wish to inform their friends and customers, that they carry on the CABINET BUSINESS, *in the town of Richmond, one door North of the Brewery,* where they keep on hand, a supply of CLOCK CASES, &c. well made, and of the best materials. . . ."

1801
SNELLING, ELLIOTT.
Cabinetmaker.

Born c. 1827, Indiana; w. 1850, New Harmony, Posey Co. (C)

1802
SNELLING, ENOCH.
Cabinetmaker.

Born c. 1824, Indiana; w. 1850, New Harmony, Posey Co. (C)

1803
SNODGRASS, ADDISON.
Cabinetmaker.

Born c. 1830, Indiana; w. 1850, Vernon Twp., Washington Co. (C)

1804
SNODGRASS, NATHAN.
Cabinetmaker.

Born c. 1818, Kentucky; w. 1850, Sugar Creek Twp., Hancock Co. Lived with George Robinson, cabinetmaker. (C)

1805
SNYDER, CHARLES C.
Chairmaker.

Born c. 1820, Germany; w. 1850, Noblesville, Hamilton Co. (C)

1806
SOUFRAIN, ISAAC. Chairmaker.
Born c. 1817, Pennsylvania; w. 1850, Wayne Twp., Wayne Co. (C)

1807
SPALDEN, WILLIAM.
Cabinetmaker.

Born c. 1821, Indiana; w. 1850, Barr Twp., Daviess Co. (C)

1808
SPARKLIN, BARTON.
Cabinetmaker.

Born c. 1817, Maryland; w. 1850, Elkhart Twp., Elkhart Co. (C)

1809
SPECHT, CHARLES.
Cabinetmaker.

Born c. 1819, Germany; w. 1850, Haw Creek Twp., Bartholomew Co. (C)

1810
SPEERS, CHENEY. Bed maker and wheelmaker.

> W. 1820, Brownsville, Fayette (now Union) Co. (MC) *See also* CHURCH, UZZIEL, and CHENEY SPEERS.

1811
SPENCER, J.—*see* SPENCER, WILLIAM & J.

1812
SPENCER, JAMES. Chairmaker.

> Born c. 1797, Pennsylvania; w. 1850, Knox Twp., Jay Co. (C)

1813
SPENCER, JOHN W. Cabinetmaker.

> Born c. 1807, Virginia; w. 1850, Orange Twp., Fayette Co. Two men worked in this shop, using machinery powered by horse. In 1850 they made 60 bedsteads, 10 bureaus, 15 tables and three dozen washboards. (C, MC)

1814
SPENCER, WILLIAM & J. Cabinetmakers.

> William Spencer was born c. 1824, Kentucky; w. 1850, Madison, Jefferson Co. Five men worked in this shop; in 1850 they made furniture valued at $4,000. (C, MC)

1815
SPERRY, GEORGE, SR. Cabinetmaker.

> Born c. 1802, Germany; w. 1850, Cambridge City, Wayne Co. (C)

1816
SPIEGLE, AUGUSTUS. Cabinetmaker.

> Born c. 1822, Germany; w. 1850, Lawrenceburg, Dearborn Co. (C)

1817
SPIEGLE, CHRISTIAN. Cabinetmaker.

> Born c. 1820, Germany; w. 1850, Lawrenceburg, Dearborn Co. (C)

1818
SPONBERG (SPONBURGER), HENRY. Cabinetmaker.

> Born c. 1810, England; w. 1850, Greenwood, Johnson Co. (C, CH 29)

1819
SPURGIN, ISACH. Cabinetmaker.

> Born c. 1808, North Carolina; w. 1850, Vienna Twp., Scott Co. (C)

1820
STANLEY, CHESTERFIELD. Cabinetmaker.

> Born c. 1818, England; w. 1850, Lynn Twp., Posey Co. (C)

1821
STANLEY, JAMES W. Cabinetmaker.

> Born c. 1829, Indiana; w. 1850, Stony Creek Twp., Henry Co. (C)

1822
STARR, JEREMIAH. Cabinetmaker.

> Born c. 1832, Maryland; w. 1850, Bluffton, Wells Co. (C)

1823
STARR, JOHN. Cabinetmaker.
Born c. 1818, North Carolina; w.
1850, Mooresville, Morgan Co.
(C)

1824
START, AUGUSTUS.
Cabinetmaker.
Born c. 1821, Massachusetts; w.
1850, Vanderburgh Co. (C)

1825
STEDE, BENJAMIN.
Cabinetmaker.
Born c. 1817, Maryland; w. 1850,
Camden, Carroll Co. In same
household, Bergen Wescoat, cabi-
netmaker. (C)

1826
STEEL, THOMAS. Chairmaker.
Born c. 1805, Kentucky; w. 1850,
Vanderburgh Co. (C)

1827
STEFFEE, JAMES.
Cabinetmaker.
Born c. 1814, Virginia; w. 1850,
Knox Co. (C)

1828
STEFFEY, CLAYTON.
Cabinetmaker.
Born c. 1816, Tennessee; w. 1850,
Mount Tabor, Monroe Co. (C)

1829
STELL (or STELT), ELI.
Cabinetmaker.
Born c. 1818, Pennsylvania; w.
1850, Harrison Twp., Miami Co.
(C)

1830
STEPHENS, GEORGE. Cabinetmaking, chairmaking, and upholstery.

W. 1838, Mishawaka, St. Joseph
Co. Adv. in *South Bend Free
Press* 16 June through 15 Septem-
ber 1838: "New Establishment—
Cabinet, Chair Making and Up-
holstery . . . New Shop . . .
Main St. . . . one door north of
Mishawaka Hotel. . . CABINET
FURNITURE, such as Side
Boards, Escritoires, Lockers &
Bookcases, Centre Tables, Dining,
Pembroke, Dressing and Work
Tables, Candle, Work & Wash
Stands, Different kinds of Bed
Steads, Mahogany & Walnut
Chairs, Windsor Rocking, Sewing
& Children's Chairs, Etc." Has
obtained in the East mahogany,
black walnut and "French Veneers,
. . . hard wove curled hair and
hair cloth."

1831
STEVENS, ELISHA.
Chairmaker.
Born c. 1824; w. 1850, Jefferson-
ville, Clark Co. Lived with
William Guy, chairmaker. (C)

1832
STEVENSON, BENJAMIN F.
Cabinetmaker.
Born c. 1802, Ohio; w. 1850, Clay
Twp., Owen Co. (C)

1833
STEVENSON, JOHN.
Chairmaker.
Born c. 1826, Pennsylvania; w.
1850, Pike Twp., Marion Co. (C)

1834
STEWART, ALLEN.
Cabinetmaker.

Born c. 1804, Pennsylvania; w.
1850, Washington Twp., Miami
Co. (C)

1835
STEWART, C. C. Cabinetmaker.
Born c. 1805; w. 1850, Lafayette,
Tippecanoe Co. (C)

1836
STEWART, CHARLES.
Cabinetmaker.
Born c. 1804, Ohio; w. 1850,
Washington Twp., Tippecanoe Co.
(C)

1837
STEWART, HILL. Chairmaker.
Born c. 1813, Ohio; w. 1850,
Mount Vernon, Posey Co. (C)

1838
STEWART, LOUIS B.
Cabinetmaker.
Born c. 1820, Crawford Co.; w.
1850, Liberty Twp., Crawford Co.
(C)

1839
STIFLER, JOHN F.
Cabinetmaker.
Born c. 1829, Pennsylvania; w.
1850, Liberty Twp., Delaware Co.
(C)

1840
STILLWAGGON, SMITH.
Chairmaker.
Born c. 1825, Pennsylvania; w.
1850, Washington Twp., Putnam
Co. In same household, Thomas
Stillwaggon, chairmaker. (C)

1841
STILLWAGGON, THOMAS.
Chairmaker.
Born c. 1830, Pennsylvania; w.

1850, Washington Twp., Putnam
Co. Lived with Smith Stillwaggon, chairmaker. (C)

1842
STITES, JOSEPH. Cabinetmaker.
Born c. 1815, Ohio; w. 1850,
Jackson Twp., Spencer Co. (C)

1843
STOCKWELL, JOHN.
Cabinetmaker.
Born c. 1815, Indiana; w. 1850,
Charlestown Twp., Clark Co. In
same household, William Cham-
bers, cabinetmaker. (C)

1844
STOCKWELL, SAMUEL.
Cabinetmaker.
Born c. 1822, Indiana; w. 1850,
Charlestown Twp., Clark Co. (C)

1845
STOGDON, BENJAMIN.
Cabinetmaker.
Born c. 1798, Pennsylvania; w.
1850, Harrison Co. (C)

1846
STONE, DANIEL C.
Cabinetmaker.
Born c. 1815, New York; w.
1850, Center Twp., Howard Co.
(C)

1847
STONE, E. S. Cabinetmaker.
Born c. 1825, Indiana; w. 1850,
Orange Twp., Fayette Co. (C)

1848
STONE, JOHN. Cabinetmaker.
Born c. 1811, Pennsylvania; w.
1850, Indianapolis, Marion Co.
(Because the "Mr. *Sloan*" of the
firm of Espy & Sloan, q.v., does
not appear in the Marion County

census of 1850, it is possible that John *Stone's* entry may be an error on the part of the census taker. *See* SLOAN, JOHN.) (C)

1849
STONEBRAKER, JOHN.
Chairmaker.
> Born c. 1805, Pennsylvania; w. 1850, Jefferson Twp., Wayne Co. (C)

1850
STONTION (or STOUTION), LEMUEL. Cabinetmaker.
> Born c. 1795, Virginia; w. 1850, Shelbyville, Shelby Co. (C)

1851
STORY, DAVID M.
Cabinetmaker.
> Born c. 1832, New York; w. 1850, Chester Twp., Wabash Co. Lived with John F. Smith, cabinetmaker. (C)

1852
STOUT, JONATHAN.
Cabinetmaker.
> Born c. 1818, Indiana; w. 1850, Stony Creek Twp., Randolph Co. (C)

1853
STOVER, DAVID.
Cabinetmaker.
> Born c. 1817, Virginia; w. 1850, Portage Twp., St. Joseph Co. Sherman Turner, cabinetmaker, lived in his household; altogether there were three men working in this shop. In 1850, they produced cabinet ware valued at $1,500. (MC) *See also* W I L S O N , ABRAHAM.

1854
STOVER, MATHIAS (MITHIAS). Cabinetmaker.
> Born 1802; 1832, arrived in South Bend, St. Joseph Co., from Virginia; w. -1838-1850-, South Bend; died 1879. Adv. in *South Bend Free Press,* April through July 1838: "Cabinet and Chair Factory . . . Keeps constantly on hand . . . cabinetware at his well known stand opposite the printing office, on Michigan St. . . . He also has connected with the above business, an extensive CHAIR FACTORY . . . keeps on hand . . . Chairs, settees, etc., made and finished in the best style, warranted good & cheap-cheap-CHEAP!!!" Free repair offered for his own merchandise if defective. Adv. *ibid.* November through December 1839: "Chair Factory and House & Sign Painting . . . Windsor, & Flag Bottom Chairs, and other articles, at Mr. M. Stover's Cabinet Shop on Mich. St. . . . Sign & House Painting, and Paper Hanging, will be attended to by him, to order, with neatness and dispatch." This advertisement was signed by Leonard Hain. *See* HAINES, LENARD.
>
> In addition to his cabinet and chair business, Mr. Stover was also a surveyor and served as the city engineer. He was an amateur composer, and in the Northern Indiana Historical Society museum is a hymn book for which he wrote either words or music for many hymns; that collection also includes a portrait of Mr. Stover. (C)

1855
STRAND, THOMAS V.
Cabinetmaker.
> Born c. 1824, Indiana; w. 1850,
> New Albany, Floyd Co. (C)

1856
STRETCHER, JOSEPH I.
Chair factory.
> W. 1836-1842-, I n d i a n a p o l i s,
> Marion Co. Adv. in *Indiana
> Democrat* 20 July 1836:
> "WANTED, TWO apprentices to
> the Chair Making and Ornamental
> Painting [business], to two good
> boys a first rate opportunity will
> be given to learn the above busi-
> ness in all its various branches.
> Apply at the third door above the
> bank at the Chair Manufactory of
> JOSEPH   J.   STRETCHER."
> Adv. in *Indiana Journal* 22 Oc-
> tober 1841: "EAGLE CHAIR
> FACTORY/The Subscriber an-
> nounces to the public that he has
> removed his Chair Establishment
> to the 2 story building on Wash-
> ington street, one door west of the
> Indiana Journal office and nearly
> opposite the Post Office, where he
> keeps constantly on hand a large
> and splendid assortment of **Fancy**
> and Windsor Chairs, as follows:
> Black Walnut Chairs; Upholstered
> do [ditto]; Large Cane back and
> Cane seat Rocking Chairs; Large
> Boston style Rocking do., The
> most approved patterns of Uphol-
> stered Rocking do.; Maple Stools,
> cane seats, for Hotels or **Canal**
> Boats; Upholstered Lounges; Cane
> seat do; Large Writing Chairs;
> Fancy Grecian Cane seat do; Fan-
> cy Grecian Flag seat Chairs; Reg-
> ular Sweep Fancy do; Round post
> Cane seat do; do do Flag do do;
> Large Windsor Rocking do;
> Small do do do; Windsor Scroll
> Top do; do Slatback do; do Com-
> mon do; do Table do; do Chil-
> dren's do; do Settees of all pat-
> terns. P.S. *Cabinet Furniture,*
> carved or plain, kept constantly
> on hand. *Sofa Springs* also kept
> constantly on hand. All orders
> from a distance will be punctually
> attended to, and neatly pack[ed].
> JOSEPH   I.   STRETCHER."
> Adv. *ibid.* 28 January 1842, for
> a cabinetmaker and a turner.

1857
STRIKER, JACOB W.
Cabinetmaker.
> Born c. 1804, New Jersey; **w.**
> 1850, Parke Co. In same house-
> hold, Vincent P. Bonsal, cabinet⸍
> maker. (C)

1858
STRINGER, LINBRIDGE (?).
Cabinetmaker.
> Born c. 1813, Kentucky; w. 1850,
> Jackson Twp., Putnam Co. (C)

1859
STRINGER, WILLIAM A.
Chairmaker.
> Born c. 1811, Kentucky; w. 1850,
> Cloverdale Twp., Putnam Co. (C)

1860
STROBELL, JOHN H.
Cabinetmaker.
> Born c. 1814, Germany; w. 1850,
> Eel Twp., Cass Co. (C)

1861
STROHM, EARNESTUS.
Cabinetmaker.
> Born c. 1810, Germany; w. 1850,
> Winchester, Randolph Co. (C)

1862
STRONG, E. B.
Chairmaker and cabinetmaker.
   Born c. 1811, New York; w.
   1838-1850, La Porte, La Porte Co.
   Adv. in *La Porte County Whig*
   20 June 1838: "CHAIR WARE
   HOUSE. The subscriber, recently from the city of N. York, would
   respectfully inform the inhabitants
   of LaPorte and vicinity, that he
   has opened a CHAIR WARE
   HOUSE . . . he warrants his
   work to be finished equal to any
   in New York city. Also sign
   painting executed with neatness
   and dispatch . . . E.B.
   STRONG." By 1850 there were
   six men working in his shop;
   paint was included in the list of
   their raw materials. That year
   they made 1,000 chairs worth
   $1,000 and cabinet furniture valued
   at $3,000. (MC)

1863
STRONG, N. R.
Cabinetmaker and chairmaker.
   Born c. 1822, New York; w.
   1850, Centre Twp., Porter Co. In
   same household, Julian Hatch, also
   cabinetmaker and chairmaker. (C)

1864
STROUP, GEORGE.
Cabinetmaker.
   Born c. 1814, Germany; w. 1850,
   Portage Twp., St. Joseph Co. (C)

1865
STUDY, MARTIN. Cabinetmaker.
   Born c. 1814, Maryland; w. 1850,
   Hagerstown, Wayne Co. (C)

1866
STUDY, SAMUEL.
Cabinetmaker.
   Born c. 1825, Indiana; w. 1850,
   Hagerstown, Wayne Co. (C)

1867
STURLTON, FREDERICK.
Cabinetmaker.
   Born c. 1821, Germany; w. 1850,
   Indianapolis, Marion Co. (C)

1868
STURNAHAN, JOHN.
Chairmaker.
   Born c. 1824, Ohio; w. 1850,
   Tippecanoe Twp., Carroll Co.
   Lived with Matthew Sturnahan,
   chairmaker. (C)

1869
STURNAHAN, MATTHEW.
Chairmaker.
   Born c. 1816, Ohio; w. 1850,
   Tippecanoe Twp., Carroll Co. In
   same household, John Sturnahan,
   chairmaker. (C)

1870
SUDLOW, PHILIP. Painter.
   Born c. 1833, Kentucky; w. 1850,
   New Albany, Floyd Co. Lived
   with George W. Porter, cabinet-
   maker. (C)

1871
SULLINGER, THOMAS.
Cabinetmaker.
   Born c. 1811, Indiana; w. 1850,
   Knox Co. (C)

1872
SULLINGER, WILLIAM.
Cabinetmaker.
   Born c. 1825, Indiana; w. 1850,
   Knox Co. (C)

1873
SUMMER, SELBY.
Cabinetmaker.
    Born c. 1805, Maryland; w. 1850,
    Sugar Creek Twp., Montgomery
    Co. (C)

1874
SUMNER, ALVA. Cabinetmaker.
    Born c. 1828, Ohio; w. 1850,
    Shawnee Twp., Fountain Co. (C)

1875
SUMPTER, SETH. Chairmaker.
    W. -1824, Brookville, Franklin Co.
    Adv. in *Brookville Enquirer*, 25
    September 1824: "LOOK OUT
    FOR WOLVES IN SHEEP'S
    CLOTHING. A Man (as he
    called himself) by the name of
    Seth Sumpter, A chairmaker by
    trade, boarded with me for five
    weeks past, and promised that I
    should have my demand for all
    incidental expenses knowing his
    employers to be men of stability,
    every attention was rendered unto
    him: Notwithstanding the afore-
    said Seth, has absconded and to
    my loss ten dollars . . . ."

1876
SUTPHEN, M. L.
Cabinetmaker.
    Born c. 1823, New York; w.
    1850, Marshall Co. (C) *See*
    SUTPHEN & HAVENS.

1877
SUTPHEN & HAVENS.
Cabinetmakers.
    M. L. Sutphen and H. H.
    Havens; w. 1850, Marshall Co.
    In 1850 they made "Bedsteads &
    Tables &c," worth $1,000. (MC)

1878
SWAIM, CHRISTOPHER.
Cabinetmaker.
    Born c. 1816, North Carolina;
    w. 1850, Spiceland Twp., Henry
    Co. Two men worked in this
    shop; in 1850 they made 32
    bureaus and 40 tables. (C, MC)

1879
SWAIM, EDWIN. Cabinetmaker.
    W. 1850, Spiceland Twp., Henry
    Co. Three men worked in his
    shop; in 1850 they made 40
    bureaus and 50 tables. (MC)

1880
SWAIN, JOB. Cabinetmaker.
    Born 1806, Tennessee; 1815, ar-
    rived in Wayne Co.; 1828, arrived
    in Muncie, Delaware Co. He was
    apprenticed to his father-in-law,
    James Hodge, and before 1848 was
    a member of the firm of Notting-
    ham & Swain, q.v. (CH 41)

1881
SWAMP, LEWIS. Cabinetmaker.
    Born c. 1820, Kentucky; w. 1850,
    Brown Twp., Ripley Co. (C)

1882
SWANK, DAVID. Cabinetmaker.
    Born c. 1805, Pennsylvania; w.
    1850, Peru, Miami Co. (C)

1883
SWRING (?), ICHOBOD W.
Chairmaker.
    Born c. 1803, New Jersey; w.
    1850, West Greenfield, La Grange
    Co. (C)

1884
SYMINGTON, JOHN.
Cabinetmaker.
    W. before 1842, Hartford City,

Blackford Co. He was the first cabinetmaker in Hartford City, but moved from there before 1842. (CH 5)

1885
TANNER, JOSEPH. Chairmaker. Born c. 1828, Pennsylvania; w. 1850, New Albany, Floyd Co. Lived with George W. Porter, cabinetmaker. (C)

1886
TATE, WILLIAM. Carpenter, lumber merchant, and forwarding agent. Born 1792, Boston; 1814, to Lawrenceburg, Dearborn Co. Died 7 October 1875. The local newspapers carried advertisements for "William Tate & Son, Lumber" in 1839; by 1846 they advertised "William Tate, Commission and forwarding merchant." Furniture known: sewing table finely made (*see* Plate VIII); child's chest, c. 1830, made of curly maple, and mention of a dresser, tilt-top table, and secretary with writing shelf (*Indianapolis Star*, 21 April 1940).

1887
TAYLOR, DAVID. Cabinetmaker. Born c. 1827, Indiana; w. 1850, Dublin, Wayne Co. Lived with Jesse Pike, cabinetmaker, q.v. (C)

1888
TAYLOR, ELEAZER H. Cabinetmaker. Born c. 1811, New Hampshire; w. 1850, Orleans Twp., Orange Co. In same household, Francis M. Taylor, cabinetmaker. (C)

1889
TAYLOR, FRANCIS M. Cabinetmaker. Born c. 1833, Indiana; w. 1850, Orleans Twp., Orange Co. Lived with Eleazer H. Taylor, cabinetmaker. (C)

1890
TAYLOR, JOHN. Cabinetmaker. W. 1820, Jackson Twp., Fayette Co. He worked alone. The prices of his products were given as follows: "Bureaus $16; desks $30; Secretaries $40; Cupboards $15; Tables $8." The census taker noted that the "Establishment is new & small and in Tolerable Condition. . . ." (MC)

1891
TAYLOR, JOHN. Cabinetmaker. Born c. 1820, Kentucky; w. 1850, Washington Twp., Washington Co. Lived with Robert Harned, cabinetmaker. (C)

1892
TAYLOR, JONATHON. Chairmaker. Born c. 1792, Massachusetts; w. 1850, North Madison, Jefferson Co. (C)

1893
TAYLOR, JOSEPH. Cabinetmaker. Born c. 1800, Ireland; w. 1850, Honey Creek Twp., Vigo Co. In same household, William Taylor, cabinetmakers. (C) *See also* TAYLOR & DAVEY, possibly same.

1894
TAYLOR, LUCIUS. Cabinetmaker and chairmaker.

W. 1830, Lawrenceburg, Dearborn Co. Adv. in *Indiana Palladium* 30 January 1830: "CABINET & CHAIR SHOP/LUCIUS TAYLOR, RESPECTFULLY informs the public, that he has opened a shop for the manufacture of all kinds of *Cabinet Furniture*. He also will make all kinds of Chairs, such as Windsor, Fancy and Split Bottom. He flatters himself, from the experience he has had in the business, and from the fact of his having employed a first rate workman, directly from New York, that he will be able to give general satisfaction."

1895

TAYLOR, LUCIUS. Chairmaker. Born c. 1797, Massachusetts; w. 1850, Center Twp., Howard Co. (C)

1896

TAYLOR, WILLIAM. Cabinetmaker.
Born c. 1834, Indiana; w. 1850, Honey Creek Twp., Vigo Co. Lived with Joseph Taylor, cabinetmaker. (C) *See also* TAYLOR & DAVEY, possibly same.

1897

TAYLOR & DAVEY. Cabinetmakers.
Joseph and/or William Taylor and John Davey; w. -1826, Terre Haute, Vigo Co. Succeeded by Davey & East, q.v.

1897a

TEAS, GIBSON. Turner and cabinetmaker.
W. -1834-, Richmond, Wayne Co. Adv. in the *Palladium,* 3 January 1834: "The subscriber continues to carry on the turning business . . . . he intends keeping on hand an assortment of bed posts ready turned, which he will sell low." Adv. 4 July 1835 that he had joined with G. S. Shearman in cabinetmaking but would still carry on his turning business.

1898

TEITHEL, AUGUST. Cabinetmaker.
Born c. 1814, Germany; w. 1850, Wayne Twp., Allen Co. (C)

1899

TEMPLETON, THOMAS. Cabinetmaker.
Born c. 1820, Ohio; w. 1850, Williamsport, Warren Co. (C)

1900

THAYER, ALVIN. Cabinetmaker. Born c. 1817, Maryland; w. 1850, Peru, Miami Co. (C) *See* LOW & THAYER.

1901

THITSET, JOHN. Cabinetmaker. Born c. 1814, Kentucky; w. 1850, Jackson Twp., Fayette Co. (C)

1902

THOM, WILLIAM W. Cabinetmaker.
Born c. 1819, Indiana; w. 1850, North Madison, Jefferson Co. (C)

1903

THOMAS, DAVID. Painter.
Born c. 1833, Pennsylvania; w. 1850, New Castle, Henry Co. Lived with John Shroyer, painter and chairmaker. (C)

1904
THOMAS, DAVID. Cabinetmaker.
Born c. 1826, Indiana; w. 1850,
Marrs Twp., Posey Co. (C)

1905
THOMAS, EDWARD B.
Cabinetmaker.
Born c. 1813, Maryland; w. 1850,
Connersville, Fayette Co. (C)

1906
THOMAS, ELIAS. Cabinetmaker.
Born c. 1829, Ohio; w. 1850,
Washington Twp., Hamilton Co.
(C)

1907
THOMAS, JAMES. Cabinetmaker.
Born c. 1831, Indiana; w. 1850,
New Garden Twp., Wayne Co.
Lived with Harvey Davis, cabi-
netmaker, q.v. (C)

1908
THOMAS, SAMUEL.
Cabinetmaker.
Born c. 1825, Ohio; w. 1850,
Ripley Twp., Montgomery Co.
(C)

1909
THOMAS, SOLOMON.
Cabinetmaker.
W. 1824-, Fountain City, Wayne
Co. (CH 34)

1910
THOMAS, WILLIAM B.
Cabinetmaker.
Born c. 1813, Ohio; w. 1850,
Ripley Twp., Montgomery Co. In
same household, William P.
Washburn, cabinetmaker. (C)

1911
THOMPSON, DAVID D.
Cabinetmaker.
Born c. 1817, Kentucky; w. 1850,
Helt Twp., Vermillion Co. (C)

1912
THOMPSON, DAVID R.
Cabinetmaker.
Born c. 1820, Tennessee; w. 1850,
Brown Twp., Washington Co.
(C)

1913
THOMPSON, G. A. Cabinetmaker.
W. 1850, Steuben Co.; three men
worked in this shop. Their raw
materials included cherry. In 1850
they produced $1,000 worth of
goods. (MC)

1914
THOMPSON, IRA. Cabinetmaker.
Born c. 1812, New York; w.
1850, Bluffton, Wells Co. (C)

1915
THOMPSON, JESSE.
Cabinetmaker.
Born c. 1828, North Carolina; w.
1850, Danville, Hendricks Co. (C)

1916
THOMPSON, LEVI.
Cabinetmaker.
Born c. 1825, New York; w.
1850, Angola, Steuben Co. (C)

1917
THOMPSON, ROBERT H.
Cabinetmaker.
Born c. 1834, Pennsylvania; w.
1850, Shawnee Twp., Fountain Co.
Lived with John Marr, cabinet-
maker, q.v. (C)

1918
THORNBURG, JONATHAN W.
Cabinetmaker.
   Born c. 1826, North Carolina; w.
   1850, Greensboro Twp., Henry Co.
   (C)

1919
THORNTON, ALPHEUS.
Chairmaker.
   Born c. 1815, New York; w. 1850,
   Portage Twp., St. Joseph Co. (C)

1920
THRASHER, WILLIAM.
Cabinetmaker.
   Born c. 1826, Ohio; w. 1850,
   Noble Twp., Noble Co. (C)

1921
THROCKMORTON, SAMUEL.
Cabinetmaker.
   Born c. 1814, New Jersey; w. 1850,
   Union Twp., Johnson Co. (C)

1922
TILFORD, HENRY.
Cabinetmaker.
   Born c. 1826, Indiana; w. 1850,
   New Washington, Clark Co. (C)

1923
TILFORD, J. M. & M. C.
Cabinetmakers and mattress makers.
   W. 1850, Madison, Jefferson Co.
   Five men employed in shop; raw
   materials listed were lumber, glue,
   varnish, and ticking. In 1850 they
   produced furniture worth $5,000
   and mattresses valued at $600.
   (MC)

1924
TILFORD, JOHN S.
Cabinetmaker.
   Born c. 1812, Indiana; w. 1841-

1850, Franklin, Johnson Co. Three
men worked in this shop; in 1850
they made furniture worth $2,000.
(C, MC, CH 29)

1925
TILFORD, JOSEPH M.
Cabinetmaker.
   Born 11 November 1811, Scott
   Co., Kentucky; 1816-1828, living
   in Jefferson Co., Indiana; 1829-
   1832, apprenticed to John G. Henderson, Salem, Washington Co.;
   1832-1850, cabinet business, Madison, Jefferson Co. From 1850 to
   1853 he ran a farm west of Hanover, and in 1853 moved to
   Indianapolis, where he became a
   publisher. He was still living in
   1876. (CH 39) See TILFORD,
   J. M. & M. C., probably same.

1926
TILFORD, MILTON C.
Cabinetmaker.
   Born c. 1819, Indiana; w. 1850,
   Madison, Jefferson Co. (C) See
   TILFORD, J. M. & M. C., proba-
   bly same.

1927
TILLER, JAMES. Chairmaker.
   Born c. 1822, Virginia; w. 1850,
   Wayne Twp., Henry Co. (C)

1928
TINKELPAUGH, WILLIAM.
Cabinetmaker.
   Born c. 1820, Pennsylvania; w.
   1850, Milford Twp., La Grange
   Co. (C)

1929
TODD, ROBERT. Cabinetmaker.
   Born c. 1815, Kentucky; w. 1850,
   Franklin Twp., Johnson Co. He
   also had a shop with William

Todd on Noble Street in Greenwood, Johnson Co., which was in operation in the 1840s and continued for twelve years. (C, CH 29)

1930
TODD, THOMAS J.
Cabinetmaker.
Born c. 1800, New York; w. 1850, Morgan Twp., Owen Co. (C)

1931
TODD, WILLIAM. Cabinetmaker. Born c. 1814, Kentucky; w. 1850, Franklin Twp., Johnson Co. He also had a shop with Robert Todd on Noble Street in Greenwood, Johnson Co., which was in operation in the 1840s and continued for twelve years. (C, CH 29)

1932
TOLLBOTT, ALLEN.
Cabinetmaker.
Born c. 1832, Indiana; w. 1850, Centerville, Wayne Co. Lived with Owen Morris, cabinetmaker. (C)

1933
TOTTEN, JAMES. Chairmaker. Born c. 1791, Virginia; w. 1850, Barkley Twp., Jasper Co. (C)

1934
TOWER, BENJAMIN H.
Cabinetmaker.
Born c. 1817, New York; w. 1850, Wayne Twp., Allen Co. His shop employed four men and in 1850 produced items valued at $3,000. He died in 1872. (C, MC)

1935
TOWNSEND, JOHN.
Chairmaker and painter.
Born c. 1801, Kentucky; w. 1850, Chester Twp., Wabash Co. (C)

1936
TRENARY, RICHARD.
Cabinetmaker.
W. -1848-, Jefferson Twp., Wells Co. Said to have made furniture for Thomas Archibald there, including basswood benches and primitive bedsteads. (CH 4)

1936a
TRICHE, CHARLES—see BALL, ISAAC.

1937
TROTTER, GEORGE W.
Cabinetmaker.
Born c. 1815, North Carolina; w. 1850, Jackson Twp., Fountain Co. (C)

1938
TROUT, SIMPSON. Chairmaker. Born c. 1826, Virginia; w. 1850, Washington Twp., Hamilton Co. (C)

1939
TROY, SAMUEL. Cabinetmaker. Born c. 1828, Ohio; w. 1850, Mount Pleasant Twp., Delaware Co. Two men worked in his shop; in 1850 they made 50 tables and bedsteads "&c," worth $500. (C, MC)

1940
TRUEMAN (TRUMAN), EDWARD. Cabinetmaker.
Born c. 1819, Kentucky; w. 1850, Jackson Twp., Washington Co. He worked alone, using machinery

powered by horse. His product in 1850 was furniture worth $800. (C, MC)

1941
TRUESDELL, JOHN.
Cabinetmaker.
   Born c. 1818, New York; w. 1850, Goshen, Elkhart Co. (C)

1942
TRUSSEL, HENRY.
Cabinetmaker.
   Born c. 1832, Ohio; w. 1850, Dalton Twp., Wayne Co. Lived with Solomon Bellhammer, cabinetmaker. (C)

1943
TUCKER, FRANKLIN.
Cabinetmaker.
   Born c. 1804, Kentucky; w. 1850, Fayette Twp., Vigo Co. (C)

1944
TUCKER, SAMUEL.
Cabinetmaker.
   Born c. 1819, Kentucky; w. 1850, Martinsville, Morgan Co. (C)

1945
TUCKER, THOMAS.
Cabinetmaker.
   Born c. 1828, Indiana; w. 1850, Henry Co. (C)

1946
TUCKER & WEAVER.
Cabinetmakers.
   ——Tucker and William W. Weaver; w. 1840, Indianapolis, Marion Co. Successors to Fleming T. Luse, q.v. Succeeded by William W. Weaver working alone, later Weaver & Williams, q.v. Adv. in *Semi-Weekly Journal* 26 November 1840: "CABINET

BUSINESS. The subscribers have taken the well known Cabinet Shop formerly occupied by Fleming T. Luse, where they will punctually attend to all orders entrusted to them . . . [offered use of hearse, made coffins] TUCKER & WEAVER."

1947
TULLOF, ERASTUS M.
Cabinetmaker.
   Born c. 1826, Ohio; w. 1850, Clinton, Vermillion Co. (C)

1948
TURNER, GEORGE. Chairmaker.
   Born c. 1814, Ohio; w. 1850, Muncie, Delaware Co. (C)

1949
TURNER, LEMUEL. Chairmaker.
   Born c. 1823, North Carolina; w. 1850, Marion, Grant Co. In the same household, William Cook, chairmaker. In 1850 Lemuel Turner reported that his establishment had made 50 dozen chairs worth $500. (C, MC)

1950
TURNER, SHERMAN.
Cabinetmaker.
   Born c. 1826, Virginia; w. 1850, Center Twp., St. Joseph Co. (C) Probably the same as man listed below.

1951
TURNER, SHERMAN.
Cabinetmaker.
   Born c. 1825, New York; w. 1850, Portage Twp., St. Joseph Co. Lived with David Stover, cabinetmaker. (C)

1952
TUSH, ELWOOD. Cabinetmaker.
Born c. 1822, Indiana; w. 1850,
Clay Twp., Hendricks Co. (C)

1953
TUTTLE, J. O. B. Chairmaker.
Born c. 1814, Ohio; w. 1850,
Centerville, Wayne Co. (C)

1954
TUTTLE, WILLIAM.
Chairmaker.
Born c. 1810, Virginia; w. 1850,
Jefferson Twp., Miami Co. (C)

1955
TUTWILER, JOHN. Chairmaker.
Born c. 1823, Pennsylvania; w.
1850, Carroll Co. In same household, Allen Braulsfort, cabinetmaker. (C) *See also* TUT-
WILER & DUNKLE.

1956
TUTWILER & DUNKLE.
Chairmakers and cabinetmakers.
John Tutwiler and Jonathan
Dunkle; w. 1850, Carroll Co.
Three men worked in this shop.
In 1850 they produced 40 bureaus,
100 bedsteads, 50 tables, 600 chairs,
and "Other Ware," totaling in
value $3,300. (C, MC)

1957
UEL—*see* ARMSTRONG & UEL.

1958
UHLER, JOHN. Cabinetmaker.
Born c. 1824, Maryland; w. 1850,
Covington, Fountain Co. (C) *See
also* UHLER & GABRIEL.

1959
UHLER & GABRIEL.
Cabinetmakers.
John Uhler and John S. Gabriel;

w. 1850, Covington, Fountain Co.
This shop employed three men;
in 1850 they made 10 bureaus and
"other shop work." (C, MC)

1960
ULLERY, GEORGE.
Turner and chairmaker.
Born c. 1814, Ohio; w. 1850,
Franklin Twp., Kosciusko Co.
(C)

1961
UNDERHILL, CLARKSON.
Cabinetmaker.
Born c. 1820, Tennessee; w. 1850,
Perry Twp., Wayne Co. (C)

1962
UNDERWOOD, JOSEPH.
Chairmaker.
Born c. 1818, New Richmond,
Ohio; w. Felicity, Ohio; w. 1846-
1849, Indianapolis, Marion Co.; w.
1849-1850-, Versailles, Ripley Co.
Made chairs, settees, cradles,
stands, hickory, wooden and woven
splint-seated chairs. Illustration of
rocking chair made by him in
1846 is in the *Indianapolis Star*
1 June 1941. (C)

1963
UNDERWOOD, JOSHUA D.
Cabinetmaker.
Born c. 1819, Indiana; w. 1850,
Westport, Decatur Co. (C)

1964
UNGER, ANDREW.
Cabinetmaker.
Born c. 1817, Pennsylvania; w.
1850, Benton Twp., Elkhart Co.
(C)

1965
UREY, JOHN. Chairmaker.
    Born c. 1830, Indiana; w. 1850,
    Carroll Co. Lived with John Cut-
    ter [Sr.], chairmaker and wheel-
    maker. (C)

1966
VAIL, J. J. Cabinetmaker.
    Born c. 1797, Ohio; w. 1850,
    Madison, Jefferson Co. (C) *See
    also* VAIL & WHITE.

1967
VAIL & WHITE. Cabinetmakers.
    J. J. Vail and ——— White; w.
    1841, Madison, Jefferson Co. Adv.
    in *Republican Banner* 12 May
    1841: "CABINET MAKING
    . . . they continue the Cabinet
    business . . . at their old stand
    on West street, near the Post
    Office, . . . We have now on
    hand a fine assortment of FURNI-
    TURE not inferior to any in the
    city . . . [have hearse, ready
    made coffins] V A I L &
    WHITE."

1968
VALENTINE, JOHN W.
Cabinetmaker.
    Born c. 1829, Indiana; w. 1850,
    Prairie Twp., Henry Co. (C)

1969
VALENTINE, LYMAN.
Chairmaker.
    Born c. 1830, New York; w. 1850,
    Mishawaka, St. Joseph Co. (C)

1970
VAN CLEAVE, MATTHIAS
MOUNT (REV.). Cabinetmaker.
    Born 1810, near Shelbyville, Ken-
    tucky; 1824, arrived 8 miles south
    of Crawfordsville, Montgomery

Co.; w. -1850-, Crawfordsville. In
1850 his shop made furniture
worth $1,000; its equipment in-
cluded a lathe, saw, and boring
machine operated by water power;
his raw materials included paint.
He was in the furniture business
22 years. He also erected a mill,
a carding mill, and a hominy
machine in the town of Browns
Valley. (MC, CH 42)

1971
VANDYKE, JOSEPH.
Cabinetmaker.
    W. 1825, Brookville, Franklin Co.
    Adv. in the *Brookville Inquirer
    and Franklin Republican* 6 April
    1825: "JOSEPH VANDYKE/
    late of the City of Cincinnati/
    WISHES to inform the citizens
    of Brookville and vicinity, that he
    has taken the shop formerly oc-
    cupied by John Brown in this
    place, and intends carrying on the
    Cabinet Business in all its various
    branches; after the newest and
    best modes. Persons wanting work
    in his line, are respectfully solici-
    ted to call and satisfy themselves;
    as he contemplates keeping con-
    stantly on hand, a general assort-
    ment of Furniture of the best
    quality." Adv. *ibid.* 25 October
    1825 for two journeymen cabinet-
    makers.

1972
VANHORN, BEVROD.
Cabinetmaker.
    Born c. 1818, Indiana; w. 1850,
    Harrison Twp., Dearborn Co. (C)

1973
VANHOY, JOHN. Cabinetmaker.
    Born c. 1831, Indiana; w. 1850,

Perry Twp., Martin Co. Lived
with Andrew S. Wood, cabinetmaker. (C)

1974
VANHUIS, HEZAKIAH.
Cabinetmaker.
Born c. 1832, Indiana; w. 1850,
New Garden Twp., Wayne Co.
Lived with Harvey Davis, cabi-
netmaker, q.v. (C)

1975
VAN PELT, NICHOLAS.
Cabinetmaker.
Born c. 1818, Ohio; w. 1850,
Tippecanoe Twp., Carroll Co. In
same household, Robert McTeer,
cabinetmaker. (C)

1976
VAUGHAN, WILLIAM.
Cabinetmaker.
Born c. 1824, Kentucky; w. 1850,
Brownsburg, Hendricks Co. (C)

1977
VEDER, NICHOLAS J.
Chairmaker.
Born c. 1796, New York; w. 1850,
Orange Twp., Fayette Co. (C)

1978
VERBACK, JOHN. Upholsterer.
Born c. 1820, Germany; w. 1850,
New Albany, Floyd Co. (C)

1979
VICKERS, CHRISTIAN S.
Cabinetmaker.
Born c. 1817, Virginia; w. 1850,
Covington, Fountain Co. (C) *See
also* ALLEN & VICKERS.

1980
VICKERS, JAMES. Cabinetmaker.
Born c. 1815, Ohio; w. 1850,
Wayne Twp., Allen Co. (C)

1981
VINES, DANIEL. Cabinetmaker.
Born c. 1813, Pennsylvania; w.
1850, Pine Twp., Warren Co. (C)

1982
VLIET, DANIEL. Cabinetmaker.
Born c. 1832, New Jersey; w.
1850, Washington Twp., Daviess
Co. Lived with Samuel A. Rodar-
mel, cabinetmaker, q.v. (C)

1983
VOSS, LORENZO. Cabinetmaker.
Born c. 1818, Tennessee; w. 1850,
Perry Twp., Lawrence Co. (C)

1984
VOSS, WILLIAM. Cabinetmaker.
Born c. 1809, Tennessee; w. 1850,
Perry Twp., Lawrence Co. (C)

1985
WABER, CONRAD. Chairmaker.
Born c. 1818, Germany; w. 1850,
Germantown, Wayne Co. (C)

1986
WACHTEL, JONATHAN.
Chairmaker.
W. 1848, Muncie, Delaware Co.
His shop was located at the west
end of Main Street in Muncie.
(CH 36)

1987
WADDING, JOHN M.
Cabinetmaker.
Born c. 1821, Ohio; w. 1850,
Parke Co. Lived with Calvin J.
Evans, cabinetmaker. (C)

1988
WADE, JOHN. Cabinetmaker.
Born c. 1827, North Carolina; w.
1850, Washington Twp., Hamilton
Co. (C)

1989
WAGHORN, CONRAD.
Cabinetmaker.
Born c. 1812, Bavaria; w. 1850,
Adams Twp., Ripley Co. (C)

1990
WAGONER, ROBERT.
Cabinetmaker.
Born c. 1830, Indiana; w. 1850,
Blue River Twp., Johnson Co.
(C)

1991
WAHL, LEWIS. Piano maker.
Born c. 1810, Württemberg, Ger-
many; w. 1850, New Albany,
Floyd Co. (C)

1992
WAINSEL (WAINSOTT),
MORGAN. Chairmaker.
Born in Kentucky; w. 1850, Mont-
gomery Twp., Jennings Co. (C)

1993
WAKEFIELD, EPHRAIM.
Chair painter.
Born c. 1809, Maryland; w. 1850,
New Albany, Floyd Co. (C)

1994
WALDEN, WILLIAM M.
Cabinetmaker.
Born c. 1818, Ohio; w. 1850,
Putnamville, Putnam Co. (C)

1995
WALKER, GEORGE B.
Cabinetmaker.
W. 1820, Connersville, Fayette
Co. Two men worked in this

shop; the raw materials included
cherry, walnut, and poplar. The
products were priced as follows:
"French Bureau $60; Clock Cases
Average $25; Desks Dto $30;
Dining Tables $12; Breakfast
Tables $6; Coffins Raised lids
large $10; Candle Stands $5;
Sugar Desks $8.50; Corner Cup-
boards $18." (MC)

1996
WALKER, JOHN. Chairmaker.
Born c. 1829, Virginia; w. 1850,
Winchester, Randolph Co. Lived
with Lewis Walker, chairmaker.
(C)

1997
WALKER, JOSEPH M.
Cabinetmaker.
Born c. 1815, Pennsylvania; w.
1850, Madison, Jefferson Co. Two
men working in this shop made
$1,000 worth of furniture in 1850.
(C, MC)

1998
WALKER, LEWIS. Chairmaker.
Born c. 1820, Virginia; w. 1850,
Winchester, Randolph Co. In 1850
his shop produced 75 sets of chairs
and 30 settees. Living in the same
household were chairmakers John
Walker and William Edwards.
(C, MC)

1999
WALKER, SAMUEL.
Cabinetmaker.
Born c. 1808, Vermont; w. 1850,
Benton Twp., Elkhart Co. (C)

2000
WALLACE, EDWARD.
Chairmaker.
Born c. 1833, Ohio; w. 1850,

Fugit Twp., Decatur Co. Lived with Samuel Moore, chairmaker, q.v. (C)

2001
WALLACE, JAMES. Chairmaker. Born 15 May 1804, Maryland; died 10 February 1879; w. 1839-1850, Lafayette, Tippecanoe Co. Adv. in *Indiana Eagle* 2 January 1839: "J. WALLACE, Windsor Chair-maker & painter, warehouse and shop on corner missouri & Columbia sts." In 1850 two men worked in this shop (Wallace's assistant was William Kerson), and they made 1,300 chairs. (C, MC, CH 8a)

2002
WALTON, JOSEPH.
Cabinetmaker.
Born c. 1814, New York; w. 1850, Whitley Co. (C)

2003
WARD, BEVERLY R.
Cabinetmaker.
Born c. 1823, Indiana; w. 1850, Harrison Twp., Howard Co. (C)

2004
WARD, OTHO W. Chairmaker.
Born c. 1821, Maryland; w. 1850, Greencastle, Putnam Co. (C)

2005
WARE, WILLIAM. Chairmaker.
Born c. 1784, Virginia; w. 1850, Posey Twp., Washington Co. (C)

2006
WARREN, JOHN. Cabinetmaker.
Born c. 1821, Indiana; w. 1850, White River Twp., Johnson Co. (C)

2007
WARREN, JOHN.
Cabinetmaker.
Born c. 1794; w. 1850, Jefferson Twp., Tipton Co. Lived with Luke C. Warren, cabinetmaker. (C)

2008
WARREN, JOHN H.
Cabinetmaker.
Born c. 1803, Virginia; w. 1850, Posey Twp., Washington Co. (C)

2009
WARREN, LUKE C.
Cabinetmaker.
Born c. 1830, Connecticut; w. 1850, Jefferson Twp., Tipton Co. In same household, John Warren, cabinetmaker. (C)

2010
WASHBURN, GEORGE.
Cabinetmaker.
Born c. 1823, Ohio; w. 1850, Monroe Twp., Pulaski Co. (C)

2011
WASHBURN, WILLIAM P.
Cabinetmaker.
Born c. 1829, Indiana; w. 1850, Ripley Twp., Montgomery Co. Lived with William B. Thomas. (C)

2012
WATSON, SAMUEL E.
Cabinetmaker.
Born c. 1808, Kentucky; w. 1850, Posey Twp., Franklin Co. (C)

2012a
WEATHERS, SQUIRE.
Chairmaker.
W. 1839-, Crawford Co. (CH 39a)

2013
WEATHERWAX (WETHER-
WAX), WILLIAM. Cabinetmaker.
Born c. 1828, New York; w. 1850,
Harrison Twp., Vigo Co. (C)
See also CONE & WEATHER-
WAX (WETHERWAX).

2014
WEAVER, GEORGE. Chairmaker.
Born c. 1794, Virginia; w. 1850,
Washington Twp., Kosciusko Co.
(C)

2015
WEAVER, JAMES. Cabinetmaker.
Born c. 1827, Kentucky; w. 1850,
Smith Twp., Posey Co. (C)

2016
WEAVER, JOSEPH.
Cabinetmaker.
Born c. 1814, Pennsylvania; w.
1850, Marion Twp., Owen Co.
(C)

2017
WEAVER, PETER. Chairmaker.
Born c. 1791, Kentucky; w. 1850,
Washington Twp., Shelby Co.
(C)

2018
WEAVER, WILLIAM W.
Cabinetmaker.
Born 14 July 1808, Philadelphia,
Pa.; learned cabinetmaking in
Philadelphia; 1829, moved to Cum-
berland, Md., where he established
a shop which burned within the
year; 1836, arrived in Indianapolis,
Marion Co. W. 1836-1877-, Indian-
apolis. 1837-1840, with Espy &
Sloan, q.v.; 1840, Tucker & Wea-
ver, q.v. Adv. in *Indiana Journal*
5 July 1842: "CHEAP FOR
CASH! CABINET WARE-

ROOM. The subscriber . . . in-
vites all those in want of furniture to give hime a call at the old
stand of Tucker & Weaver, on
Washington street, . . . where he
is always ready to accommodate
those who may call upon him with
any article in his line at the shortest notice . . . [mentions coffins
and hearse] WILLIAM W.
WEAVER."
  1844-1850-, Weaver & Williams,
q.v. Still working in 1877. His
shop was located on Washington
Street between Illinois and Tennessee streets. His shop was the
first in Indianapolis to use two-
horse hearses and to furnish carriages for funerals. A local his-
torian of 1877 commented on his
undertaking activities, "It is certainly some consolation and will
ameliorate the pangs of death to
know that we will be taken care
of by the genial and clever W. W.
Weaver." Living with Mr. Weaver in 1850 was Abraham Charles,
cabinetmaker. (C, CH 39)

2019
WEAVER & WILLIAMS. Cabi-
netmakers, undertakers and coffin
makers.
  William W. Weaver and Charles
W. Williams; w. 1844-1850, Indianapolis, Marion Co. Adv. in *Indiana State Sentinel* 11 January 1844
that William W. Weaver's new
partner was Chas. Williams; they
were operating a Cabinet ware-
room. Adv. *ibid.* 7 January 1844,
that they were undertakers and
coffin makers. In 1850, six men
worked in this establishment, and
that year they made "100 pairs

Bedsteads, 100 Tables, and Other articles. (MC) *See also* TUCKER & WEAVER.

2020
WEBB, JOHN W. Chairmaker.
Born c. 1824, Virginia; w. 1850, Warsaw, Kosciusko Co. (C)

2020a
WEBER, CONRAD. Chairmaker.
W. 1844, Centerville, Wayne Co.
Adv. in *Wayne County Record,* 3 July 1844: "CHAIRS!! The subscriber respectfully informs his friends, former customers and the public generally, that he continues to carry on the *Chair Making Business,* at his shop on *Milton Street* . . . where he will make and keep constantly on hand a variety of Fancy and Common Windsor Chairs Settees, &c., &c."

2021
WEBSTER, RICHARD.
Cabinetmaker.
Born c. 1829, Indiana; w. 1850, New Castle, Henry Co. (C)

2022
WEBSTER, S. Cabinetmaker.
Born c. 1814, New York; w. 1850, Benton Twp., Elkhart Co. (C)

2023
WEED, JAMES. Chairmaker.
Born c. 1829, New York; w. 1850, La Porte, La Porte Co. (C)

2024
WEEKLEY, JOHN. Cabinetmaker.
Born c. 1800, Kentucky; w. 1850, Addison Twp., Shelby Co. (C)

2025
WEEKLY, JEREMIAH.
Cabinetmaker.
Born c. 1827, Kentucky; w. 1850, Shelbyville, Shelby Co. (C)

2026
WEESONER, JOHN.
Cabinetmaker.
Born c. 1816, North Carolina; w. 1850, Harrison Twp., Henry Co. (C)

2027
WEIR—*see* McCOLLOUGH & WEIR.

2028
WEIR, D. T. Cabinetmaker.
W. 1827, Salem, Washington Co.
Adv. in *Annotator of News, Politics and Literature* 24 November 1827: "Cabinet Work. The subscriber has on hand a considerable supply of finished work, and wishes to inform the citizens of Salem and its vicinity, that they can be accommodated on as good terms as any where in the Western Country. His work is warranted to be good, and neatly executed, and not inferior to any. His shop is kept at No. 2 Depauw's row all kinds of produce is taken in exchange. D. T. WEIR."

2029
WEIR, DAVID B.
Cabinetmaker.
Born c. 1823, Indiana; w. 1848-1850, Fairbanks Twp., Sullivan Co. Firm was known as D. B. Weir & Co., and had three

employees. In 1850 they made furniture worth $2,000. (C, MC, CH 52)

2030
WEIR, TRAVANIAN.
Cabinetmaker.
　Born c. 1829, Indiana; w. 1850, New Albany, Floyd Co. Lived with William M. Weir, cabinetmaker. (C)

2031
WEIR, TRAVANIAN L.
Cabinetmaker.
　Born c. 1834, Indiana; w. 1850, New Albany, Floyd Co. Lived with William M. Weir, cabinetmaker. (C)

2032
WEIR, WILLIAM.
Cabinetmaker.
　Born c. 1832, Indiana; w. 1850, New Albany, Floyd Co. Lived with William M. Weir, cabinetmaker. (C)

2033
WEIR, WILLIAM D.
Cabinetmaker.
　Born c. 1826, Indiana; w. 1850, Fairbanks Twp., Sullivan Co. In same household, David Crosby, cabinetmaker. (C)

2034
WEIR, WILLIAM M.
Cabinetmaker and undertaker.
　Born c. 1808, Kentucky; w. 1826-1850-, New Albany, Floyd Co. Died 1862. In 1850, assisted by Travanian Weir, Travanian L. Weir and William Weir, his shop produced furniture worth $3,000. (C, MC, CH 7)

2035
WELLINGTON, MARTIN.
Cabinetmaker.
　Born c. 1820, Germany; w. 1850, Evansville, Vanderburgh Co. (C)

2036
WELLMAN, ELEXAS.
Cabinetmaker.
　Born c. 1831, Indiana; w. 1850, Clinton, Vermillion Co. Lived with Ephraim Dewitt, cabinetmaker. (C)

2037
WELLMAN, ISAM.
Cabinetmaker.
　Born c. 1819, Indiana; w. 1850, Posey Twp., Washington Co. (C)

2038
WELSH, JOHN. Cabinetmaker.
　Born c. 1815, Ohio; w. 1850, Greensburg, Decatur Co. (C)

2039
WELSH, JOHN. Cabinetmaker.
　Born c. 1818, Delaware; w. 1850, Whitley Co. (C)

2040
WESCOAT (WESCOTT), BERGEN. Cabinetmaker.
　Born c. 1828, Indiana; w. 1850, Camden, Carroll Co. In the same household was Benjamin Stede, cabinetmaker. (C)

2041
WEST, BASSETT. Cabinetmaker.
　Born c. 1804, Pennsylvania; w. 1850, Peru, Miami Co. (C)

2042
WEST, GEORGE W.
Cabinetmaker.
　Born c. 1828, Ohio; w. 1850, Harrison Twp., Vigo Co. (C)

2043
WEST, H. C. Chairmaker.
Born c. 1826, Pennsylvania; w.
1850, Princeton, Gibson Co. (C)

2044
WEST, JESSE. Cabinetmaker.
W. 1823, Corydon, Harrison Co.
His cabinet shop burned in March
1823 but re-opened in August of
the same year. (*See* pp. 17-18.)

2045
WEST, LUCIUS A.
Cabinetmaker.
Born c. 1808, Vermont; w. 1850,
Germantown, Wayne Co. (C)

2046
WEST, WILLIAM H.
Cabinetmaker.
Born c. 1824, Ohio; w. 1850,
Harrison Twp., Vigo Co. In 1850,
two men worked in this shop and
made 7 bureaus, 75 bedsteads, 30
tables, and other articles. (C, MC)

2046a
WEST & DILL. Cabinetmakers.
W. 1835, Centerville, Wayne Co.
Adv. in *The People's Advocate*,
18 September 1835, for cabinetmaking and also that "they have
a mourning hearse and will furnish coffins." *See also* DILL,
ALEXANDER C.

2047
WHEAT, JAMES E. Chairmaker.
W. -1835-, Indianapolis, Marion
Co. Worked for A. McClure &
Co. (q.v.) until 29 June 1835 when
p a r t n e r s h i p was dissolved
(*Indiana Democrat*). Adv. *ibid.*
29 June 1835: "INDIAN-
APOLIS FANCY AND WIND-
SOR CHAIR M A N U F A C-
TORY AND *Cabinet Furniture
Warehouse*. The subscriber respectfully informs his friends and
the public generally that he has
obtained the sole management of
the CHAIR FACTORY formerly
owned by A. McClure & Co.
where he intends carrying on the
Chair Making Business in all its
branches. He will be able to
furnish parlor sets of every kind
of CHAIRS, SETTEES, &C. at
short notice. Orders from a
distance punctually attended to.
An apprentice wanted to the above
business. . . Also, may be found
at the above establishment, a large
and general assortment of CABI-
NET FURNITURE." W. 1838,
Brookville, Franklin Co., as member of firm of Hartley, Wheat &
Co., q.v.; January 1839 in firm
of Wheat & Longe, q.v.; July
1839-, worked alone in Brookville.

2048
WHEAT & LONGE. Chairmakers.
James E. Wheat and Jasper
Longe; succeeded firm of Hartley,
Wheat, & Co. c. 25 January 1839,
Brookville, Franklin Co.

2049
WHEELER, FRANCIS.
Cabinetmaker.
Born c. 1814, England; w. 1850,
Lafayette, Tippecanoe Co. (C)

2050
WHEELER, JOHN R.
Chairmaker.
Born c. 1834, New York, N.Y.;
w. 1850, Van Buren Twp.,
Kosciusko Co. (C)

2051
WHISLER, JACOB, JR.
Cabinetmaker.
  Born c. 1818, Pennsylvania; w.
  1850, Marion, Grant Co. Died
  1875. Although one man was listed
  as working in this shop, Samuel
  Whisler, cabinetmaker, lived in
  the same household. In 1850 the
  shop produced furniture worth
  $700. (C, MC, CH 45)

2052
WHISLER, SAMUEL.
Cabinetmaker.
  Born c. 1827, Pennsylvania; w.
  1850, Marion, Grant Co. Lived
  with Jacob Whisler, cabinetmaker.
  (C)

2053
WHITAKER, HIRAM.
Cabinetmaker.
  Born c. 1816, Pennsylvania; w.
  1850, Goshen, Elkhart Co. (C)

2054
WHITAKER, JAMES.
Cabinetmaker (?).
  This name and the date 1847
  appear on a cupboard in the Van
  Nuys house, Johnson County. No
  information is known about James
  Whitaker and it is possible that
  the name is merely that of a
  previous owner of the cupboard.

2055
WHITCOMB, ISAAC G.
Cabinetmaker.
  Born c. 1827, New York; w. 1850,
  Spencer Twp., Jennings Co. (C)

2056
WHITE—see VAIL & WHITE.

2057
WHITE, ALLEN. Chairmaker.
  Born c. 1825, Indiana; w. 1850,
  Connersville, Fayette Co. (C)

2058
WHITE, IRVIN. Chairmaker.
  Born c. 1825, Ohio; w. 1850,
  Union Twp., Montgomery Co.
  (C) See also WHITE & ROB-
  INSON.

2059
WHITE, ISAAC. Chairmaker.
  Born c. 1784, Virginia; w. 1850,
  Liberty, Union Co. (C)

2060
WHITE, JOHN. Chairmaker.
  Born c. 1811, North Carolina; w.
  1850, Clay Twp., Pike Co. (C)

2061
WHITE & ROBINSON.
Furniture makers.
  Irvin White and William Robinson; w. 1850, Union Twp., Montgomery Co. Three men worked in
  this shop which included paints
  in its list of raw materials. In
  1850 they made furniture valued
  at $2,200. (C, MC)

2062
WHITEMAN, FRANKLIN.
Cabinetmaker.
  Born c. 1825, Delaware; w. 1850,
  Jennings Twp., Crawford Co. (C)

2063
WHITESILT, CHARLES.
Cabinetmaker.
  W. 1820, Jennings Twp., Fayette
  Co. Two men worked in this shop.
  Their products were priced as
  follows: "Wheat fans larger $25;
  Patent Dto $16; Desks $25; Cup-

boards $18; Tables from $3 to 10 Dollars; Candlestands $4." The census taker remarked, "Establishment new and not finished yet but in tolerable condition . . . but sales are verry dull." (MC)

2064
WHITLOCK, JOHN T.
Cabinetmaker.
Born c. 1811, New York; w. 1845-1850, Rising Sun, Ohio Co. In 1850 Enos Gray and James Scott worked with him to produce furniture worth $2,000. The Whitlock shop was on the west side of Main Street, opposite the Presbyterian Church, in 1845. (C, MC, CH 26)

2065
WHITMAN, GEORGE.
Cabinetmaker.
W. 1839, Cambridge City, Wayne Co. He built the stairway and much of the furniture used in the Conklin house in Cambridge City, which was built in 1839. (FWP)

2066
WHITMAN, JAMES T.
Cabinetmaker.
Born c. 1825, Vermont; w. 1850, Portage Twp., St. Joseph Co. (C)

2067
WHITSALL, ANDREW.
Cabinetmaker.
Born c. 1810, Pennsylvania; w. 1850, Abington, Wayne Co. (C)

2068
WHITTAKER, JAMES.
Cabinetmaker.
Born c. 1812, Indiana; w. 1850, Sparta Twp., Dearborn Co. (C)

2069
WHITTENBERGER, JACOB.
Cabinetmaker.
Born c. 1818, Pennsylvania; w. 1850, Henry Twp., Fulton Co.(C)

2070
WIAMER, JOSEPH.
Cabinetmaker.
Born c. 1830, Ohio; w. 1850, Wayne Twp., Randolph Co. (C)

2071
WICKS, ADISON. Chairmaker.
Born c. 1809, Virginia; w. 1850, Jackson Twp., Wayne Co. (C)

2072
WILBRAHAM, JOSHUA H.
Cabinetmaker.
Born c. 1828, Pennsylvania; w. 1850, Aurora, Dearborn Co. (C)

2073
WILES, JOSEPH. Cabinetmaker.
Born c. 1825, Ohio; w. 1850, Spiceland Twp., Henry Co. (C)

2074
WILEY, ALEXANDER.
Chairmaker.
Born c. 1825, Pennsylvania; w. 1850, Wayne Twp., Allen Co. (C)

2075
WILEY, HARRISON.
Cabinetmaker.
Born c. 1828, Ohio; w. 1850, Jonesboro, Grant Co. (C)

2076
WILEY (WHILY), WILLIAM C.
Cabinetmaker.
Born c. 1816, North Carolina; w. 1850, Clinton Twp., Vermillion Co. Three men worked in his shop;

in 1850 they made bureaus, tables, and bedsteads worth $1,200. (C, MC)

2077
WILHITE, WILLIS H.
Cabinetmaker.
   Born c. 1825, Kentucky; w. 1850, Plainfield, Hendricks Co. (C)

2078
WILKINS, THOMAS.
Cabinetmaker.
   Born c. 1814, Ohio; w. 1850, Center Twp., Howard Co. (C)

2079
WILKINSON, JOHN.
Cabinetmaker.
   Born c. 1784, Pennsylvania; w. 1850, Johnson Twp., Ripley Co. (C)

2080
WILKLEY (?), CHANSY C.
Cabinetmaker.
   Born c. 1810, Ohio; w. 1850, Green Twp., Noble Co. (C)

2081
WILLIAMS, CHARLES W.
Cabinetmaker.
   Born c. 1812, Pennsylvania; w. 1844-1850, Indianapolis, Marion Co. In the same household, Robson Harrison, cabinetmaker. (C) See also WEAVER & WILLIAMS.

2082
WILLIAMS, JEROME.
Cabinetmaker.
   Born c. 1830, Indiana; w. 1850, Blue River Twp., Johnson Co. (C)

2083
WILLIAMS, JONATHAN.
Cabinetmaker.
   Born c. 1800, Kentucky; w. 1850, Franklin Twp., Johnson Co. (C)

2084
WILLIAMS, LEWIS G.
Cabinetmaker.
   Born c. 1829, Ohio; w. 1850, Muncie, Delaware Co. (C)

2085
WILLIAMS, SAMUEL L.
Cabinetmaker.
   Born c. 1831, Tennessee; w. 1850, Franklin Twp., Montgomery Co. (C)

2086
WILLIAMS, SYLVESTER.
Cabinetmaker.
   Born c. 1815, Delaware; w. 1850, Harrison Twp., Vigo Co. In the same household, John Codzenbaugh, cabinetmaker. In 1850 there were three men working in this shop; they made 50 bedsteads and tables, 40 coffins, 20 cupboards and bureaus, and other articles not enumerated. (C, MC)

2087
WILLIAMS, THOMAS.
Cabinetmaker.
   Born c. 1826, Ohio; w. 1850, Franklin Twp., Johnson Co. (C)

2088
WILLIAMS, WILLIAM.
Cabinetmaker.
   Born c. 1808, Tennessee; w. 1850, Jackson Twp., Porter Co. (C)

2089
WILLIAMSON, ISAAC.
Cabinetmaker.

Born c. 1806, New Jersey; w. 1850, Clay Twp., Dearborn Co. (C)

2090
WILLMOT, DANIEL.
Cabinetmaker.
Born c. 1806, New York; w. 1850, Rockport, Spencer Co. Three men working in this shop used machinery powered by horse; in 1850 they produced 100 bedsteads, 50 tables, 6 bureaus, 12 presses, and 6 cupboards. In same household, Nicholas Oberhousen, cabinetmaker. (C, MC)

2091
WILLS, S. H. Cabinetmaker.
Born c. 1791, North Carolina; w. 1850, New Albany, Floyd Co. In the same household, Robert F. Budlett, cabinetmaker. (C)

2092
WILLSON, WILLIAM.
Cabinetmaker.
Born c. 1799, Maryland; w. 1850, Moral Twp., Shelby Co. (C)

2093
WILS, GEORGE. Cabinetmaker.
Born c. 1830, Ohio; w. 1850, Jackson Twp., Hamilton Co. (C)

2094
WILSEN, I. B. (or G.).
Cabinetmaker.
Born c. 1818, Kentucky; w. 1850, Milford, Decatur Co. (C)

2095
WILSON, ABRAHAM.
Cabinetmaker.
Born c. 1805, Pennsylvania; w. -1846-1850, South Bend, St. Joseph Co. Adv. in *St. Joseph Valley Register* December 1846 that he was in partnership with Alfred Wright, a painter, doing cabinetmaking and offering coffins and the services of a hearse. Adv. *ibid.* May 1848 and later, that he was in partnership with David Stover doing cabinet work and making coffins. (C) *See also* WILSON & BOND; LANDON, ROBERT.

2096
WILSON, ALEXANDER.
Cabinetmaker.
Born c. 1801, Pennsylvania; w. 1850, Franklin Twp., Johnson Co. In same household, James and William Wilson, cabinetmakers. (C)

2097
WILSON, CHARLES G.
Chairmaker.
Born c. 1815, Indiana; w. 1850, Indianapolis, Marion Co. (C)

2098
WILSON, DAVID.
Cabinetmaker.
Born 1794, Ireland; 1808, to Philadelphia, where he learned cabinetmaking and woodcarving; 1818, to Kentucky and shortly thereafter arrived in Madison, Jefferson Co., Indiana. He was still working in Madison in 1850. (C) *Antiques*, XLVIII, No. 4 (October 1945), p. 219, discusses his career and illustrates a silhouette portrait of him attributed to Charles Willson Peale, as well as a cherry bureau-desk he made in late Sheraton style. Two other pieces of his work are known:

a mahogany sideboard with four rope-carved pilasters, and a mahogany pedestal side table with four winged-paw feet. The single Indiana cabinetmaker listed in Ethel Hall Bjerkoe, *The Cabinetmakers of America* (Garden City: Doubleday & Company, Inc., 1957), p. 235, is given incorrectly as John Wilson, David Wilson's father, who is not known to have been a cabinetmaker or to have come to Indiana.

2099
WILSON, DAVID D.
Cabinetmaker.
    Born c. 1828, Indiana; w. 1850, Lexington Twp., Scott Co. (C)

2100
WILSON, DUNKEN C.
Cabinetmaker.
    Born c. 1813, North Carolina; w. 1850, Greensboro Twp., Henry Co. (C)

2101
WILSON, I. P. Cabinetmaker.
    Born c. 1792, Pennsylvania; w. 1850, Jeffersonville, Clark Co. (C)

2102
WILSON, JACOB. Cabinetmaker.
    Born c. 1810, Pennsylvania; w. 1850, Tobin Twp., Perry Co. (C)

2103
WILSON, JAMES.
Cabinetmaker.
    Born c. 1823, Ohio; w. 1850, Harrison Twp., Clay Co. (C)

2104
WILSON, JAMES. Cabinetmaker.
    Born c. 1828, Kentucky; w. 1850, Franklin Twp., Johnson Co. Lived with Alexander Wilson. (C)

2105
WILSON, JESSE. Cabinetmaker.
    Born c. 1831; w. 1850, Monroe Twp., Howard Co. (C)

2106
WILSON, JOHN—*see* WILSON, DAVID.

2107
WILSON, RICHARD.
Cabinetmaker.
    Born c. 1819, Maryland; w. 1850, Blooming Grove Twp., Franklin Co. (C)

2108
WILSON, SAMUEL.
Cabinetmaker.
    Born c. 1817, Kentucky; w. 1850, Princeton, Gibson Co. (C)

2109
WILSON, THOMAS.
Cabinetmaker.
    Born c. 1777, Scotland; listed as cabinetmaker and pauper in 1850 census of Centre Twp., Wayne Co. (C)

2110
WILSON, WILLIAM.
Cabinetmaker.
    Born c. 1812, North Carolina; w. 1850, Charlestown Twp., Clark Co. (C)

2111
WILSON, WILLIAM.
Cabinetmaker.

Born c. 1830, Indiana; w. 1850, Franklin Twp., Johnson Co. Lived with Alexander Wilson, cabinetmaker. (C)

2112
WILSON, WILLIAM. Cabinetmaker.

W. 1850, Madison Co. Two men worked in this shop, using hand power to make an annual product valued at $700. (MC)

2113
WILSON & BOND. Cabinetmakers.

Probably Abraham Wilson and ——Bond; w. 1832, South Bend, St. Joseph Co. Adv. in 1832 in the *Northwestern Pioneer* that they were makers of "something that's nice . . . bureaus, Bedsteads, Tables, Stands, etc." Their shop was opposite Benjamin Coquillard's hotel.

2114
WIMLEN, OLIVER. Chair painter.

Born c. 1827, Pennsylvania; w. 1850, Madison, Jefferson Co. (C)

2115
WING, A. M. Cabinetmaker.

Born c. 1812, New York; w. 1850, Mishawaka, St. Joseph Co. In same household, Michael Miller, chairmaker. (C)

2116
WINN, JAMES H. Cabinetmaker.

Born c. 1823, Kentucky; w. 1850, Center Twp., Hancock Co. (C)

2117
WINN, JOHN. Cabinetmaker.

Born c. 1826, Indiana; w. 1850, Center Twp., Hancock Co. (C)

2118
WINSHIP, JOHN. Cabinetmaker.

Born c. 1831, Indiana; w. 1850, Lafayette, Tippecanoe Co. Lived with James Roberts, cabinetmaker, q.v. (C)

2119
WINSHIP, SAMUEL. Cabinetmaker.

Born c. 1829, Virginia; w. 1850, Carroll Co. (C)

2120
WINTERS, ANDREW. Chairmaker.

Born c. 1816, Pennsylvania; w. 1850, Haddon Twp., Sullivan Co. (C)

2121
WINTERS, CHARLES. Cabinetmaker.

Born c. 1810, Switzerland; w. 1850, Highland Twp., Vermillion Co. Two men worked in this shop; in 1850 they made furniture valued at $1,000. (C, MC)

2122
WISE, GEORGE W. Cabinetmaker.

Born c. 1824, Virginia; w. 1850, Fall Creek Twp., Henry Co. (C)

2123
WISEHART, CHARLES W. Cabinetmaker.

Born c. 1816, Kentucky; w. 1850, Carroll Co. (C)

2124
WITHEROW, DAVID.
Cabinetmaker.
Born c. 1800, Pennsylvania; w.
1850, Carroll Co. (C)

2125
WOOD, ANDREW S.
Cabinetmaker.
Born c. 1826, Indiana; w. 1850,
Martin Co. In the same household,
James Wood and John Vanhoy,
cabinetmakers. In 1850 this shop
produced cabinet work valued at
$1,000. (C, MC)

2126
WOOD, CHARLES. Chairmaker.
Born c. 1800, North Carolina; w.
1850, Metamora Twp., Franklin
Co. (C)

2127
WOOD, DAVID. Cabinetmaker.
Born c. 1777, Massachusetts; w.
1850, Greencastle, Putnam Co.
(C)

2128
WOOD, JAMES. Cabinetmaker.
Born c. 1830, Indiana; w. 1850,
Perry Twp., Martin Co. Lived
with Andrew S. Wood, cabinet-
maker. (C)

2129
WOOD, PETER. Cabinetmaker.
Born c. 1813, North Carolina; w.
1850, Fayette Twp., Vigo Co. (C)

2130
WOOD, SILAS F. Cabinetmaker.
Born c. 1825, New York; w. 1850,
Mishawaka, St. Joseph Co. (C)

2131
WOOD, WILLIAM. Cabinetmaker.
Born c. 1829, Indiana; w. 1850,
New Albany, Floyd Co. (C)

2132
WOODBECK, WILLIAM.
Cabinetmaker.
Born c. 1819, Virginia; w. 1850,
Rush Co. (C)

2133
WOODRUFF, ALFRED.
Chairmaker.
Born c. 1828, Ohio; w. 1850,
Union Twp., Montgomery Co.
Lived with Ephraim Woodruff,
chairmaker. (C)

2134
WOODRUFF, CHARLES.
Chairmaker.
Born c. 1835, Indiana; w. 1850,
Union Twp., Montgomery Co.
Lived with Ephraim Woodruff,
chairmaker. (C)

2135
WOODRUFF, DAVID.
Chairmaker.
Born c. 1795, New Jersey; w.
1850, Union Twp., Montgomery
Co. (C)

2136
WOODRUFF, EPHRAIM.
Chairmaker.
Born c. 1824, Ohio; w. 1850,
Union Twp., Montgomery Co. In
same household, chairmakers Al-
fred, Charles and Oath Wood-
ruff. (C)

2137
WOODRUFF, JOHN W.
Chairmaker.
  Born c. 1797, New Jersey; w. 1850, Wayne Twp., Noble Co. (C)

2138
WOODRUFF, OATH.
Chairmaker.
  Born c. 1826, Ohio; w. 1850, Union Twp., Montgomery Co. Lived with Ephraim Woodruff, chairmaker. (C)

2139
WOODS, JACKSON.
Cabinetmaker.
  Born c. 1820, Kentucky; w. 1850, Washington Twp., Brown Co. (C)

2140
WOODSON, WILLIAM T.
Chairmaker and cabinetmaker.
  Born c. 1825, Virginia; w. 1850, Michigan City, La Porte Co. His raw materials included paints. In 1850 his shop produced 600 chairs, 18 bureaus, 50 bedsteads, and 30 tables in addition to other items not listed. (C, MC)

2141
WORLEY, BLUFORD.
Cabinetmaker.
  Born c. 1823, Indiana; w. 1850, Perry Twp., Lawrence Co. (C)

2142
WORNER, CHARLES.
Cabinetmaker.
  Born c. 1822, Germany; w. 1850, Indianapolis, Marion Co. (C)

2143
WORRELL, PRESTON S.
Cabinetmaker.
  Born c. 1825, Indiana; w. 1850, Orleans Twp., Orange Co. (C)

2144
WORTS, PETER. Cabinetmaker.
  Born c. 1823, Pennsylvania; w. 1850, Jackson Twp., Shelby Co. (C)

2144a
WRIGHT—*see also* RIGHT.

2145
WRIGHT, ALFRED. Painter.
  W. 1846-, South Ben, St. Joseph Co. Adv. in *St. Joseph Valley Register* December 1846 and later; in partnership with Abraham Wilson, cabinetmaker, q.v.

2146
WRIGHT, ELWOOD.
Chairmaker.
  Born c. 1823, Tennessee; w. 1850, Harrison Twp., Henry Co. (C)

2147
WRIGHT, JAMES. Chairmaker.
  Born c. 1826, Indiana; w. 1850, Madison, Jefferson Co. (C)

2148
WRIGHT, JAMES. Cabinetmaker.
  Born c. 1811, New York; w. 1850, Swan Twp., Noble Co. (C)

2149
WRIGHT, WILLIAM E.
Cabinetmaker.
  Born c. 1826, Indiana; w. 1850, Liberty Twp., Parke Co. (C)

2150
WURSTEIN, DAVID.
Cabinetmaker.

Born c. 1810, Germany; w. 1850, Wayne Twp., Allen Co. In same household, Dominic Kneche, cabinetmaker. (C)

2151
WURSTEN, JACOB.
Cabinetmaker.
  Born c. 1812, Germany; w. 1850, Wayne Twp., Allen Co. (C)

2152
WYATH, ELASTIN.
Cabinetmaker.
  Born c. 1782, Massachusetts; w. 1850, Riley Twp., Vigo Co. (C)

2153
WYLAND, JOHN. Cabinetmaker.
  Born c. 1820, Ohio; w. 1850, Jackson Twp., Elkhart Co. (C)

2154
WYLEY, THOMAS.
Cabinetmaker.
  Born c. 1825, New York; w. 1850, Lawrenceburg, Dearborn Co. (C)

2155
YELVINGTON, THOMAS.
Cabinetmaker.
  Born c. 1819, Virginia; w. 1850, Williamsburg, Wayne Co. Two men worked in this shop; in 1850 they made 75 bedsteads, 20 tables, and 12 bureaus. (C, MC)

2156
YERGUS, CHRISTOPHER.
Cabinetmaker.
  Born c. 1810, Germany; w. 1850, Wayne Twp., Wayne Co. (C)

2157
YODER, JOHN. Cabinetmaker.
  Born c. 1826, Virginia; w. 1850, Clay Twp., Miami Co. (C)

2158
YORK, CYRUS F. Cabinetmaker.
  Born c. 1809, Kentucky; w. 1850, Indianapolis, Marion Co. (C)

2159
YORK, J. P. Cabinetmaker.
  Born c. 1811, Ohio; w. 1850, Laurel Twp., Franklin Co. (C)

2160
YOUNG, BARTLETT.
Cabinetmaker.
  Born c. 1831, Indiana; w. 1850, Salem, Washington Co. Lived with Elijah Gossett, cabinetmaker, q.v. (C)

2161
YOUNG, EDWARD.
Cabinetmaker.
  Born c. 1820, Ohio; w. 1850, Benton Twp., Elkhart Co. (C)

2162
YOUNG, EPHRAIM D.
Cabinetmaker.
  Born c. 1816, Ohio; w. 1850, Center Twp., Hendricks Co. (C)

2163
YOUNG, JOHN.
Chair manufacturer.
  W. 1845, Rising Sun, Ohio Co. His shop was located on the west side of Main Street nearly opposite the Presbyterian Church. (CH 26)

2164
YOUNG, MARTIN.
Cabinetmaker.
    Born c. 1803, Pennsylvania; w.
    1850, Dearborn Co. (C)

2165
YOUNG, R. & Z. Chair factory.
Robert Young and probably Zebulon Young; w. 1850, Rising Sun, Ohio Co. Three men worked in this shop; their raw materials included paints. In 1850 they made 100 dozen chairs worth $1,200. (C, MC)

2166
YOUNG, ROBERT. Chairmaker.
Born c. 1808, New York; w. 1850, Rising Sun, Ohio Co. (C) *See* YOUNG, R. & Z.

2167
YOUNG, SAMUEL. Cabinetmaker.
Born c. 1817, Virginia; w. 1850, Patoka Twp., Crawford Co. (C)

2168
YOUNG, WILLIAM.
Cabinetmaker.
    Born c. 1801, Maryland; w. 1850, Whitley Co. (C)

2169
YOUNG, WILLIAM B.
Cabinetmaker.
    Born c. 1829, Ohio; w. 1850, Kent, Jefferson Co. (C)

2170
YOUNG, ZEBULON. Chairmaker.
Born c. 1827, New York; w. 1850, Rising Sun, Ohio Co. (C) *See* YOUNG, R. & Z.

2171
YOUNGMAN, JACOB.
Cabinetmaker.
    Born c. 1821, Kentucky; w. 1850, Van Buren Twp., Shelby Co. (C)

2172
ZEIGLER, JONAS. Cabinetmaker.
Born c. 1826, Ohio; w. 1850, Franklin Twp., De Kalb Co. (C)

2173
ZIMMERMAN, JOSEPH T.
Cabinet shop.
    Born c. 1825, Pennsylvania; w. 1850, Washington Twp., Hendricks Co. In 1850 his shop produced furniture worth $500. (C, MC)

2174
ZINCK, GEORGE C.
Cabinetmaker.
    Born c. 1819, Germany; w. 1850, Utica Twp., Clark Co. This shop utilized horse and hand power. In 1850 it produced 15 bureaus, 20 desks, 60 stands, and other items. (C, MC)

2175
ZINCK, J. C. Cabinetmaker.
Born c. 1818, Germany; w. 1850, Utica Twp., Clark Co. (C)

2176
ZINCK, LEONARD.
Cabinetmaker.
    Born c. 1832, Germany; w. 1850, Utica Twp., Clark Co. (C)

BIBLIOGRAPHY

1. Barrows, Frederic Irving (ed.), *History of Fayette County, Indiana* . . . (Indianapolis: B. F. Bowen & Co., 1917).
2. Bash, Frank Sumner (comp.), *History of Huntington County, Indiana* . . . (2 volumes. Chicago: Lewis Publishing Co., 1914).
3. Beckwith, Hiram W. (comp.), *History of Montgomery County* . . . (Chicago: H. H. Hill and N. Iddings, 1881).
4. *Biographical and Historical Record of Adams and Wells Counties, Indiana* . . . (Chicago: Lewis Publishing Co., 1887).
5. *Biographical and Historical Record of Jay and Blackford Counties, Indiana* . . . (Chicago: Lewis Publishing Co., 1887).
6. *Biographical and Historical Record of Kosciusko County, Indiana* . . . (Chicago: Lewis Publishing Co., 1887).
7. *Biographical and Historical Souvenir for the Counties of Clark, Crawford, Harrison, Floyd, Jefferson, Jennings, Scott and Washington, Indiana* (Chicago: John M. Gresham & Co., 1889).
8. *Biographical Memoir of Greene County, Ind., with Reminiscences of Pioneer Days* (3 volumes. Indianapolis: B. F. Bowen & Co., 1908).
8a. *Biographical Record and Portrait Album of Tippecanoe County, Indiana* (Chicago: Lewis Publishing Co., 1888).
9. Bradsby, Henry C., *History of Vigo County, Indiana* . . . (Chicago: S. B. Nelson & Co., 1891).
10. Branson, George, *Archeological and Historical Survey of Parke County* (Indianapolis: Indiana Historical Bureau, 1927).
11. Cauthorn, Henry S., *A History of the City of Vincennes, Indiana* (Terre Haute: Moore & Langen Printing Co., 1902).
12. *Counties of La Grange and Noble, Indiana. Historical and Biographical* . . . (2 parts. Chicago: F. A. Battey & Co., 1882).
13. Daniels, Eugene D., *A Twentieth Century History and Biographical Record of La Porte County, Indiana* (Chicago: Lewis Publishing Co., 1904).

14. Deahl, Anthony (ed.), *A Twentieth Century History and Biographical Record of Elkhart County, Indiana* . . . (Chicago: Lewis Publishing Co., 1905).

15. DeHart, Richard P., *Past and Present of Tippecanoe County, Indiana* (2 volumes. Indianapolis: B. F. Bowen & Co., 1909).

16. Dufour, Perret, *The Swiss Settlement of Switzerland County, Indiana* (*Indiana Historical Collections*, XIII. Indianapolis: Indiana Historical Bureau, 1925).

17. Dunn, Jacob Piatt, *Greater Indianapolis* . . . (2 volumes. Chicago: Lewis Publishing Co., 1910).

18. Dunn, Jacob Piatt, *Memorial Record of Distinguished Men of Indianapolis and Indiana* (Chicago: Lewis Publishing Co., 1912).

19. Elliott, Joseph P., *A History of Evansville and Vanderburgh County, Indiana* . . . (Evansville: Keller Printing Co., 1897).

20. Greene, George E., *History of Old Vincennes and Knox County, Indiana* (2 volumes. Chicago: S. J. Clarke, 1911).

21. Griswold, Bert J., *Builders of Greater Fort Wayne* (Fort Wayne, 1926).

22. Hadley, John V., *History of Hendricks County, Indiana* . . . (Indianapolis: B. F. Bowen & Co., 1914).

23. Harden and Spahr (comps.), *Early Life and Times in Boone County, Indiana* . . . (Lebanon, Ind., 1887).

24. Harding, Lewis A., *History of Decatur County, Indiana* (Indianapolis: B. F. Bowen & Co., 1915).

25. Helm, Thomas B., *History of Cass County, Indiana* . . . (Chicago: Brant & Fuller, 1886).

26. *History of Dearborn and Ohio Counties, Indiana* . . . (Chicago: F. E. Weakley & Co., 1885).

27. *History of Fayette County, Indiana* . . . (Chicago: Warner, Beers & Co., 1885).

28. *History of Huntington County, Indiana* . . . (Chicago: Brant & Fuller, 1887).

29. *History of Johnson County, Indiana* . . . (Chicago: Brant & Fuller, 1888).

30. *History of Miami County, Indiana* . . . (Chicago: Brant & Fuller, 1887).

31. *History of Montgomery County, Indiana* . . . (2 volumes. Indianapolis: A. W. Bowen & Co., 1913).

32. *History of Parke and Vermillion Counties, Indiana* . . . (Indianapolis: B. F. Bowen & Co., 1913).

33. *History of the Ohio Falls Cities and Their Counties* . . . (2 volumes. Cleveland: L. A. Williams & Co., 1882).

34. *History of Wayne County, Indiana* . . . (2 volumes. Chicago: Inter-State Publishing Co., 1884).

35. Hodges, Laura Fletcher, *Early Indianapolis* (Indiana Historical Society *Publications,* VII, No. 2, Indianapolis, 1923).

36. Kemper, G. W. H. (ed.), *A Twentieth Century History of Delaware County, Indiana* (2 volumes. Chicago: Lewis Publishing Co., 1908).

37. *Manufacturing and Mercantile Resources and Industries of the Principal Places in Wayne, Henry, Delaware and Randolph Counties, Indiana* . . . (n.p. Historical and Statistical Publishing Co., 1884).

38. Montgomery, Marcus W., *History of Jay County, Indiana* (Chicago: Church, Goodman & Cushing, 1864).

39. Nowland, John H. B., *Sketches of Prominent Citizens of 1876* (Indianapolis: Tilford & Carlon, 1877).

39a. Pleasant, Hazen P., *A History of Crawford County, Indiana* (Greenfield, Ind.: Wm. Mitchell Printing Co., 1926).

40. *Portrait and Biographical Record of Boone, Clinton and Hendricks Counties, Ind.* . . . (Chicago: A. W. Bowen Co., 1895).

41. *Portrait and Biographical Record of Delaware and Randolph Counties, Indiana* . . . (Chicago: A. W. Bowen & Co., 1894).

42. *Portrait and Biographical Record of Montgomery, Parke and Fountain Counties, Indiana* . . . (Chicago: Chapman Bros., 1893).

43. Reifel, August J., *History of Franklin County, Indiana* . . . (Indianapolis: B. F. Bowen & Co., 1915).

44. Richman, George J., *History of Hancock County, Indiana* . . . (Indianapolis: Federal Publishing Co., 1916).

45. Shinn, Benjamin G. (ed.), *Blackford and Grant Counties, Indiana* . . . (2 volumes. Chicago: Lewis Publishing Co., 1914).

46. Spahr, Walter E., *History of Centerville, Indiana* (Richmond: Wayne County Historical Society, 1966).

47. Stormont, Gilbert R., *History of Gibson County, Indiana* . . . (Indianapolis: B. F. Bowen & Co., 1914).

48. Strouse, Isaac R., *Parke County, Indiana, Centennial Memorial 1816-1916* (Rockville: Rockville Chautauqua Association, 1916).

49. Sulgrove, Berry R., *History of Indianapolis and Marion County* (Philadelphia: L. H. Everts & Co., 1884).

50. Travis, William, *A History of Clay County, Indiana* . . . (2 volumes. Chicago: Lewis Publishing Co., 1909).

50a. Whallon, Arthur, "Indiana Cabinetmakers and Allied Craftsmen, 1815-1860," in *Antiques,* XCVIII, No. 1 (July 1970), pp. 118-25.

51. Whitson, Rolland L. (ed.), *Centennial History of Grant County, Indiana* . . . (2 volumes. Chicago: Lewis Publishing Co., 1914).

52. Wolfe, Thomas J., *A History of Sullivan County, Indiana* (2 volumes. Lewis Publishing Co., 1909).

53. Young, Andrew W., *History of Wayne County, Indiana* . . . (Cincinnati: Robert Clarke & Co., 1872).

INDEX TO CHECKLIST BY COUNTY

969, 1045, 1082, 1243, 1322, 1388, 1590, 1808, 1941, 1964, 1999, 2022, 2053, 2153, 2161

Fayette County, 141, 279, 290, 331, 361, 380, 381, 382, 392, 394, 437, 441, 451, 485, 557, 980, 1036, 1037, 1039, 1138, 1139, 1265, 1273, 1277, 1314, 1359, 1407, 1410, 1458, 1539, 1613, 1735, 1739, 1810, 1813, 1847, 1890, 1901, 1905, 1977, 1995, 2057, 2063

Floyd County, 20, 143, 205, 216, 243, 330, 350, 357, 432, 457, 466, 500, 508, 540, 541, 542, 552, 801, 884, 903, 987, 1005, 1035, 1137, 1194, 1224, 1225, 1231, 1235, 1395, 1429, 1469, 1537, 1547, 1548, 1557, 1578, 1611, 1686, 1687, 1693, 1699, 1722, 1740, 1744, 1768, 1773, 1774, 1784, 1786, 1787, 1855, 1870, 1885, 1978, 1991, 1993, 2030, 2031, 2032, 2034, 2091, 2131

Fountain County, 14, 22, 97, 174, 217, 218, 363, 564, 672, 673, 981, 1012, 1091, 1097, 1134, 1212, 1213, 1244, 1330, 1731, 1777, 1874, 1917, 1937, 1958, 1959, 1979

Franklin County, 100, 144, 155, 171, 194, 260, 288, 409, 620, 622, 628, 704, 812, 825, 914, 933, 1201, 1257, 1268, 1271, 1306, 1323, 1466, 1483, 1631, 1697, 1776, 1780, 1875, 1971, 2012, 2048, 2107, 2126, 2159

Fulton County, 186, 1150, 1234, 1453, 1467, 1655, 1665, 1679, 2069

Gibson County, 167, 208, 494, 581, 597, 692, 726, 876, 877, 922, 998, 1008, 1541, 1781, 2043, 2108

Grant County, 66, 238, 391, 589, 652, 766, 833, 888, 917, 918, 919, 920, 986, 1208, 1337, 1417, 1544, 1555, 1949, 2051, 2052, 2075

Greene County, 151, 152, 153, 203, 249, 424, 821, 874, 878, 893, 977, 1027, 1147, 1171, 1580, 1582, 1619

Hamilton County, 176, 177, 286, 400, 468, 478, 607, 649, 650, 666, 683, 690, 691, 770, 839, 961, 962, 965, 1108, 1229, 1230, 1316, 1805, 1906, 1938, 1988, 2093

Hancock County, 43, 110, 604, 656, 768, 796, 871, 1088, 1089, 1158, 1601, 1643, 1647, 1797, 1804, 2116, 2117

Harrison County, 302, 565, 606, 706, 1041, 1075, 1098, 1099, 1122, 1177, 1194, 1291, 1301, 1305, 1320, 1403, 1404, 1420, 1440, 1509, 1520, 1549, 1612, 1614, 1615, 1747, 1845, 2044

Hendricks County, 160, 161, 250, 314, 316, 317, 369, 412, 413, 417, 554, 713, 840, 990, 1024, 1087, 1146, 1242, 1379, 1449, 1599, 1641, 1915, 1952, 1976, 2077, 2162, 2173

Henry County, 8, 18, 26, 29, 38, 47, 76, 86, 115, 136, 210, 211, 267, 268, 269, 291, 320, 325, 407, 603, 611, 617, 662, 729, 769, 820, 827, 838, 845, 867, 868, 911, 939, 1010, 1038, 1133, 1135, 1188, 1195, 1298, 1437, 1531, 1542, 1543, 1546, 1567, 1685, 1746, 1760, 1821, 1878, 1879, 1903, 1918, 1927, 1945, 1968, 2021, 2026, 2073, 2100, 2122, 2146

Howard County, 56, 117, 913, 931, 953, 964, 1077, 1365, 1366, 1421, 1422, 1496, 1570, 1846, 1895, 2003, 2078, 2105

Huntington County, 405, 406, 643, 644, 694, 912, 1031, 1124, 1227, 1228, 1288, 1433, 1562, 1587, 1712

415, 416, 664, 693, 718, 809, 818, 826, 895, 896, 897, 975, 1033, 1034, 1222, 1282, 1284, 1406, 1413, 1460, 1522, 1650, 1671, 1681, 1698, 1716, 1795, 1873, 1908, 1910, 1970, 2011, 2058, 2061, 2085, 2133, 2134, 2135, 2136, 2138

Morgan County, 101, 373, 555, 717, 860, 984, 1106, 1239, 1321, 1385, 1386, 1423, 1444, 1640, 1717, 1823, 1944

Newton County—not organized until 1860.

Noble County, 191, 237, 420, 550, 559, 560, 630, 822, 1013, 1113, 1126, 1167, 1343, 1391, 1392, 1394, 1424, 1561, 1635, 1651, 1661, 1920, 2080, 2137, 2148

Ohio County, 10, 72, 584, 742, 762, 783, 908, 909, 910, 1114, 1117, 1236, 1237, 1238, 1701, 2064, 2163, 2165, 2166, 2170

Orange County, 354, 447, 530, 985, 1129, 1143, 1280, 1294, 1387, 1642, 1711, 1798, 1888, 1889, 2143

Owen County, 65, 81, 224, 254, 422, 472, 515, 578, 763, 1136, 1145, 1168, 1172, 1199, 1261, 1319, 1324, 1332, 1378, 1551, 1700, 1705, 1832, 1930, 2016

Parke County, 15, 16, 140, 175, 227, 282, 307, 418, 484, 583, 601, 602, 613, 645, 646, 859, 865, 866, 934, 956, 1002, 1022, 1028, 1069, 1074, 1115, 1127, 1252, 1283, 1398, 1482, 1713, 1714, 1857, 1987, 2149

Perry County, 828, 950, 1560, 1676, 2102

Pike County, 95, 948, 1278, 1464, 1465, 2060

Porter County, 60, 524, 832, 1046, 1415, 1863, 2088

Posey County, 477, 579, 748, 942, 1000, 1068, 1161, 1162, 1163, 1246, 1666, 1702, 1801, 1802, 1820, 1837, 1904, 2015

Pulaski County, 705, 2010

Putnam County, 105, 147, 229, 233, 271, 309, 332, 347, 440, 518, 526, 528, 594, 665, 854, 1043, 1065, 1084, 1085, 1093, 1095, 1203, 1206, 1241, 1264, 1303, 1338, 1339, 1342, 1502, 1597, 1778, 1840, 1841, 1858, 1859, 1994, 2004, 2127

Randolph County, 21, 58, 62, 91, 157, 305, 365, 529, 571, 588, 625, 723, 728, 819, 841, 887, 967, 1120, 1121, 1142, 1154, 1311, 1352, 1353, 1357, 1358, 1495, 1618, 1750, 1753, 1782, 1852, 1861, 1996, 1998, 2070

Ripley County, 89, 251, 452, 759, 761, 830, 988, 1078, 1534, 1881, 1962, 1989, 2079

Rush County, 30, 57, 164, 166, 185, 209, 275, 280, 358, 385, 534, 655, 780, 782, 791, 861, 936, 992, 1001, 1049, 1123, 1132, 1175, 1176, 1215, 1223, 1227, 1312, 1362, 1411, 1435, 1584, 1675, 1762, 1763, 1794, 2132

St. Joseph County, 77, 230, 232, 273, 284, 304, 324, 338, 342, 344, 562, 593, 598, 648, 775, 776, 788, 993, 1079, 1100, 1153, 1254, 1255, 1286, 1295, 1307, 1558, 1559, 1728, 1830, 1853, 1854, 1864, 1919, 1950, 1951, 1969, 2066, 2095, 2113, 2115, 2130, 2145

Scott County, 28, 32, 36, 75, 119, 120, 121, 154, 327, 371, 372, 516, 721, 808, 817, 886, 924, 1604, 1606, 1607, 1645, 2099

1082A, 1083, 1159, 1198, 1256, 1258A, 1258B, 1259, 1349, 1356, 1364A,1418, 1419, 1450, 1500, 1503, 1518, 1525, 1532, 1533, 1536, 1565, 1607A, 1733, 1763A, 1770, 1779, 1800A,1806, 1815, 1849, 1865, 1866, 1887, 1897A, 1907, 1909, 1932, 1942, 1953, 1961, 1974, 1985, 2020A, 2045, 2046A, 2065, 2067, 2071, 2109, 2155, 2156

Wells County, 128, 183, 184, 605, 623, 851, 1131, 1173, 1313, 1471, 1690, 1691, 1745, 1769, 1822, 1914, 1936

White County, 376, 849, 850, 1598

Whitley County, 364, 367, 556, 574, 678, 800, 1677, 1678, 1706, 1748, 1749, 2002, 2039, 2168

APPENDIX I

Unnamed Cabinetmakers and Chairmakers, working in Clark County, Indiana, in 1820, as Listed in the 1820 Industrial Census

Jeffersonville	1 man 1 Sett of Cabinet maker Tools & lathe Product: Cabinet work $1000
Utica	Turning Lathe &c 1 Sett Product: Windsor Chairs 100 @ $12 per ½ Dozen
Jeffersonville	1 Sett of Cabinet makers Tools Raw materials: 2000 ft. lumber Product: Cabinet Work $3000
Charlestown Township	Turning Lathe &c. 1 Sett Raw materials: 400 feet of plank &c Product: Windsor Chairs 150 at $15 p ½ Dozen
New Washington	1 man 1 Sett of Cabinet Tools Raw materials: Plank & Scantling 2000 feet $35.00 Product: Cabinet Work $500
New Washington	1 Sett of Cabinet Tools Raw materials: Plank & Scantling Product: Cabinet Work [no value given]
Charlestown Township	1 man 1 Sett of Cabinet Tools Raw materials: Plank & Scantling 3000 ft. $80 Product: Cabinet Work &c $400
Jeffersonville Township	1 man 1 Boy 1 Sett of Cabinet Tools & turning lathe Raw materials: Plank & Scantling 300 [feet] $35 Product: Cabinet Work $300

Charlestown

2 men   2 boys
two Lathes &c
Raw materials: Lumber $50; paint $300;
   & oil 80 gal $100
Product: Chairs & Painting $1200

Charlestown

3 men
1 Sett of Cabinet Tools
Product: Cabinet Work $1500

Charlestown

5 men
5 Setts of Cabinet Tools
Product: Cabinet Work $4000

Charlestown

2 men
Product: Spinning Wheels Bedsteds &c
   $800

Charlestown

2 men
Shop tools 2 Setts
Product: Cabinet Work $1600
Remarks: in good repair

APPENDIX II: A List of All the Forms of Objects Made by Craftsmen Mentioned Herein

Bed
High post
French, Frenchpost
Fancy
Plain; common
Trundle
Patent screw
Curtain
Low post
Field
Cot
Day bed
Turn up
Paneled headboard
Cornice for
Tester for

Book case
With glass doors
For store

Bureau
Circular
Columned
French
Dressing
Projecting block front
Half column
Half column,
　7 drawers
Plain front
Common and fancy,
　6 drawers
Paneled

Chair
Common
Family
Fancy
Windsor (plain,
　fancy, scroll top,
　slat back

Arm
High
Rocking (Boston,
　fancy, uphol-
　stered, cane back,
　cane seat, sew-
　ing)
Sewing (with
　drawer, Wind-
　sor, fancy)
Writing (Windsor,
　fancy)
Slat back
Scollop top
Grecian cane seat
Grecian flag seat
Bannister back
Split bottom
Cane and rush bot-
　tom
Children's; chil-
　dren's rocking
Spring back
Upholstered

Chest
"3 foot chest with
a draw"

Clock case

Coffin

Commode

Cradle
Crib cradle
Rocking crib
Cradle settee
Tester for cradle

Crib	Tester for crib Crib cradle	*Stool*	Foot Cane seat, for boats and hotels
Cupboard	Corner Portable Safe For desk	*Table*	Breakfast Dining Side, end Square Large
Desk	Sugar Writing desk for store Case of pigeon holes Counting house Escritoire		Toilet Center Card Writing Kitchen Office
Dresser	Washing		Round top Tip [tilt top] Twist reeded legs
Lockers			Dressing Work; lady's work
Looking Glass			For priest 3 feet [long] 3½ feet [long]
Piano			with turned legs 3 feet square
Press	China Wardrobe; clothes With drawer	*Wardrobe*	
Secretary	Columned Plain	*Miscel- laneous*	Wash sink Clothes horse;
Settee	Cradle Fancy Windsor		clothes rack Mop handle Spice pot
Sideboard			Bread tray; bread board; bread shovel
Sociable			Churn dasher
Sofa	Upholstered lounge Cane seat lounge		Washboard Fork handle, han-
Stand	Candle Wash Work [sewing] Work, 2 drawers		dles for all kinds of tools Clothes closet

Fireboard
Instrument box for
    doctor
Picture frame;
    map frame
Bird cage; squirrel
    cage
Bathing tub; box
    and barrel for
    bath
Washing machine
Brackets and roller
    for towel
Press board
Dough tray
Salt box
Checkers
Mace sticks
Corset boards

Painted trunk
2 lions' heads
Whip handle
Child's wagon
Parts for printing
    press
Hat molds
Brick molds
Quilting frames
Boat pump
Ruler, yardstick
Sausage stuffer
Rolling pin
Spinning wheel,
    wool wheel
Wheat fan
Wool carding ma-
    chine

PLATE I. Horse power being used to operate a cider mill.
From *Illustrated London News,* 14 December 1850.

PLATE II. Dog-powered machinery being used to raise water.
From *Ballou's Pictorial Drawing Room Companion,* 1855.

PLATE III. Corner cupboard made by Thomas Lincoln in Hardin County, Kentucky, prior to 1816. Cherry with inlay of lighter wood. In J. B. Speed Art Museum, Louisville.

PLATE IV. Mark of Thomas Lincoln with date inside cupboard.

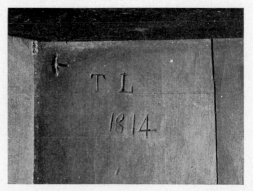

PLATE V. Cradle made by Benjamin F. Price, South Bend, in collection of the Northern Indiana Historical Society.

PLATE VI. Cradle made in shop of Andrew Gardner, Vincennes, in William Henry Harrison Mansion.

PLATE VII. Clock made by Humphrey Griffith, Indianapolis (working 1825-1835), in case undoubtedly made by a local craftsman. Owned by Mr. and Mrs. John L. Goldthwaite, Indianapolis.

PLATE VIII. Sewing table of curly maple, made by William Tate, Lawrenceburg. Owned by Caroline Dunn, Indianapolis.

PLATE IX. Chest made by Andrew Gardner, in William Henry
Harrison Mansion, Vincennes.

PLATE X.   Desk attributed to Dennis Pennington, in old
Capitol Building, Corydon.

PLATE XI.   Chest made by Samuel Boicourt, Gibson County,
for Eleanor Robb Embree, possibly 1828.   Owned by
Mrs. Morton C. Embree, Princeton.

PLATE XII. Child's
rocking chair made by
John Burns of Marion
County, 1829. In col-
lection of Children's
Museum, Indianapolis.

Kenny Strathman

PLATE XIII. Child's chair
made by Espy & Sloan,
Indianapolis, 1847. In collection of Children's Mu-
seum, Indianapolis.

Kenny Strathman

PLATE XIV. Elaborately carved arm chair made by John Ott, Indianapolis, c. 1850. Reproduced courtesy Mrs. C. B. Zeller.

PLATE XV. Original sketch for the eagle heads on the arm chair made by John Ott shown above, from original in Ott's drawing book. Reproduced courtesy Mrs. C. B. Zeller.